The Complete Guide to Second Homes for Vacations, Retirement, and Investment

GARY W. ELDRED

John Wiley & Sons, Inc.

New York • Chichester • Weinheim • Brisbane • Singapore • Toronto

Published by John Wiley & Sons, Inc.
Published simultaneously in Canada.

Library of Congress Cataloging-in-Publication Data:

Eldred, Gary W.
    The complete guide to second homes for vacations, retirement, and
investment / Gary W. Eldred.
      p.   cm.
    Includes index.
    ISBN 0-471-34967-4 (pa. : alk. paper)
    1. Real estate investment—United States. 2. Second homes—United
States. I. Title.
HD255.E375   1999
643′.2—dc21   99-35191

Printed in the United States of America.

10 9 8 7 6 5 4 3 2 1

Contents

Introduction

Should You Own a Second Home?

Thinking about owning a second home? Good for you. You're about to join one of the fastest growing trends in the United States and around the globe. Studies show that more than 30 million Americans and perhaps another 100 million people worldwide are expected to enter the second-home market within the coming decade. In fact, second-home ownership keeps setting new record highs. In many of the most popular locations, realty agents continuously voice concern over the shortage of homes available for sale.

Hot Second-Home Markets

"I'm begging owners to list with me," Vermont Realtor Rob Sherwood told the *New York Times*. "In 1991, we had fifty-two units for sale in one ski complex. Now we have seven. We're remarkably busy with hopeful buyers. This last weekend, I didn't have time to see them all."

In the Southeast, agent Dorothy Robeck says, "People have been telling us for years: You people on the coast watch out, the boomers are coming. Well, they're here. In the last eighteen months, the market has changed so fast that we're begging people for listings. Last year we had forty beachfront condo listings. This year we have two."

In the South Michigan woods, the Mammoth Lake area of California, the Colorado Rockies, and even Branson, Missouri, the story's the same: Demand for second homes is large and growing. "For years we've noticed," agent Bill Kesller tells the *Atlanta Constitution*, "baby boomers are buying preretirement homes younger and younger in order to capitalize on low interest rates, peak salaries, and unprecedented appealing housing options." In Sarasota, Florida, the *Herald Tribune* recently headlined an article, "A Vanishing Market: Longboat Key's last new home project marks the end of an era—get 'em before they're gone."

I could go on and on quoting articles, Realtors, and second-home buyers themselves. All around the country, and throughout many parts of the world, the number of people who want a second home for vacations, getaways, investment, and retirement just keeps going up.

Yet, after taking notice of the hot and growing markets for second homes, you still may be mulling over many questions such as:

- Should we really take the plunge and buy that second home?
- How much will it cost?
- How much can we afford?
- How can we be sure that we're getting good value for our money?
- Will the home appreciate?
- How much rental income will it generate?
- Will we use the home enough to justify ownership?
- What should we know to get the best deal on financing?
- What tax rules apply?

These are the questions you need to ask, and you'll find the answers to them throughout the book. But before getting into the specifics, let's preview ten reasons why so many people are buying now.

Ten Reasons to Buy and Own a Second Home Now

By surveying these ten motivating factors, you can begin to think more clearly about why you would like to own a second home.

1. Gain appreciation potential
2. Create value (through home improvements)
3. Generate rental income
4. Save on taxes
5. Reserve your place in the sun
6. Secure easier mortgage financing
7. Enjoy that feeling called home
8. Vacation free worldwide (almost)
9. Boost your business
10. Diversify your investments

Gain Appreciation Potential

"The Market for Second Homes Heats Up," writes *Golf Magazine*, "Prices for Housing Have Risen Dramatically." At long last, the real estate second-home market downturn of the late 1980s and early 1990s is now a topic for the history books. As *Golf Magazine* and dozens of other publications point out, today's second-home markets—as well as their future prospects—look very bright. Likewise, the *New York Times* has recently written that "Everything has fallen into place. Second-home prices are up by 10 to 20 percent this year nearly everywhere from the South Jersey Shore to Emerald Isle, North Carolina." In the West, "pricey second homes are driving up housing costs from Aspen, Colorado, to Park City, Utah."

The Trend in Prices Is Up

By declaring that "everything has fallen into place," the *Times* is referring to a variety of factors that will be driving second-home prices to new heights for at least the next ten to twenty years. If you want appreciation, here's why your second home will give it to you:

Demographics. Chief among these driving factors, of course, is demographics. Those same baby boomers who drove up housing prices everywhere from Georgetown to Lincoln Park to Pacific Heights during the 1970s and 1980s are now entering the second-home and retirement-home market in vast numbers. They will continue to do so until well past the year 2020.

But it's not just baby-boomer demographics that must be considered. Senior citizens experiencing better health and increased longevity are also stimulating demand for second homes. Forty years ago, most people over age 60 (if they were lucky enough to live that long) thought retirement meant a rocking chair on the front porch. Today, millions of these seniors can be found on Florida golf courses and Colorado hiking trails.

Strong second-home demand, too, can be expected from the post-boomer generation. Today, millions of credentialed young male *and* female college graduates with their J.D.s, M.D.s, M.B.A.s, Ph.D.s, C.P.A.s, and B.S.E.E.s are marrying each other. It's now commonplace to see families with both spouses under age 40 who enjoy household incomes that exceed $100,000 per year. With second-home ownership fast emerging as the newest symbol of status, the best way to reduce stress, and a direct route to quality family time, this younger generation will further fuel demand for second homes and push up housing prices in desirable locations.

The Wealth Factor.   When purchasing his family's second home in Ocean City, New Jersey, Douglas Johnson explained that "It was the right time. The strength of the stock market is something that helped us make the decision." One economic fact is certainly true: Millions of Americans like Doug Johnson have now accumulated enough money through their stock portfolios, partnership bonuses, business profits, and home equity to provide them sufficient funds to fulfill their dream of owning a second home. As these Americans continue to realize this dream, they will continue to push prices up.

Foreign Demand.   Americans aren't the only people who are increasingly attracted to second homes. The British, French, Japanese, Chinese (Hong Kong, Singapore), Dutch, and Canadians, as well as affluent citizens of many other countries are shopping the globe for good locations. They, too, want the three Rs (rest, recreation, retirement). Already, overseas investors have pushed up home prices in popular spots such as Vancouver, Vail, Maui, San Francisco, Manhattan, Brisbane (Gold Coast), Tuscany, and Dublin. Hundreds of South Florida condominium communities fly the Maple Leaf right alongside the Stars and Stripes.

People Need More Quality Time. Every study shows that Americans are working harder, longer, and with more stress. Add to that a rushed personal and family life, a never-ending list of things to do, and reduced opportunities for quality family time at home. Together these facts of life are motivating many people to seek shelter from the everyday world, to find a place of refuge from their hectic pace. No longer does a whirlwind of tourism and travel sound quite so appealing (especially for those who travel frequently for work). Instead, heading off to a second-home getaway is becoming increasingly popular. More than ever before, the lifestyles and attitudes of Americans (and other nationalities) are pulling them toward a second home.

Get Ready for Jumps in Second-Home Prices

When thinking about appreciation potential for a second home, gaze into that crystal ball that clearly reveals a rapidly growing number of people with the desire, income, wealth, and borrowing power for acquiring second homes. Sure, over the next twenty years, we will see some up and down cycles. But second-home prices in desirable locations will definitely trend up—sometimes quite steeply. There's little doubt that in the future, the prices of properties that are located in popular areas will make today's prices look like bargains—just as today we look back on the home prices of the 1960s and 1970s and view them as ridiculously cheap. (For more proof, see Chapter 7.)

Create Value (through Home Improvement)

Would you like to see your second home appreciate significantly—without waiting for market forces to push prices up? Then create value through creative improvements. Consider the experience of Raymond Brown and his wife, Annie B. When this couple bought a vacation retreat home, which they named Woodpecker Haven, Raymond recalls that he "thought it was a done property. It was only five years old."

Annie B., though, viewed the home from a different perspective. With years of experience in interior design and a vivid imagination, she saw great potential in the home. As Raymond proudly points out, "Here are some of the improvements my enterprising wife accomplished to transform a pleasantly livable property into an exquisite home":

- Landscaped the front and rear yards.
- Installed a drip irrigation system.
- Built a stone fence around the pool.
- Added decks around the rear of the house.
- Installed french doors in both bedrooms to open out to the decks.
- Remodeled the guest bedroom and bath to create a master bedroom for visitors.
- Built in a fireplace, bookshelves, cabinets, and track lighting in the living room.
- Trimmed overgrown trees and shrubs to enhance a picture-perfect lake view from the front porch.

Although Raymond and Annie B. invested $75,000 in these and other improvements, they added around $175,000 in value—throughout a falling market. "We bought our Sonoma retreat," says Raymond, "in August 1988 just as home prices were peaking, and sold five years later, two months before prices bottomed out . . . . Yet we made a $100,000 profit. Our secret? Woodpecker Haven was a fixer-upper. We renovated inside and out." Want to build equity fast? Look for a fixer that you can remodel, renovate, or romance.

How can you recognize such homes? How do you know which improvements will pay off? Good questions. They are answered in Chapter 6.

Generate Rental Income

A second home is one of those few pleasures in life that can actually pay for itself, at least in part. If you shop for locations and compare properties based on their ability to bring in rental income, you can substantially reduce (or eliminate) your annual out-of-pocket costs of ownership.

Surprisingly, though, most owners of second homes don't come close to realizing their home's full rental potential. Some owners don't want the bother of dealing with tenants. Others fear property damage.

And many owners don't know how to market their properties effectively. However, each of these (and other) concerns can easily be solved with know-how and foresight. Follow the rental advice set forth in Chapter 13. You'll profit from your second home and enjoy it, too.

Save on Taxes

Owning a second home opens an array of possibilities for additional federal tax deductions and tax-sheltered (or tax-free) income. In some cases, you can even reduce or eliminate various property taxes, income taxes, and other fees and costs levied by state and local governments. Naturally, you must discuss your own situation and tax-saving possibilities with competent tax counsel. Tax questions that arise out of the ownership of second homes can become quite technical and complex. Nevertheless, arrange your affairs appropriately and you'll find that owning a second home permits you to lighten your tax burden. Chapter 14 provides more insight into these tax issues and alerts you to a variety of income and property tax-saving techniques.

Reserve Your Place in the Sun

"The time to start making your move [to buy a second home] is now," writes Jerry Edgerton in a recent article in *Money Magazine*. He advises you to buy "before baby boomers inflate the prices of vacation homes the way they did those primary homes in the 1970s and 1980s . . . . As boomers begin to swell the rank of those preretirement buyers, increases in the prices of second homes will accelerate." Edgerton is looking at home appreciation—except he is looking at it from the buyer's perspectives of affordability and availability.

In other words, if you don't buy now, you may miss your opportunity forever. It's quite likely that home prices in choice areas will jump faster than most people's ability to pay for them. As late as 1988, for example, you could still buy a single-family home in Aspen for $300,000. Ten years later, you needed at least a cool million. But even if you can afford to pay, there is still the question of availability.

In many areas, properties in the best locations seldom come on the market—and when they do they're snapped up quickly, sometimes before they even make it into M.L.S. Obviously, home prices shoot up because too many hopeful buyers are chasing after too few properties. In those markets, you will need more than a fat bank account. You'll need an inside track to learn of properties as soon as (if not before) the for sale sign goes up in the front yard. Reserve now so that you won't face the "woulda, coulda, shoulda" regrets that will torment those who let today's opportunities pass them by.

Secure Easier Mortgage Financing

Until four or five years ago, most mortgage lenders shied away from financing second homes. Fearful of defaults, these lenders either refused to make such loans or they applied tougher requirements for down payments, qualifying standards, and appraisals. Also, in contrast to primary homes, lenders charged higher closing costs and interest rates for mortgages on second homes.

Today, the financing conditions have changed for the better. Although some differences still exist (especially if you plan to treat your second home as a rental), everyone agrees that securing a mortgage on a second home is easier and less costly than ever. In addition, two other new trends in mortgage financing make it easier to borrow money to finance a second home: home equity loans and reverse annuity mortgages. Great financing opportunities for second homes (see Chapter 11) give you another good reason to become a second-home owner.

Enjoy That Feeling Called Home

Countrywide Funding, one of the largest mortgage lenders in North America, puts out a marketing video entitled *A Feeling Called Home*. Although aimed at first-time homebuyers, this video really leads all homeowners to better appreciate the strong emotional benefits of owning. No place on earth can provide the feelings of warmth, comfort, relaxation, status, and security that most people feel when they are nestled on a sofa within a home that they own.

Increasingly, we find that many families are becoming second-home owners because they want to maintain these homey feelings whether they are at home or on vacation. No motel, hotel, or even luxurious rented condo can satisfy this basic desire to be surrounded by personal belongings. In addition, sometimes we can't choose the location where we're offered the best income potential, and thus need to maintain a primary residence, but we can choose an aesthetically appealing, climate-friendly, second-home location where we're able to wind down and remove ourselves from the stresses of job and daily aggravations.

Vacation Free Worldwide (Almost)

Perhaps the idea of owning a second home appeals to you, but you hesitate to settle on one because you don't want a long-term commitment to a single destination. Don't worry. Your concern is so common that the practice of home exchanging has become widespread. Numerous directories, publications, exchange services, and the World Wide Web provide thousands of possibilities for home exchanges practically anywhere in the world.

Consider the following comments from an exchanger:

> *After six years of vacation home exchanging in New England, New Jersey, Florida, and various cities in England, Germany, Spain, and Switzerland—with repeat exchanges in almost every instance—my wife and I have reached a unique position . . . over the years we have developed close friendships with half a dozen exchangers in the United States and Europe.*
>
> *These people know our vacation home's open to them. They can spend a couple or three weeks at our condo anytime it's not occupied, and we feel quite comfortable picking up the phone and saying, "We'd like to come to Cape Cod (or London, Cannes, Berlin, or wherever) in the spring, say for three weeks. How does your exchange schedule look?" We usually connect on choice one; if not, we're a sure bet for choice number two.*

You don't need to limit home exchanges to "like for like." Some exchangers swap golf-course condos for RVs, houseboats, in-city townhouses, mountain cabins—or any other type of trade that makes sense to all parties. One frequent business traveler to Chicago swaps several weeks of his family's Hilton Head condo for the recurring right to stay in an exchange partner's Lincoln Park carriage house. This exchange provides the traveling businessman more spacious and comfortable accommodations each time he visits Chicago. It also saves him $150 to $200 per diem in hotel bills and meal expenses.

You can learn more about home exchange practices, possibilities, and precautions in Chapter 13. For now just keep in mind that owning a second home doesn't limit your getaway opportunities. Instead, it opens the door to a world of possibilities and adventures.

Boost Your Business

Would you like to boost your business? Why not use a second home to strengthen your relationship with clients or customers; reward the exceptional performance of key employees; or, perhaps, express appreciation for your valued suppliers? By making your second home available to people in your business on whom you depend, you can generate considerable good will at little cost to yourself.

If your second home is located a convenient distance from your business, you also could use it to hold strategic planning sessions, holiday parties, or summer/winter breaks. Many businesses use some such type of retreat to overcome burnout, develop fresh strategic perspective, focus on looming problems without interruption, or even generate ideas for a business promotional campaign.

While you primarily may want a second home to get away from the concerns of work, many second-home owners do find that they can profitably use their vacation properties to help advance their business interests. It's certainly a benefit to keep in mind.

Diversify Your Investments

With strong appreciation of second-home prices expected in many locations, you might reasonably consider diversifying your investment portfolio away from stocks and into real estate—especially real estate that will add happiness to your life.

Rather than risk holding inflated financial assets (which are actually nothing more than electronic digits), doesn't it make sense to convert some amount of that artificial wealth into tangible wealth, such as a second home? Based on the sky-high prices of stocks vis à vis second homes, a well-selected second home can offer balanced protection against a loss in the value of your net worth. If the stock market drops, your second home will not only give you a place to get away to and have fun, it will help preserve your net worth.

Two Disadvantages

Overall, based on my experience as a real estate market consultant, educator, and investor, I am bullish on all types of real estate that are located in desirable areas with natural or legal constraints on land development and home construction. In other words, I am forecasting strong investment performance for real estate that's situated in areas where the emerging growth in demand is likely to exceed the possible growth in supply. But there's no doubt that buying a second home does present two disadvantages: cyclical downturns and the costs of ownership.

Cyclical Downturns

Although demographic trends signal large price increases over time, no one has yet repealed the law of real estate cycles. Undoubtedly, on our way to the future, our economy will experience recessions. People will again close their wallets to spending. Interest rates and credit standards may increase. And an upward spike in unemployment may temporarily push more property sellers into the market at the same time potential buyers head into retreat. Most families who buy second homes do so with discretionary funds. They can postpone buying until they're more comfortable with their financial security. Even super-rich Aspen suffered falling prices during the severe Colorado economic downturn of the mid- to late 1980s. So, to avoid running into difficulties, follow these time-tested rules: (1) don't stretch yourself thin; (2) don't place yourself into a position where a financial setback will force you to liquidate in a down market; (3) keep a reserve of ready cash. Although your income now may have hit new highs, don't plan to pay for your second home with earnings that you can't firmly count on.

In later chapters, I show you how to tell if you're getting good value and whether market conditions signal a "buy quick" or a "wait and see" strategy. But no one can perfectly anticipate peaks and valleys. That's why you should choose to play it safe. Look to the long term. Use only income or wealth that you're sure you won't need to support your family's lifestyle essentials.

Costs of Ownership

As a homeowner you already know that a home requires care. To maintain its condition and enhance its value, you need to put in time, money, and effort. As a precaution before you buy, take a reality check. Answer these questions:

- How much work will your second home require each year?
- How much will you have to pay others to perform the upkeep that you don't want to or can't provide?
- What amounts will you have to budget for materials and replacement items?
- Will you personally use the property enough to justify the required upkeep (time and money)?

Even if you don't personally use your second home enough to justify its costs, remember that you might still justify ownership by bringing in rental income, exchanging the home with others around the country or around the world, advancing your business interests, or by making it available to friends and family members. Nevertheless, the issue of low usage rate is one you want to carefully consider. Surveys repeatedly show that many owners to not gain nearly as much from their second homes as they could. (Perhaps that's why timeshares, partial ownership, and group buying are the fastest growing types of second-home ownership. (These options are discussed in later chapters.)

Are You Ready?

Buy your second home with both left-brain and right-brain thinking. Dampen your emotional enthusiasm with a dose of reality. For most people who can afford it, a second home makes a wise purchase. But they're not for everyone. What do you think? Will your benefits of ownership outweigh the disadvantages?

I strongly believe in the enjoyment and investment value of second homes (I have owned and profited from several), otherwise I would not have written this book. Yet, admittedly, ownership presents some downside. But you can learn to manage these potential problems to minimize hassle, reduce risk, and maximize your rewards. How? Take full advantage of the knowledge and information that you can gain from the chapters that follow. Decide on the home-ownership benefits and priorities you wish to emphasize. Have some fun. Explore a variety of areas. Discover neighborhoods, locations, and homes. Imagine the lifestyle that your second-home possibilities can provide. Then choose, enjoy, and profit.

PART I

Exploring Possibilities and Priorities

CHAPTER 1

Open Your Horizons

Do you think you know the location and type of property that you want for your second home? Perhaps so. But wait. Before you commit, ask yourself whether you have really thought through all of your possibilities. When you open your horizons, you may bring into view other properties or locations that would enhance both your pleasures and your profits.

Discovering Possibilities

Too many second-home buyers choose an area with which they are familiar and don't explore other options. Or they fix their sights on a property without first ranking their priorities. In other words, for lack of thought or system, many second-home buyers overlook locations, properties, and priorities that would have given them more value for their money.

Avoid Tunnel Vision

When you buy a primary home, your choices are generally constrained by concerns such as schools, shopping, and commuting distance to work. In buying a second home, your potential choices expand dramatically. So why not take full advantage of this luxury? Let me illustrate.

Captiva Island and Siesta Key are two popular Florida locations for second-home buyers. Captiva is located over the north-end bridge of Sanibel Island about forty-five to sixty minutes from Fort Myers. Siesta Key is located about fifteen minutes from downtown Sarasota. To my way of thinking, Siesta Key offers superior value. It has prettier beaches, less traffic congestion, a greater choice of nearby restaurants, and a more convenient location than Captiva. It's closer to major shopping and commercial districts, health-care facilities, a major airport, and other attractive resort and vacation destinations such as Busch Gardens, Disney World, and an excellent selection of golf and tennis clubs. Both Siesta and Captiva prohibit major commercial development. Lush vegetation beautifies the environment of both areas. And homeowners in both areas enjoy a sense of isolation, privacy, and security.

Yet, even though a feature-to-feature comparison seems to favor Siesta, home prices on Captiva run 50 to 100 percent higher than Siesta. Why? The only explanation that I have discovered is that Captiva has become more popular with the so-called in-crowd. Several recent visits by celebrities and famous multimillionaires have raised its national profile. Likewise (although its prices are somewhat lower and properties more abundant) for Captiva's sister island of Sanibel.

In fact, I asked recent second-home buyers on both Captiva and Sanibel whether they had considered Siesta Key. None that I talked to had made a systematic comparison or, for that matter, had even visited Siesta. On the other hand, when I asked several Siesta Key homebuyers (I visit both locations frequently) whether they were familiar with Sanibel/Captiva, they said yes. They had explicitly chosen Siesta because of its location and other advantages.

It seems that because of its greater national visibility and much larger number of time-share rentals, more people vacation at Sanibel/Captiva. They fall in love with the area and then decide to buy—

without any attempt to discover whether other possibilities would offer them a more attractive package of benefits relative to costs.

Even if you think you now know where you would like to buy a second home, explore other possibilities. You may find much better value. Should you decide to follow through on your original inclinations, you can make your choice with far greater confidence. Bringing more potential choices into view insures you against the "woulda, coulda, shoulda" regrets that often arise when your decisions jump the gun and fail to incorporate clear thinking and more extensive knowledge.

Avoid Decision Traps

In their eye-opening book, *Decision Traps: The Ten Barriers to Brilliant Decision-Making and How to Overcome Them*, Edward Russo and Paul Schoemaker discuss the following ten traps that can keep people from making the best decisions:

1. *Plunging in*: gathering information before you've really identified your most important issues.
2. *Frame blindness*: applying decision criteria without first identifying and ranking priorities.
3. *Lack of frame control*: randomly mixing decision criteria without focus, or letting others unduly influence your criteria.
4. *Overconfidence*: failing to search out information because you're sure your current and often unstated assumptions, opinions, and conclusions couldn't possibly be wrong.
5. *Shortsighted shortcuts*: trusting rules of thumb or second-hand information without verifying accuracy and applicability.
6. *Disorganized thinking*: failing to systematically write out and compare information and priorities, or winging it by trying to keep track of everything in your head.
7. *Group failure*: forgetting to adequately weigh the concerns of everyone who must live by your decision.
8. *Ignoring feedback*: discounting or throwing out facts that contradict or fail to support your predetermined decision.
9. *Relying on "experts"*: abdicating your decision to others (lawyers, realty agents, mortgage advisors, etc.) without questioning their facts, biases, or understanding of your priorities.

10. *Failure to audit and control your decision process*: unconsciously or impulsively changing priorities midstream and placing excessive emphases on selected favorable (or unfavorable) facts.

Of course none of us can ever go through a perfect decision-making process. We can never "systematically compare all possible options," but, as Russo and Schoemaker's list suggests, we certainly can *improve* our decision making. By paying attention to potential traps and by making sure we have really identified and ranked our priorities according to our longer-term objectives, we can enjoy a fuller life without encountering quite so many potholes and detours.

Revisit Benefits and Priorities

Naturally, then, since buying a second home involves so much information relating to priorities and potential outcomes, as a first step toward a rewarding experience, it would help to develop an organized checklist. What benefits of buying and owning a second home are most important to you? Let's review the list discussed in the Introduction:

- Gain appreciation potential
- Create value (through home improvements)
- Generate rental income
- Save on taxes
- Reserve your place in the sun
- Secure easier mortgage financing
- Enjoy that feeling called home
- Vacation free worldwide (almost)
- Boost your business
- Diversify your investments

As you continue reading this book, you will discover various ways to achieve each of these benefits. In most cases, however, you may have to make trade-offs. Always remember, "You can have *anything* you want, but you can't have *everything* you want." If you want to earn substantial income by renting out your second home, you'll probably have to pay more for your financing and meet tougher qualifying standards. If you want to actively use your second home in a national l or international vacation exchange program, you may want to relax your personal preferences for location or property features. Instead, you should favor those features that are most desirable to other exchangers.

Obviously, many types of trade-offs will present themselves as you emphasize certain desired benefits over others. Yet, some people do find a second home where "everything falls into place." But to make this happen, you can't really count on luck. You must know what you're looking for, otherwise you won't recognize it when you see it. Or even worse, you'll never even see it because your "order-taker" real estate agent simply shows you properties without first fully exploring your possibilities and priorities.

Beware of Order Takers

When it comes to "order takers," you know the type: The agent merely asks you to describe the property features, neighborhood, and price range you're looking for. Then he or she chauffeurs you around showing you "only the properties that meet your needs." Unfortunately, when you specify "needs" only in terms of property features, personal preferences, and price range—as opposed to the full assortment of benefits and goals you would like to achieve—you will probably end up with far fewer choices than you could have otherwise.

Consider Possible Trade-Offs

As you begin to shop for a second home, decide how much you want to emphasize personal preference over other potential benefits. Think about how you might answer these questions:

- Would you buy a "fixer" if you could create $40,000 in added value during the next two years?
- Would you buy a home with an accessory apartment if it would provide a caretaker for your property and $6,000 in annual rental income?

- Would you buy a home that's too small, too large, or too ugly if you could get it for, say, $25,000 under market?
- Would you be willing to buy into a larger condo complex than you wanted if it meant more possibilities for rentals or exchanges?
- Would you be willing to use your second home for rental and business purposes if these uses generated significant tax deductions?
- Would you be willing to choose Florida, even though you preferred North Carolina, because Florida offers strong tax advantages?

These questions only scratch the surface of the many issues and opportunities that the following chapters address. But they illustrate the gains you can achieve by opening your horizons. Redefine your search. You can often discover better possibilities that you might otherwise have overlooked.

Second Home, Retirement Home, or Both?

"Our biggest market," says David Everett of Belfair, a private club community in South Carolina, "is the pre-retiree who does not plan to fully retire for another 5 to 10 years." Likewise, David Sarka, of the Vacation Rental Managers Association, notes the trend. "More second-home buyers are looking at vacation homes with retirement in mind," he points out.

Increasingly, as people realize that many of the best locations are selling out, more second-home buyers are shopping with "double vision"—a great place for leisure activities now, plus an attractive location for more extended (or even year-round) living at some future date.

The Present versus the Future

Does this plan appeal to you? If so, think through not only your present needs and wants, but also those that will concern you later. Does the location offer quality health-care services, convenience to shopping, and good public services (libraries, parks, police, fire, etc.)? Would you enjoy the weather patterns throughout the entire year (or at least during the months you intend to live there)?

Consider the cost of living. As a second-home owner in your years of strong earnings and investment gains, you may be less sensitive to living costs. But what about during retirement? At that time will you want to scale back? Would you prefer a good selection of restaurants where dining for two is easily available for less than $25? What about greens fees, lift tickets, tennis court time, and marina costs? How much will you need to spend on groceries? Pay attention to gasoline prices and yard-care services. How do these prices and costs compare to other locations—and to your future budget?

Advantages of "Double Vision"

If you buy now with an eye on the future, you not only will be able to reserve your place in the sun (in mountains or woods, lakeside, on the ocean shore, near the golf course, etc.), but you also will begin to make friends (and perhaps business relationships) that will ease your transition into a permanent relocation. You might also benefit from a change in residency for purposes of state and local taxation. For example, Florida does not impose a state income tax on residents and taxes estates much more lightly than, say, New York.

The new federal capital gains exclusion might also benefit you. Some people are now buying a second home with plans for substantial long-term appreciation. At some point in the future, they will sell their principal home, take up to $500,000 in tax-free gains, move into their "second" home for two years (possibly less), and then sell and again escape taxation on the gains.

Up-and-Coming Areas

When many people think of second or retirement homes, they think of popular locations like Aspen, Lake Tahoe, Naples (Florida), Hilton Head, and Scottsdale. Unfortunately, most home prices in these locations are well beyond the means of typical second-home buyers. The same may be true of other well-known locations that are on your dream list of places where you would like to own. If that's the case, perhaps you should consider an up-and-coming area.

"As the market for second homes in the Sun Belt heats up," reports *Golf Magazine*, "prices have risen dramatically." To maximize value, smart home shoppers are scouting up-and-coming areas that offer quality golf courses and prime amenities—without the bull market prices. "One of the rising starts in this category is Mesa and the East Valley, located 12 miles east of Phoenix Sky Harbor International Airport," the report continues. Although Mesa offers fewer restaurants and golf courses than its rich cousin, Scottsdale, it also provides a less hectic pace and free-flowing traffic. Its views of Superstition Mountain remain unbeatable and a variety of master-planned golfing communities surrounding Mesa still offers newly built homes within the price range of $115,000 to $200,000. And, as in Scottsdale, Mesa residents enjoy low humidity and more than 300 days of sunshine each year.

Expand Your Search

Can you locate a lower-priced "rising-star" area near your otherwise first-choice location? Several years ago (but much less today), Snowmass Village, Colorado, offered relatively low prices compared to its nearby rich cousin, Aspen. Even now, you still can own in Breckenridge for substantially less than in Aspen or Snowmass. And while Breckenridge doesn't offer quite the same glamour or beauty as Aspen, its restaurants are priced more reasonably and (unless you're arriving by private jet) it surpasses Aspen in terms of convenient accessibility.

In many cases, too, the rising-star location will not only offer lower home prices and a lower cost of living, it also may provide a higher quality of life. Few long-term residents of Aspen, Scottsdale, Jackson Hole, Martha's Vineyard, the Hamptons, and other premier second-home communities are pleased with the changes their towns have incurred during the past twenty to thirty years. Many residents long for the less congested, quieter times of bygone days. Rather than regret the unaffordability of marquee locations, why not search out a community that still displays a true sense of itself?

In other words, don't fix your sights on just one brand-name location. Look around. Investigate and discover. The law of real estate markets says that as home prices increase beyond reason in a given area, smart home buyers will expand their horizons. They will scout for the next up-and-coming location.

Stay Alert to Revitalized Locations

In addition to setting your radar to discover newly emerging second- and retirement-home locations, a variety of up-and-coming areas are really a blast from the past. Some faded areas that were once popular are showing (or about to show) a new vitality.

Consider Mammoth Mountain. This once booming resort area is located in the Eastern High Sierra Mountains of California. It offers world-class hiking, fishing, and mountain-biking in the nearby John Muir and Ansel Adams Wilderness areas; championship golf; downhill and cross-country skiing; and easy access to Yosemite National Park. With such strong recreational amenities, Intrawest, a Canadian development company, is investing more than $500 million to revitalize this resort area. Their plans include a resort village with new shops, restaurants, and lodging; a gondola to connect the center of town to the heart of the mountain; and a variety of on-mountain improvements.

Upon entering first-phase sales for its planned vacation homes, Intrawest was met with the "remarkable response" of 129 home sales in its opening weekend. "The demand we see today shows tremendous support and enthusiasm for Mammoth's master plan," says Dana Sevey, an Intrawest vice president. "These buyers are not just purchasing real estate, they are buying into the new and improved Mammoth still to come." As an indicator of the strong emerging demand for Mammoth Mountain vacation homes, Intrawest's first-weekend sales volume of $36 million nearly equaled the $38 million of resale volume for existing homes during the entire preceding year.

Of course, whenever you are buying "still-to-come" planned improvements, watch out for the fine print and proceed with caution. Big promises often fall short. It will pay you to ask questions such as: "Are plans underway to redevelop or revitalize any 'faded glories' that might appeal to us?" As currently premier spots continue to escalate in price, alert development and resort companies are scouting for once popular locations that they can bring back to life. Such a location may give you the opportunity you are looking for.

Brand-Name "Bargains"

What should you do if, after searching up-and-coming and revitalized areas, you still long for the unaffordable brand-name location? In that case, you may want to try to find a bargain-priced property. Remember, when you hear about those "outrageous" prices, the figures cited may represent averages, not low-end prices.

Look for the Low End

On a recent trip to Aspen, I heard everyone saying that entry-level home prices started at $1,000,000. True, for single-family homes in the West End. But on personal investigation, I found condominium units priced as low as $100,000. Granted, those so-called apartments were little more than rooms with a bath, bed, microwave, and sink. They had been converted into condos from a Holiday Inn motel. Still, the apartments carried an Aspen address. And with rental income, the units were certainly affordable to singles or couples with middle-income wages.

Likewise in high-priced La Jolla, California, another favorite spot for vacations and second homes. As of my visit last summer, a few small condominium units (actually real apartments, not converted motel rooms) were available for less than $100,000. I also was able to find a small two-bedroom house with a partial view of the Pacific Ocean located fewer than 200 yards from the beach priced at around $300,000. Entry-level single-family home prices in La Jolla generally start upwards of $400,000.

Consider the Wrong Side of the Tracks

Nearly every city and neighborhood has certain perimeter markers such as "inside the beltway," "west of the trail," "walk to the village," "one bridge to the bay," that in some sense separate higher-priced, preferred locations from their supposed inferiors. The trick is to find one of these "inferior" locations that offers almost the same advantages as the more prestigious area, but at a fraction of the higher price.

I used this "wrong side of the tracks" strategy when I bought my first Florida home 20 years ago. I wanted lakefront; a Winter Park address, zip code, and telephone exchange; and convenient access to Park Avenue shops and restaurants. Unfortunately, homes in the preferred locations (Lake Virginia, Lake Sue, Chain-of-Lakes) that met these criteria were double the price I could afford. Yet, by extending my search just 5 minutes to the west—on the "wrong" side of Interstate 4—I located and bought a 3,200 square foot lakefront house on an acre lot with 165 feet of shoreline. It wasn't Chain-of-Lakes, but I got a Winter Park address, a larger house and lot, faster access to downtown Orlando, and easy access to Park Avenue, and I paid only 50 percent as much as a similar property would have cost on the more prestigious Lake Virginia or Lake Sue. I might add that this house enjoyed spectacular lake views from eight of its nine rooms—far better views than any other home I had looked at. Today, that "inferior" property is worth at least three times what I paid for it.

The Lesson

The lesson from these experiences is clear. If you can't afford—or don't want to pay—the prices of premier homes in premier locations, don't give up. Open your horizon. Bring into view homes with low-end prices. Or, alternatively, step just across the "tracks" (highway, bridge, zip-code line, municipal boundary, etc.). Quite often you can find better value at a more acceptable price.

City Seconds

Exhausted from the never-ending commute between suburbia and your downtown office? Would you like more weekends in the city that combine shopping, theater, night life, museums, and great restaurants? The answer to your dilemma may be a second home in the city. As Bill Rumbler of the *Chicago Sun-Times* has discovered, "A reversal is taking place. Used to be that when people bought a second home it was in the country, a place to go to escape the hectic urban pace. [But] nowadays, people are buying second homes in the heart of the city from Lincoln Park to the South Loop. Instead of running away from the urban experience, they are embracing it."

From London to San Francisco

This trend to city seconds isn't just limited to Chicago. It's happening throughout the United States and Europe. "At seven o'clock every Friday evening," reports the *Daily Telegraph*, "the M4 and M40 are crammed with Londoners fleeing to their second homes for [the traditional] weekend in the countryside. [Yet] the other side of the carriage way is crowded with country dwellers, eager to forgo the country air and Sunday in the garden for the cultural buzz of London."

"More people than ever before," continues the *Telegraph*, "are choosing to buy a second home in the capital. Some wish to avoid the daily drudge of commuting, or buy for investment. But many others see London, one of the world's greatest cultural and culinary centers, as the perfect place to spend free time."

Atlanta, Paris, Manhattan, Miami, Vancouver, and Rome are all experiencing this urban revival. In fact, when friends of mine recently sold their Pacific Heights co-op, none of the five bidders (in the then hot San Francisco market) planned to live in the unit. All planned to use it only for weekend or business visits to the city.

A Feeling Called Home

Why buy a city second home when hotel rooms and other types of accommodations are plentiful? The answer to that question includes cost, convenience, and the feeling called home. "I used to stay in bed-and-breakfasts," says one city second buyer, "but it was expensive and uncomfortable. I wanted someplace I could relax and not move in and out of on every visit. In other words, I wanted a place of my own."

Of course, the price-per-square-foot of living area for city homes tends to run higher than for homes located farther out. On the other hand, you won't need a large apartment since your primary goal is to roam out and about. What if the kids stay too? Put them on an air mattress on the floor. And when you own, you can eliminate your worry over what to do with the family Fido. Bring him with you.

Ruralize Your Dreams

In the old television sitcom, *The Beverly Hillbillies*, Jed Clampett asked his cousin Pearl whether the family should pick up and move from their country life to the city of Beverly Hills. Cousin Pearl answered, "Jed, how can ya ever ask? Look around ya. Yer eight miles from your nearest neighbor. Yer overrun with skunks, possums, coyotes, and bobcats. Ya use kerosene lamps fer light and ya cook on a wood stove summer and winter. Yer drinkin' homemade moonshine and washin' with homemade soap. And yor bathroom is fifty feet from the house and ya ask, 'Should I move?'" Jed responds, " I reckon yer right. A man'd be a dang fool to leave all of this."

Well, if you're like Jed Clampett with a hankering for the country life, you're not alone. Increasingly, Americans (and Europeans) are buying up the countryside. Many want to flee from the crime, congestion, and crowds of urban living. Hundreds of thousands of families have chosen to ruralize their dreams.

Nearly 30 years ago, Alvin Toffler was among the first popular writers who noted this growing trend. In his book, *Future Shock*, Toffler lamented the decline of cities and the "escape from chaos" that was driving movement to the country. Yet, even now with urban revival upon us, the country trend continues. In their book, *Megatrends 2000*, John Naisbitt and Patricia Aburdene write,

> *In the United States, for the first time in 200 years, more people are moving to rural areas than urban—many more. In the Northeast, West, Great Plains, and Southwest, everywhere. . . . people are abandoning cities for quality of life reasons: low crime rates, comparatively low housing costs, recreational opportunities, and perhaps most of all, a search for community values.*

Of course, "ruralizing your dreams" can actually refer to a number of quite different living experiences. You might choose a farm and acreage; a small town in New England; a mountain community in Virginia, North Carolina, or Colorado; a cabin in the woods of Michigan or Minnesota; a place out "at the lake"; or maybe even a ranchette in Wyoming, Montana, or Texas. In searching for a rural second-home getaway, your choices are limited only by your imagination and budget.

A Place on the Water

Across the United States, small riverfront communities are being redis-covered. In some towns, the population doesn't even reach 1,000. In other instances, rural waterfront homes sit isolated, uncared for, and rarely used. But one fact seems clear: These types of properties (often just cottages that need modernizing) are becoming increasingly popular.

A Cottage in Haddam (Population 7,200)

"The view is phenomenal," reports John Romano, who owns a second home on Little Meadow Road in the small riverfront community of Haddam, Connecticut. "I just love to be here when the sun shines."

Romano first noticed his property-to-be as he was boating on the Connecticut River. Returning to Haddam by car, he then viewed what he realized would serve as a great vacation home where he could have some fun with his grandchildren. The price: For his cottage with a deck and dock situated on a 1.3 acre riverfront lot, Romano paid just $70,000.

"A few years ago, you couldn't give these properties away," notes another Haddam property owner. "But local people started buying the properties and putting their boats in the river out in back of their cot-tages. People who wanted a place on the water have now discovered the possibilities of Haddam."

"People are fixing up their homes and bringing back some of the good old times," says long-time resident Ray Bogdan. Dorothy Piper, another admirer of Haddam, says, "In the autumn, the leaf change is beautiful. It's one of the simple pleasures that makes life so enjoyable down here on the river."

Southern Michigan Chain-of-Lakes

In areas of southern Michigan, not far from Detroit and Ann Arbor, "The demand for rural waterfront is overwhelming," says Realtor Tim Przysiecki. "I've got a ton of very qualified buyers and very few places to show them." Rustic lakefront cabins can run up to $150,000 and waterfront homes suitable for year-round occupancy are selling for much more. "It seems that just a week or two vacation in a rural get-away is giving second-home prospects the itch to buy a cottage of their own. In addition, since this rural area (near Pickney) is within an hour or two of heavily populated metro areas, it definitely beats driving to some of the more widely known locations (such as Mackinac Island) 300 miles to the north."

Thankful for the easy escape from daily stress, cabin owners Marv and Julie Howe remark how great they feel after they arrive "home." "Time really slows down here," says Julie. "We love the chance to make an attitude adjustment, to unwind and downshift from the pressure of business. Besides, the home draws the family together and enables us to spend quality time with the kids."

Home or Dock

I might note one other point that relates not just to rural locations, but to nearly all types of waterfront homes. Dock space itself has become a much sought after amenity. As marinas have become far more crowded and expensive, boat-owning second-home buyers are especially looking for properties that offer on-site docking.

Even if you don't boat (and don't plan to), you might still attach high value to this feature. With much tighter Environmental Protection Agency and U.S. Corps of Engineer regulations now in force, the demand for dock space will surely outpace the building of new facilities. (More on these restrictions in Chapter 6.) Future buyers may bid up the price of your property—not because they love the home, but because they are willing to pay a large premium to secure a convenient place to dock their boat.

Country Houses and Acreage

In contrast to going after rural waterfront properties, thousands of families are returning to the land. They dream of a home in the country surrounded by at least enough land to keep the neighbors well outside of shouting distance. If a creek runs through the wooded area on the property, so much the better.

Gene's Place in the Country

When author Gene GeRue (*How To Find Your Ideal Country Home*) began his search for a place in the country, he really opened his horizons. As a first step he applied the following criteria to all of the lower forty-eight states:

- ☐ Mild winters, but four seasons
- ☐ Topography of wooded hills and valleys
- ☐ Clean air and water
- ☐ Relatively affordable land prices and property taxes
- ☐ Minimal land-use regulations and government bureaucracy
- ☐ At least 20 miles out from major cities, highways, and rail traffic, yet within an hour's drive of a four-year college

After careful review, Gene narrowed his search to seven states. He contacted more than twenty Realtors and racked up 2,000 miles of driving as he canvassed various locations. All told, he inspected dozens of potential properties. How did all of this effort pay off?

"Wonderfully," says Gene, an urban burnout from California who has now settled into early retirement in the Missouri Ozarks. "I got everything I wanted except the four-year college, which is two hours away. Everything else is so great that I have no regrets. In fact, because some areas are growing so rapidly, I am glad I landed further out in the boondocks than I planned. Had I bought closer to Springfield, I might now find my tranquillity destroyed by the growth of Branson, and the bumper-to-bumper summer traffic."

Farmhouses in Round Top

With her youngest daughter out the door and off to college, Lenore Winston set off to ruralize her dream for a farmhouse and acreage. But after buying a house on 30 acres, she found another farmhouse she liked better. So what did Lenore do? She bought and moved the farmhouse to her property in the trendy area of Round Top, Texas. Although it's now restored and serving as a combination second home and bed and breakfast, Lenore and her physician husband, Barry, plan to make it their permanent home after retirement.

Buying in a rural area now for later retirement is one trend the Winstons are participating in. In addition, they have joined the house-moving trend. With a resident population of just 100, Round Top, an emerging center for artworks, antiques, and music festivals, is surrounded by green fields, the Texas Hill Country, and old farmhouses—many built more than 100 years ago by the German immigrants who originally settled the area.

Increasingly, weekenders, second-home buyers, and retirees from nearby Houston, as well as other areas as far as Connecticut and Florida, are buying the old and often abandoned acreage and dwellings. As it turns out, frequently they can buy, move closer to Round Top, and restore these farmhouses for substantially less than the cost of building new. Plus, as Dick and Sherry Peck, two recent mover-restorers point out, "The charm of an old house is something that cannot be built into a new one. We desire a slower-paced life, the rocking chair flavor, the porches—all of a bygone era. The kids are married, I'll [Sherry] be 52 this year. Living in Round Top, we'll be able to walk to the post office, the bank, and to neighbors for visiting."

Trends versus Trendiness

Quite likely, Gene GeRue wouldn't care for the "trendiness" of Round Top and the "gentleman farmers" who are buying up the land. He prefers the original, local rural atmosphere and culture. But for others, Round Top offers a rural escape with culture and community, without isolation.

Of course, Round Top doesn't stand alone in this category of trendy rural escapes. If somewhat similar locales appeal to you, nearly every state has a variant of Round Top—from Ashland, Oregon, to Nashville, Indiana, to Williamsburg, Virginia, to St. Augustine, Florida—or maybe even Branson, Missouri. Places where you can live in a nearby rural locale, yet still enjoy easy access to restaurants, festivals, arts and crafts shops, and people who originate from all points east, west, north, and south.

CHAPTER 2

More Popular Locations

"It may be shaping up as another record year for vacation-home sales in beach communities in the Northeast," reports the *New York Times*. And with record sales, come record prices—not just in the Northeast, but in most beach communities from Kennebunkport to Key West, from Naples to Brownsville, from San Diego to Vancouver. Nearly everywhere, inventories are low and the lists of buyers are long. Beach areas seem to rank as the most desired places for second homes.

Americans Love Their Oceans, Bays, and Gulfs

Most Americans who can afford their choice of second and vacation homes are choosing properties on or near the coastlines. Why such popularity? Long beach walks—especially at sunrise or sunset—beach volleyball, boating, beach cookouts, sandcastles, swimming, fresh seafood restaurants, village shopping, night life, and a casual, easy-going ambiance. All of these delights combine to make seaside visits a time for relaxation, fun, and long-remembered get-togethers with friends and family.

In addition, many seaside vacation/second home destinations are noted for their championship golf courses and abundant tennis courts. Hilton Head Island, Myrtle Beach, and Padre Island are several examples. Other coastal communities offer world-class art galleries and exquisite shopping (La Jolla), casino gambling and entertainment (Atlantic City), miles of bike trails (Longboat Key), mountain hiking, hang-gliding, downhill and cross-country skiing (Vancouver–Grouse–Whistler), scuba diving (Fort Lauderdale), country music theaters (Myrtle Beach), and deep-sea fishing (Atlantic Ocean, Pacific Ocean, Gulf of Mexico, Gulf of Alaska).

At one time, most seaside vacationers were pretty much restricted to fun in the sand and surf. Today, that's no longer true. For no matter what other activities members of your family would like to enjoy, you're sure to find a good selection of coastal locations that offer something for everyone.

Price: The Great Obstacle

In many favorite coastal areas, second-home buyers flush with stock market gains, executive bonuses, and six- to seven-figure annual earnings have dramatically pushed up the prices of properties. In 1990, says sales agent Penny Day, a small cottage in Nantucket on a tiny (not waterfront) lot would have sold for $120,000. Today, a similar cottage would sell for close to $200,000. For properties that actually include a shoreline, prices upwards of $1 million are the norm. In California, Florida, Maryland, and South Carolina the story is much the same: If you want to own a lot on the ocean, gulf, or bays, prices of $500,000 or more are becoming the norm.

Affordable Alternatives

Do such high prices mean people of lesser means are excluded from coastal areas—especially waterfront properties? No. If popular coastal areas give you sticker shock, stay cool. You do have alternatives.

Partnerships

You might bring in partners (friends or family) to share ownership. Since you won't be using the property every week of the year, why not split the costs with others? Some years back when condominiums were first built in Myrtle Beach, I knew a group of ten golfing buddies who put up $3,000 each to buy a very nice $30,000 two-bedroom, two-bath unit. (This was the 1970s. So that price now seems ridiculously low.)

Partnership arrangements are explored in more detail in Chapter 11, but here I can say that my friends' agreement did work well. They remain friends to this day. Through the years, as circumstances changed, some partners sold their shares and new partners entered the agreement. Once in doesn't necessarily mean you're in for life or until the unit is sold in total.

Timeshares (Interval Ownership)

Timesharing, sometimes known as interval ownership, is another possibility that you might use to own a premier coastal location at an affordable price. In a sense, timesharing forms a partnership ownership agreement, but does so on impersonal and commercial terms.

As you probably know, under most timesharing arrangements, a developer owns or builds an apartment complex or hotel. Then, rather than sell each unit to just one family (or partnership), the developer slices ownership into as many as fifty one-week periods. In contrast to actually owning real estate, as a practical matter, many timeshare buyers merely obtain the right to occupy a unit during a specified period, for example, June 15 to June 22 every year for, say, forty years. Timesharing really dilutes the benefits of ownership, but you do get a much lower price.

Nevertheless, whatever its drawbacks, timesharing now claims more than 4 million owners worldwide. Recently, timeshare sales have topped $6 billion a year. Apart from providing affordable vacationing in a specific location, timesharing attracts vacationers and second-home owners who want to participate in the now highly organized, worldwide timeshare exchange program.

Timesharing is covered in depth in Chapter 12. For now, keep in mind that through interval ownership, you may be able to enjoy a premier oceanfront property at a price that is lower than staying in a hotel or paying for the privileges and benefits of full ownership.

Areas of Less Visibility or Popularity

Keep in mind, too, that by looking in areas close to where you would most like to own, you may find an undiscovered gem. Paul Grover, a broker and part owner of a real estate firm in the Cape Cod town of Osterville, says that record high prices for waterfront homes in Osterville have eliminated many would-be buyers. Consequently, savvy shoppers are shifting their search to the nearby communities of Centerville and West Hyannisport.

In Centerville, for example, Grover reveals that "just minutes away from the village of Osterville, a two-bedroom bungalow located within a block of Craigville Beach is listed for $135,000. In West Hyannisport on an inlet of Nantucket Sound, a quaint Cape Cod beach house with views of the water is priced at $299,000. And if buyers are willing to go north on Route 28, they can find even better deals because prices there have not completely recovered from the 'soft' market of several years ago."

Price Categories

You should also be aware that not all price categories move up (or down) at the same speed. "While prices of luxury properties on the east end of Long Island have soared," reports sales-agent Tim Davis, "houses in the more moderate price ranges are holding steady, or at least increasing at a more reasonable rate." On Martha's Vineyard, Kathy Burton has noticed that "The high 300s are not moving as swiftly as anything that comes on the market under $200,000—unless the upper range is a rare or unusual waterfront property. Those sell immediately."

Various Markets

Once again, this advice holds: By comparing various locations and price ranges you can expand your possibilities. You may not only find ways to buy more for less, you might even discover properties or locations that permit you to achieve a greater number of your ownership goals. More than any other second-home market, home prices in coastal communities vary widely according to what may be subtle distinctions. I have seen $3,000,000 properties located just several blocks away from $300,000 properties.

Cottages situated on oceanfront lots frequently sell for much more than large houses right across the street. "South of the highway" or "one bridge to the bay" may add (or subtract) $50,000 to $100,000 of pricing power. So, if you run up against the problem of affordability, adjust your focus. Explore, discover, and compare. You may surprise yourself and find nearly everything you need (if not everything you want) at an attractive and manageable price.

Mountain Retreats

Running a close second to the popularity of coastal areas are mountain resorts and retreats. Booming second-home and retirement markets in North Carolina, New Mexico, and Colorado attest to that fact. Although historically popular for winter skiing, today many mountain areas are promoting recreational activities such as hiking, biking, fishing, golfing, camping, horseback riding, and rock climbing. Arts and music festivals also are increasingly common.

In Aspen, the summer calendar is enlivened with a roster of nationally prominent speakers and conferences sponsored by the Aspen Institute. Following suit, other mountain towns such as Snowmass Village, Beavercreek, Whistler, Keystone, and Big Sky also are setting up noted conferences and festivals.

The North Carolina Advantage

Among all the second-home mountain areas in the United States, more people seem to be choosing western North Carolina. Although the mountain peaks and ski slopes of the Appalachians cannot rival those of the Rockies or the Sierras, the state of North Carolina does offer many advantages such as easy accessibility from southern and East Coast population centers; scenic beauty; cool summers without severe winters; abundant golf courses; respectable universities (Duke, Wake Forest, the University of North Carolina); a rural ambiance; numerous festivals; multiple outlets for antiques, arts and crafts; whitewater rafting; oceanfront weekend visits; a good selection of lakes for boating; mountain trout streams for fishing; and relative affordability.

Compared to Aspen, Telluride, Jackson Hole, Santa Fe, and Tahoe, western North Carolina offers bargain-basement home prices. (Of course, if you want to spend $1 million or more, builders will accommodate you.) "In the trendy, upscale area of Cashiers Highlands, some premium building lots sell for as much as $150,000 to $400,000. Yet, in nearby Franklin, at a lower elevation, you can still find one- or two-acre sites bordering a trout stream for $25,000 to $30,000," says Don Hazazer of Hazy Acre Realty in Franklin. Nevertheless, as more second-home buyers discover its advantages, you can expect to soon hear that familiar refrain: "The reality is there aren't that many homes left—at least not at an affordable price," reports a discouraged looker.

Several new home developments in the Cashiers Highlands area include The Trillium and Wade Hampton. The Trillium is nestled on 700 acres that border the 1,500-acre Lake Glenville and its 26 miles of shoreline. The community consists of several village centers, town squares, and retail shops all interconnected by streets, lanes, and footpaths. In creating the Trillium, the developers were intending to bring back "neighborly" neighborhoods. For golfers, Trillium Links offers a new, rugged 6,505-yard course that wraps around grand vistas, meandering creeks, and spectacular changes in elevation. Home prices start at $225,000. Small, so-called intimate ("postage-stamp" size) homesites start at $45,000 and move up quickly.

The new Wade Hampton community also sits on 700 acres, but build-out is limited to 300 single-family homes. This development is somewhat pricier and more exclusive than Trillium. The Wade Hampton golf course was designed by Tom Fazio. *Golf Magazine* ranks it among the top 100 courses in the United States and it is acclaimed as one of the nation's best mountain courses. Surrounded by 28,000 acres of national forest, the Wade Hampton development provides residents and golfers magnificent views of Chimney Top, Whiteside, and Rock mountains.

These two developments are merely samples of the broad variety of popular areas and developments in the Jackson County area of North Carolina. In addition, nearby mountainsides, streams, and lakes offer thousands of freestanding homes and potential homesites. Yet, to a large degree, the residential growth of the area does not (yet) intrude upon its natural tranquillity and scenic beauty.

As for commercialization, forget it. "Tradition-bound and rich in the folklore of the Scottish clans that first settled here, Cashiers Highlands bears none of the marks of a tourist town," writes *Golf Magazine*. No chain retailers or chain restaurants are welcome. When, several years back, a businessman tried to construct an unobtrusive stone and wood building for use as a Burger King, the townspeople raised such a ruckus that he withdrew his plans.

What Can You Discover?

I have traveled through North Carolina dozens of times (my brother owns a home on Sugar Mountain in Banner Elk). I have lived in the neighboring states of Virginia and South Carolina. Yet, until I began writing this book, I knew next to nothing about the Cashiers Highlands area. Then, when I did make my first visit to Jackson County, I was awed and amazed. Awed because of the beauty and peaceful ambiance. Amazed as I asked myself how I could have previously missed it.

Could you be missing something similar in the Berkshires, Poconos, Adirondacks, Cascades, Catskills, Great Smokies, or some other mountain retreat? In fact, the good news is that in some of the mountain communities of the Northeast and New England, home prices have not yet fully recovered from the downturn of the last recession.

About an hour east of Pittsburgh lies the Laurel Highlands, which includes the mountain resorts of Hidden Valley and Seven Springs. In addition, the area is well stocked with cottages and homes on scenic streams and lakes. Home prices there are still quite affordable as the McCarthys of Fox Chapel recently discovered. This fiftyish couple bought a great vacation home for family getaways and get-togethers. Their find features three bedrooms, a loft, two baths, and plenty of driveway parking to accommodate the cars of six children and a myriad of guests. The price: $144,000. Still, if that price level doesn't work for you, other selections in the Hidden Valley area are available from $38,000 up to $429,000.

College Towns

"With 'lifelong learning' a boomer buzzword," writes T. J. Becker in the *Chicago Tribune*, "college towns are becoming another magnet that's attracting second-home buyers and retirees. In addition to advancing intellectual and educational interests, academic communities offer character, charm, and culture."

Having chosen to live nearly all of my adult life in college towns, I can readily appreciate all of the advantages that such towns offer. For the most part, my college communities have included Champaign-Urbana, Illinois (University of Illinois); Palo Alto, California (Stanford); Berkeley, California (University of California Berkeley); Charlottesville, Virginia (University of Virginia); Williamsburg, Virginia (College of William and Mary); and Gainesville, Florida (University of Florida). Other college towns that I like include Chapel Hill, North Carolina (University of North Carolina, Duke); Austin, Texas (University of Texas); Ann Arbor, Michigan (University of Michigan); Bloomington, Indiana (Indiana University); and Madison, Wisconsin (University of Wisconsin).

What Is a College Town?

By using the term "college town," I am referring to a city or town where campus life, college attitudes, and college activities noticeably influence the ambiance of the community. Admittedly, I can sketch only a rough standard. Austin, Texas, for example, not only is home to the University of Texas, but also serves as the state capital. Moreover, it is fast emerging as a center for technology companies. Yet, even with all the growth from government and industry this city has experienced, the university remains integral to the character of Austin.

In a sense, "college town" refers to no easily defined objective standards. To a large degree, it's the feeling the town gives. When you're in Gainesville, Champaign, Eugene, Oregon (University of Oregon), Bloomington, Madison, Charlottesville, Athens, Georgia (University of Georgia), Boulder (University of Colorado), Hanover, New Hampshire (Dartmouth), or Oxford, Mississippi (University of Mississippi), you know you're in a college town. You can just feel it.

For contrast, consider Denton, Texas, Terre Haute, Indiana, and Tallahassee, Florida. Although these cities give homes to colleges with large student enrollments, I would never advise anyone who wants a college-town ambiance to buy a home in any of these locations. They are merely cities where colleges happen to be located.

What Are the Benefits of College Towns?

What benefits should you look for in a college town? Why should you consider buying a second home in a college community—especially if you're shopping with "double or triple vision": (1) a place for rest, relaxation, and recreation; (2) a place for retirement living; and (3) a place for the kids to live while they're getting their college degrees? While no list of benefits applies equally across the board, following are some advantages that you might enjoy.

Campus Activities (Free or Low Cost)

Colleges today offer an unlimited variety of free or low cost, open-to-the-public activities, events, and speakers. During any given week, you might spend a Saturday afternoon at a tailgate party and football game; attend a play; listen to a music recital; visit a university museum or art gallery that's featuring a national touring exhibit; and participate in a political rally with leading state or national candidates or office holders.

Leaders from the Professions

You might also attend a talk by a national or international business leader. Bill Gates, for example, recently spoke at Indiana University. The University of Washington business school got Bill Gates and Warren Buffett to share their words of wisdom and experience on the same program. If you choose a college town that houses a well-recognized school of business, you can bet that during the year a dozen or more entrepreneurs, executives, and investing luminaries will be sharing their knowledge and experiences.

Should your interests run to law or other professions, you'll find similar opportunities to listen to—and sometimes meet—leading practitioners within the field. While serving on the faculty at the College of William and Mary, I met and talked with U.S. Supreme Court associate justices O'Connor, Scalia, and Kennedy. The conferences and receptions where these meetings occurred were held with little or no charge and were open to the public. Dan Rather spoke this year at the University of Florida school of journalism. Author/television/ movie satirist Michael Moore (*Roger and Me*) spoke at an event sponsored by the University of Florida department of labor and industrial relations.

Recreational Facilities

If you're up for golf, tennis, squash, or swimming, a college campus is the place to be. For that matter, name any type of recreational or exercise activity from weight-lifting to boating and chances are the college has facilities to accommodate you. To gain admission to a golf course or indoor facilities, you will probably have to pay a fee. However, compared to private golf, health, and racquet clubs of comparable quality, the costs of usage are generally quite reasonable.

At the University of California, Berkeley, for example, members of the public could buy a membership in its outstanding facility (swimming, squash, racquetball, sauna, basketball, exercise equipment of every kind) for $650 per year. At the University of Texas, with sponsorship of a faculty member, a member of the public could join its "health and racket club" for just $250 annually. At the College of William and Mary, my regular squash partner (from the community of Williamsburg) paid only $2 per visit. At the University of Florida, admission is open and without charge to outdoor swimming (Broward pool), tennis courts, squash, and racquetball.

If you find a college that excludes or restricts members of the public from using its recreational facilities, you could sign up for a class or two, pay a modest student fee, and gain privileges.

Libraries

Do you enjoy reading? Most colleges will grant library cards to members of the local community. In addition to millions of books that permit in-depth research, college libraries offer dozens (often hundreds) of specialized academic journals from every field; dozens (often hundreds) of professional magazines and journals applicable to every profession; and dozens of newspapers from around the nation and around the world. Increasingly, too, college library computers will connect you to a variety of on-line full-text information services. Unlike older, highly limited retrieval systems, the newer systems permit you to instantly locate all database articles that use any key word or term you designate.

Lifetime Learning

As T. J. Becker points out, college towns have become an important draw for people who wish to pursue "lifetime learning." With convenient access to conferences, seminars, workshops, and classes, you can enliven your intellect and interest in practically any subject from English literature to constitutional law.

Or if you're more ambitious, maybe you would like the satisfaction of gaining a graduate degree in law, business, or creative writing. Today, many colleges are reaching out to attract nontraditional students. In addition to formal programs, colleges offer many informal or nonstructured learning opportunities—everything from one-on-one talks with nationally acclaimed professors to various specialized noncredit workshops, seminars, clubs, and organizations. If, as you get older, you want to remain intellectually curious and engaged, you should definitely consider owning a home in a college town.

Restaurants, Movies, Nightlife

Do you want to escape the downside of big city living but still live in town where you can see independent and foreign films such as *Shall We Dance?* Do you want a variety of unique local and ethnic restaurants? How about quirky used bookstores as well as the chain superstores? Do you enjoy clubs that feature jazz, bluegrass, or folk music?

Although most college towns can't match Chicago, Los Angeles, Boston, or D.C., they typically do offer a much greater selection of restaurants, nightlife, theater, dance companies, movies, bookstores, coffeehouses, and similar culture than do non-college towns of comparable—or even much larger—populations. College town attitudes and demographics (middle- to upper-middle income, well-above average education, catholic tastes, eclectic individualism, national to international orientation) tend to create a local culture that fits pleasantly in between the crowded and expensive big city cornucopia and the parochial boredom of many small- to mid-size towns and cities.

What about the Living Costs in College Towns?

In welcome contrast to big cities and popular resort or vacation areas, college towns permit you to buy a nice home and pursue a full calendar of events and activities without spending the family fortune. With certain exceptions (such as Berkeley and Palo Alto), in most college towns you can buy a substantial three- or four-bedroom home for less than $200,000—sometimes much less (e.g., in Gainesville, Champaign, Bloomington, Lawrence, Kansas, Norman, Oklahoma, Williamsburg, Virginia). Also, you frequently can find condominiums and townhouses priced in the range of $60,000 to $125,000.

Groceries, restaurants, plays, movies, nightlife, and other activities also tend to fall well below the costs of major urban or vacation areas. And, as noted earlier, campus-sponsored events often are free or priced moderately. I also have found that most college towns support excellent public facilities such as libraries, parks, and schools. Overall, this fact is pretty clear: Increasingly, second-home buyers, retirees, and preretirees are finding that college towns combine relatively moderate living costs with a superb package of benefits.

Even better, many popular college towns (such as Athens, Gainesville, Boulder, Chapel Hill, Madison, Eugene, Williamsburg, Charlottesville) offer convenient access to some combination of mountains, forests, lakes, and the seashore. Choose to live in Eugene, for example, and you will enjoy not only the college town culture, but also the Pacific Ocean, the Willamette National Forest, and the Cascades.

Naturist Resorts and Communities

Do you want to stop worrying about what clothes to take, what clothes to wear? Then consider Club Paradise at Paradise Lakes or one of several hundred other naturist (nudist) communities located throughout the United States and many other countries. Growing as a popular choice for vacations, second homes, retirement homes, and year-round living, naturist resorts and residential communities typically offer affordable housing and a full complement of recreational activities.

As an example, consider Club Paradise. Located on 73 acres of beautiful subtropical lakefront property just north of Tampa, Florida, this combination resort–residential community was visited by more than 80,000 people in 1998. Activities and recreational amenities include a nightclub and lounge (Club Fred), restaurant, snack bar, boating, three swimming pools, two hot tubs, sauna, tennis courts, shuffleboard, volleyball, and children's playground. It also offers several retail shops, a beauty salon, recreational vehicle sites, and hotel and apartment rental accommodations.

You shouldn't think that R&R in naturist resorts stands for raunchy and ribald. While everyone admits that some hanky-panky occurs, in general, naturist communities maintain strict rules against lewd or lascivious conduct or appearance. They are populated by all ages from infants to retirees over 70. Residents and visitors include many families with children. "Nudists go to great lengths to be very middle-class, very normal, very nonsexual about our nudism," reports one resident. "We are trying to escape from the stigmatism that naked means sexual looseness."

For those who want to call Club Paradise home, the 350 residential properties offer a selection of single-family houses, a mobile home park, and several clusters of condominiums. Current home prices range from $49,000 up to $310,000. For other choices of naturist resorts and communities, contact either the American Association for Nude Recreation at (800) 879-6833 or the Naturist Society at (414) 231-9950.

At first, I hesitated to include this section on naturist resorts and communities. I believed this option would be of interest to very few readers. But on further investigation, I discovered that several million Americans (and millions more worldwide) favor clothing-optional beaches, resorts, and residential developments. If you were previously unaware of this housing possibility, at least now you know. For vacations, second homes, or retirement living, naturist communities offer an option that is increasingly popular.

CHAPTER 3

Comparing Locations

Would you prefer the beach or the mountains? The woods or the village? A college town? Or maybe even a naturist resort? Do you want a low maintenance condominium or an old farmhouse on acreage? A log cabin or a riverfront cottage? A tightly restricted development or a complex with kids and dogs?

As you search for the place and property that's best for you, here's a suggestion: Prepare to ask many questions. Develop an organized system for comparing locations and housing possibilities. Even when you think you know an area, step back for a moment. Detach yourself. Act as though you have just arrived from another planet.

Why take this precaution? Because it will protect you from making faulty assumptions. "It's the things we know that just aren't so," that often lead us into sloppy decision making. Partial familiarity breeds overconfidence. In addition, when second-home buyers systematically question and investigate, they often discover opportunities (and sometimes potential problems) that they would not have thought of otherwise. Here are some questions that can guide your investigations:

- What's the weather?
- What activities are available?
- Who are the people who already live in the area?
- Are there concerns for property or personal safety?
- Is the area easily accessible?
- How strong is the local economy?
- What types of properties are available?
- How high (low) is the cost of living?
- What government facilities and services are available?
- What restrictions apply?
- What about health care and other services?
- What does the future hold?

Of course, depending on your goals and priorities, you will want to answer some of these questions in more detail than others. But, remember the benefit: As you become more informed, you increase the probability that you will discover the property and location that's best for you.

A Cautionary Word about Rating Guides

Each year a variety of new books and magazine articles rate places. Such guides typically rank the "best small towns," "best places to live," "best places to retire," "lowest-cost places," "best vacation spots," "most popular places for second homes," and so on, ranking everything from ski resorts to camping areas, from golf courses to hiking trails.

While such guides can definitely help you open your horizons, don't accept their conclusions as the gospel. Every rating guide develops its own unique criteria and methods of weighing various features. Moreover, accurately collecting and interpreting the enormous volume of data from which these ratings are constructed can challenge even the most thorough and thoughtful researcher. Use "places rated" lists to give you ideas, but don't accept their facts or conclusions without question. To find the place and property that's best for you, think through your own preferences. Then, collect the facts necessary to help you make a smart decision.

What's the Weather Like?

Before you buy a second home, think carefully about the types of climate and weather patterns that you can expect. Although this advice seems obvious, a surprisingly large number of people don't really do their homework on year-round weather patterns. Nor do they adequately investigate typical variance in day-to-day, week-to-week changes.

Temperature

Some years ago, I bought a new, custom-built home in South Carolina. The couple who sold me the house had built it as their retirement dream home. Yet, they only lived in the home six months. As recent migrants from Illinois, the couple was looking forward to a four-season climate with mild winter days. They expected South Carolina's January and February temperatures to be in the 50s and 60s. But after experiencing a 15-inch snowstorm and subfreezing cold, the couple quickly decided to head further south to Naples, Florida.

This couple mistook "average" temperatures for "certain" temperatures. In point of fact, January in South Carolina can produce temperatures of 75°F or 15°F. The "average" is often reported as mid-50s, but it is subject to substantial variance. Beware of so-called averages. To further show the misleading effect of averages, would you believe that San Francisco and St. Louis both report an average annual temperature of 57°F? But, of course, their range of temperatures differ substantially. Temperatures in San Francisco seldom drop below 40°F and seldom rise above 80°F; whereas in St. Louis, temperatures regularly fall within the much wider range of 0°F to 100°F. To really investigate temperature, look at a temperature chart that actually reveals the day-to-day, month-to-month, year-to-year ups and downs that the area experiences.

Rainfall

Vancouver, British Columbia, and Gainesville, Florida, both receive approximately 40 inches of annual rainfall. But, Vancouverites suffer through more than 100 rainy days each year, whereas Gainesville residents typically experience fewer than 12 rainy days. (By "rainy day" I mean those dreary, wet, cloud-covered days that depress the spirits.)

In Vancouver, it may rain (mist) for three or four days and yet accumulate fewer than 2 inches. In Gainesville, the sun may shine from dawn until 3:00 P.M. Then a cloudburst lets go a 2-inch downpour, and by 5:00 P.M. the sun is shining once again. So, look beyond "average" annual rainfall. Far more important to consider is when and how often the rain falls and clouds block the sun.

Fog, Humidity, Snowfall, Winds

Regardless of whether we're talking temperatures, rainfall, fog, humidity, days of sunshine, snowfall, or wind frequency and velocity, it pays to look beyond averages, totals, and other potentially misleading aggregate measures. Instead, think of the specific weather patterns that will exist day to day, week to week, season to season. Think how many days a year you'll be able to enjoy being outdoors.

On paper, the weather of Dallas, Texas can look reasonably attractive. In reality Dallas has the worst weather of any sunbelt place I have ever lived. Unbearable heat during the summer, unpleasantly chilly winters, bone-rattling thunderstorms, floods, hail storms, ice storms, frequent wind speeds in excess of 20–25 miles per hour. My guess is that Dallas enjoys fewer than 50 days each year where being outside is a pleasure to cherish.

In contrast, the number of beautiful "outside days" in Florida approaches 300 or more (perhaps 275 for those who absolutely cannot stand humidity). I don't mean to offend my many Texan friends who wouldn't live anywhere else, but I do want to emphasize the importance of discovering in detail how the year-round weather of your chosen location will affect your ability to emotionally and physically enjoy the area.

Microclimates

Although most people tend to think that weather patterns apply equally across an area, that's not always true. Whenever you are located near a valley, deserts, mountains, large lakes, bays, oceans, or even tall buildings, the weather (wind, sunshine, temperature, fog, rain) can vary substantially over distances of just a few miles. (Sometimes a distance of even a half mile can make a noticeable difference.)

Consider the San Francisco Bay Area. Within the city, Cow Hollow and the Marina District enjoy more sunshine and less fog than other neighborhoods located near the zoo and the Pacific Ocean. Go several miles east across the Bay Bridge and the temperatures jump 10°F with the fog seldom creating a problem. Go a few more miles east through the Caldecott tunnel and you'll experience less rain, less fog, and even warmer temperatures.

Somewhat similarly, when it's near freezing in Boston, 45 miles to the southeast on Cape Cod, golfers may be out playing thirty-six holes. In the Los Angeles area, Ventura residents breathe (relatively) clean air. Yet, closer to the desert in Palmdale, residents suffer as many as 150 smog-day warnings a year.

Finding Out If You Will Like the Weather

To most buyers of second homes, weather patterns set the stage for pleasant living and outdoor activities. Make sure you get the specific facts. Be wary of the hype put forth by the local government's department of tourism or the local Chamber of Commerce. (I once read a travel brochure from Edmonton, Alberta, that described its brutal weather in terms so glowing that it would have put a politician's spin-meister to shame.)

Look for actual day-to-day recorded patterns. Pay attention to potential variance and rapid changes. (Within twenty-four hours Boulder, Colorado, temperatures can drop 50 degrees with wind speeds hitting 80 miles per hour or more.) Also, stay on the lookout for locations with microclimates. For better or worse, the microclimate weather can deviate significantly from the weather pattern of the general area.

Experience Counts

When possible, before you buy a second home visit the area at different times of the year. Nothing substitutes for experience. You won't really know whether you can stand the wet chilly winters, high winds, or summer humidity until you feel it for yourself. (In fact, many of Florida's immigrant retirees from the northern states are now buying second homes in North Carolina so they can escape the July–August Florida heat.)

Having previously visited Florida only in the snowbird season, these retirees didn't anticipate how uncomfortable they would feel during the summers. On the other hand, some North Carolina retirees now find that although they enjoy the summer mountain climate, they greatly dislike navigating icy mountain roads during the winter. No location enjoys perfect weather, but imperfection need not spoil your enjoyment. Just learn ahead of time what to expect, and what trade-offs you're most willing to live with.

What Activities Are Available?

Generally, the more activities an area offers, the more you, your family, and your friends will appreciate your second home. Even if you are one of those obsessed golfers who cares nothing about any other activity, it can still pay you to take note of any activity that makes the area desirable.

Who knows what the future holds? Maybe your interest or your health will change. If you plan to rent out or exchange your home, a wider variety of things to do will certainly add to your second home's marketability. And don't forget friends and family members. How will they spend their time while you're on the links struggling to break 80?

Outdoor Life

As a starting point, you may want to inventory an area's outdoor activities. I would suggest investigating several characteristics: (1) availability, (2) quantity and quality, and (3) convenience.

Availability

Find out if the area offers any of the following activities and note others not listed:

☐ Golf   ☐ Horseback riding
☐ Tennis   ☐ Fishing

☐ Swimming	☐ Camping
☐ Parks	☐ Hiking
☐ Reserves (forest, animal)	☐ Walking
☐ Boating	☐ Running
☐ Rafting	☐ Hunting
☐ Rock climbing	☐ Birding
☐ Biking	☐ Skiing
☐ Tourist attraction	☐ Wildlife sanctuaries
☐ Recreation areas	☐ Hang gliding
☐ Beaches	☐ Mountain trails
☐ Rodeos	☐ Racing (dogs, horses, cars)
☐ _____	☐ _____
☐ _____	☐ _____
☐ _____	☐ _____

I suspect that in some parts of the country (and world), people find pleasure in outdoor leisure pursuits that I have never heard of—but may be quite fun. You might find them fun, too. So, give your inquiries free rein. Put some new excitement in your life. What other kinds of outdoor activities can you discover?

Quantity and Quality

Beyond mere availability, you will want to rate the outdoor activities you discover in terms of quantity and quality. Must you play the same crabgrass-ridden golf course every day? Or can you choose from a dozen or more top-flight courses? How many beaches can you find? Are they wide, beautiful, secluded white-sand beaches? Or must you go to a narrow, rocky beach that's crowded with blaring boom boxes and littered with beer cans and hot dog wrappers? How many ski runs? How many high-speed lifts? Can you ski 40 inches of powder? Or will you find (at best) a surface coating of icy slush?

No matter what outdoor sports or recreational activities an area offers, identify how many and what quality. Whether it's fishing, hunting, skiing, boating, swimming, surfing, golfing, hiking, or even walking, look for variety. Look for a level of quality and interest that will please the most die-hard aficionados. Virtually any area can boast about its wide-ranging variety of outdoor activities, but "available" doesn't necessarily translate into "enjoyable."

Again, I caution you to make sure you learn how frequently the weather permits enjoyable use. I know of one area that claims 300 golfing days a year. While it's true that on 300 days of the year some crazed golfer shows up to play, it's also true that *most* people don't consider days with 35 mile per hour winds, rainstorms, or 45°F or 100°F temperatures as good golfing days. (If those types of days were subtracted from the hyped-up 300 days, the true total would fall below 100 days.)

Certainly, "more" is not always better than "less," but by uncovering all of the choices, you'll be able to make a better decision.

Convenience

In terms of convenience, you might rate various activities according to how long it will take you to drive (bus, walk, bike) from your second home to the desired location:

- ☐ Fewer than thirty minutes
- ☐ Thirty to sixty minutes
- ☐ Day trip
- ☐ Weekend trip

Don't forget to measure travel times during those periods when you're most likely to travel. As you are probably aware, traffic congestion during peak hours can create unhappy delays. Trying to "get off the island" at 5:00 P.M. can get you stuck in traffic for an hour or more.

Also, another potential hassle you should check pertains to tee times, court times, and other activities that require scheduling. How difficult? How much wait? How long are the lines? Are the campsites fully booked three months in advance? Must you arrive by 9:00 A.M. on Sundays to stake out a good spot on the beach?

Should you buy a second home in an area where crowds and congestion take away a good part of your enjoyment? Or would you prefer a less popular, but perhaps a more relaxing and accommodating environment?

Cultural Life

Increasingly, second-home buyers are choosing locations that offer a good variety of cultural activities. They're looking for touring artists and exhibits, dance companies, theater companies, art festivals, galleries (photo, painting, and sculptures), institutes, conferences, speakers, and author readings and signings. Charity events, street performers, Fourth of July extravaganzas, and New Year's Eve gala celebrations also add cultural interest and excitement to an area.

What else? Virtually any activity or gathering that involves community sponsorships and participation. "The Run for the Cure" in Aspen brings out nearly 2,000 residents and visitors to raise money for breast cancer research. But it's also a fun time with music, breakfast, a 5K run or walk, awards, and an evening barbecue and dance. A true community spirit runs through the event.

How much culture would you like? What cultural events, activities, and facilities does your second-home location offer?

Restaurants, Entertainment, and Music

Does a tour of area restaurants treat you to the food of nearly every country of the world? Or do chain restaurants and fast-food franchises dominate the commercial strips? Read through the arts and entertainment section of the metro newspaper, or sometimes even better—when available—collect a sampling of those smaller, alternative newspapers that you can pick up free at coffeehouses, bookstores, and corner newsracks. Papers like the *Montecito Journal*, the *Del Mar Times*, the *Aspen Times, West Coast Woman*, the *Pelican Press*, the *Longboat Observer*, *Martha's Vineyard News*, or the *Islander* are some examples. By surveying these types of alternative papers, you can generally get a good sense of an area's restaurant, entertainment, and nightlife scene. (The local library may even carry back issues.) These papers also will feature movie listings and reviews, often giving notable attention to independent and foreign films and the theaters (or other outlets) that exhibit them.

You are also likely to find in these types of papers, gallery showings, museum exhibits, garden tours, live theater listings and reviews, film series and festivals, arts and crafts fairs, dog shows, ballet, casino gaming, and even psychic readings and acupuncture clinics. By reviewing these and other sources of information (yellow pages, visitor centers, real estate firms, personal exploration, conversations with residents and vacationers), you can develop the knowledge necessary to rate and compare areas on the basis of "things to do," "places to eat," "where to go," and "what's happening."

Shopping

In some areas, you can experience a full range of conveniently located shopping options. But if you choose the North Michigan woods or North Captiva Island, you'll have to drive or ferry thirty minutes or more just to go to a well-stocked grocery.

What's included in the term "full-range" shopping? Here are some examples:

- *Routine shopping*: groceries, hardware, bookstores, pharmacies, and everyday clothing.
- *Bargain shopping*: discount malls, factory outlets, and clearance stores.
- *Fun shopping*: antique shops, art and photo galleries, souvenir stores, specialty clothing, sports, and hobby shops.
- *Upscale shopping*: stores that feature designer labels, galleries that feature high-priced originals and prints.
- *Specialty shopping*: wine and cheese stores, tobacconists, bakeries, international newsstands, coffee and tea outlets (e.g., Starbucks, Barney's).

Which of these types of shopping options are located conveniently within the area(s) you're rating? Where does it fall between "full range" and "virtually isolated"?

What Services Are Available?

As with outdoor, cultural, entertainment, and shopping options, the variety and quality of services among areas can differ markedly. More specifically, you might especially want to investigate health care, government services, and private services.

Health Care

Perhaps most important to look into fully is health care. If you (or members of your family) may need continuing or acute treatment for health problems, verify whether the area offers appropriate specialists, technology, and facilities. Or, less desirably, does the area offer helicopter transport for medical emergencies?

You might also want to verify that your health insurance plan will offer adequate coverage. Some plans limit "out of area" or out-of-country coverage in both reimbursement amounts and eligible treatments.

Government Services

If you are used to urban living, you may take government services for granted. But in many areas, government does not provide such ordinary basics as sewer and water, police and fire protection, and trash pickup. In addition, some of the services government does provide (schools, libraries, parks, snow removal) may fall far below the quality that you would find reasonable and necessary.

On the other hand, some communities offer high quality and a great variety of services and activities such as recreation centers, public transportation, swimming pools, organized leagues (soccer, baseball, basketball) for kids, parks and outdoor entertainment. When you buy a second home, you will pay property taxes, so it's wise to ask beforehand: What services will government provide (quantity and quality) to justify its taxes?

Private Services

Granted, private services seldom rate as critically important as health care or government services. Yet, as a matter of convenience, you are better off with a good selection. By private services, for example, I refer to the following:

- Dry cleaners
- Tax specialist/financial planners
- Hair stylist (barbers and beauty shops)
- Spas
- Health and fitness clubs
- Racket clubs
- Taxi or limousine service
- Banking/financial service
- Auto repair
- Private airports
- Catering/party planners
- Secretarial
- Computer repair
- Appliance repair
- Yard care and landscaping
- Home repair
- Telecommunications

What services do you typically require? Which ones would you want available or on call? What services would you add to the list? How would you rate the area that you're considering?

What's the Cost of Living Like?

Perhaps you're a member of that fortunate minority who makes buying decisions without concern for costs. On the other hand, if you're like the rest of us, you'll probably want to compare and rate areas according to their costs of living.

Housing Costs

As noted previously, high housing prices (and, correspondingly, high property taxes) can sometimes eliminate areas as possibilities. However, don't prematurely dismiss an area as too expensive. By applying one or more buying and financing techniques that can stretch affordability, you may pleasantly surprise yourself. (In later chapters I show you how to buy at a bargain price; buy with partners; buy a "fixer" and create instant appreciation; and buy a property that can help pay for itself through rentals and exchanges.)

Housing Types and Price Ranges

Remember that the price you pay for housing may vary considerably depending on its location, neighborhood, size, and amenities. A gulf-front villa on Siesta Key (Sarasota) may carry a price tag of up to $1.5 million. But if you go 8 to 10 miles west, you can buy a mobile home in a reasonably nice park for $15,000. If you insist on gulf-front, you can find a one-bedroom or studio condominium for less than $100,000.

I recently checked out a fantastic-looking duplex with two 1,800-square-foot units located just a stone's throw from Siesta Village and the Gulf of Mexico. Although at $375,000, the price tag wasn't cheap, the purchaser will be able to generate somewhere between $20,000 and $36,000 a year in rental income from the property (depending on the amount of personal use). After a $50,000 to $100,000 down payment, the property would almost pay for itself. If rent escalations continue in the area as they have in the past, after five years, this duplex may even yield a positive cash flow.

Housing Needs versus Housing Wants

Do you really need as much house as you want? How much time will you spend within the home? Should you really pay for those extra bedrooms that will only be used on rare occasions when the kids or friends visit? Moreover, can't the kids just sleep on the floor? Sure a large garage and extra rooms for storage are great. But it's usually cheaper to place the stuff in a miniwarehouse.

I know from experience that it's easy to confuse want for need. It's easy to slip into saying, "Well, we might get by with three bedrooms, but we really need four." Back up. Reevaluate *need*. Could you live happily with one or two? When faced with trading off first-choice location for home size, think for a moment. Could you make do with less? I once downsized from 3,200 square feet of living space to 1,700 square feet. As it turned out, I enjoyed living in the smaller house more than the larger one. Maybe you would, too.

Townhomes and Condominiums

If you're like me, you strongly prefer a single-family house over town-homes and condominiums. But when I lived in Williamsburg, Virginia, I chose to live in a townhouse and enjoyed it very much. I feared that noise could come through the adjoining walls (which I detest). Fortunately, I never heard my neighbors. I also appreciated the enhanced security of the unit during my frequent travels and the "no-worry, no work," yard care and maintenance.

Although many condo and townhouse complexes do suffer from noise, poor upkeep, financial mismanagement, contemptuous busybodies, and absurd rules, many others do not share this unhappy fate. So don't summarily dismiss this lower-cost housing option without inquiry. You may be able to find a complex to enjoy as much as I did my townhome in Williamsburg.

Routine Necessities

As another cost of living concern, make sure your area investigation includes price comparisons for routine necessities such as groceries, gasoline, utilities, pharmacy items, household cleaning and maintenance, and other goods and services your family typically uses. If you discover unreasonably high prices are you willing to pay them? Although you might be able to bring many items you need with you from home, for services you will probably have to pay local prices.

I recently visited a resort/vacation area where gasoline was priced at $1.67 a gallon, auto mechanics billed at $90 an hour, and groceries cost 40 percent more than back home. As you might suspect, area merchants were protected against competition through very restrictive zoning laws and the relative isolation of the community.

Activities, Restaurants, Entertainment

In the resort location just mentioned, restaurant dinner prices (including entrée, one drink, tax, and tip) *started* at around $40 per person— although I did find one early-bird special fixed price at $25. But do you want to eat dinner before 6:00 P.M.?

There's no question that in many popular locations for second homes, leading a full life of golf, tennis, dining, theater, and nightclubbing quickly can get expensive. For a once-a-year, two-week vacation, OK. But for longer stays or more frequent visits, the high price of going out may prompt you to cocoon more than you really want to. As you inventory "things to do" and "places to go," take note of prices. Would a steady diet of activities soon trim the fat out of your bank account?

Tactics to Reduce Your Costs of Living

Would you like to boost your ability to buy a second home and enhance the quality of your life? Then reduce your costs of living. Consider these six suggestions:

1. *Never pay full retail.* Discount malls, clearance stores, promotional coupons, two-for-one sales, and closeouts now proliferate. Instead of shopping regularly for what you need, buy what you need only on those occasions when you find that prices have been slashed. Then, buy in quantity.
2. *Shop the Web.* Cutthroat competition among Web merchants is driving down the price of everything from books to computers. As of this writing, the website buy.com is offering a full range of products at wholesale cost.
3. *Never buy a new car.* New cars not only cost thousands more in price, they result in higher sales and property taxes, higher insurance premiums, and large depreciation charges. Lower maintenance and repair costs? Not necessarily. Today's higher quality cars and extended warranties mean that most vehicles will deliver more than 100,000 miles of dependable, trouble-free driving.
4. *Buy used clothing.* With the Goodwill and Salvation Army thrift shops in mind you might quickly reject this suggestion. But wait. Are you aware that most major cities now offer outlets that feature preowned (sometimes never worn) upscale clothing at prices 40 to 80 percent less than new? For example, try Boys to Men in La Jolla or Gently Owned in Atlanta.
5. *Eliminate costly habits.* Do you routinely drink with lunch or dinner? Do you smoke? Do you buy on impulse? Do you subscribe to magazines and newspapers you rarely read? Rethink your costly habits. You will not only save money, you may also save your health.
6. *Downsize your principal housing.* Friends of mine recently cut their outgo by $5,000 a month. A little over $4,000 was saved by selling their principal home for $780,000. They then took their $330,000 in equity and paid cash for another home—not quite as nice, but almost as large. In the swap, they

also gained a swimming pool, tennis court, and quicker commute to work.

Match Your Priorities to Your Spending

More than 20 million Americans say they plan to buy a second home sometime within the next ten years. But will they be able to afford the home they like in the area they prefer? Maybe, maybe not. For many it will depend on whether they rethink their spending in terms of the pleasures they value most. Remember, "You can have *anything* you want. But, you can't have *everything* you want."

In his terrific book, *How To Gain Control of Your Time and Your Life*, Alan Laiken shows readers how they can accomplish far more in their lives with less effort and anxiety. Before working on any task, he urges individuals to continually ask this simple question: "Is this the highest and best use of my time?" Likewise, before you spend your cash or your credit line, ask this question, "Is this expenditure the highest and of best use of my money?"

The true art of budgeting doesn't mean scaling back your spending per se. It means spending (and investing) in ways that advance you toward your most important goals. So, as you rate places for their cost of living, also rate yourself. That more expensive place or property you like best may actually lie within your means—if you really get control of your money and your life.

CHAPTER 4

Taking a Closer Look

Once you decide that you find an area's weather, activities, services, and cost of living attractive and affordable, you next might want to take a closer look at the types of people who populate the area and how easily you can travel to and from your second home from your primary residence. Then, when you're satisfied the place you've chosen meets all (or most) of your important buying criteria, you can start to explore the housing choices that are available and appealing to you.

Who Are These People?

"It's a pretty sad moment for Aspen—a clear sign that too many of us have forgotten who we once were, and what it was like to be kids and have fun in the sun listening to music in the great outdoors." This quote appeared in an editorial in the *Aspen Times*. The editorial went on to call some Aspen residents "mean-spirited bullies" and a "noisy coalition." What was the dispute about? Some young people wanted to camp out near the base of Buttermilk Mountain during a scheduled music festival.

The "mean-spirited" residents objected. They pressured the county commissioners to enact an ordinance that banned overnight outdoor sleeping in the area. According to the editorial, by knuckling under to politics as usual, "the commissioners pounded another nail into Aspen's community coffin, confirming that Aspen is not for you unless you are loaded with money."

Ironically, the music festival had been named, the Concert for Harmony.

Rural Idylls Lose Local Life

As the Aspen dispute illustrates, when areas become popular, they often change their character. The result may be culture clash. Longtime residents array against newcomers; the rich seek to exclude those of more moderate means; the old rail against the young; and, year-round residents and merchants express dismay as once-vibrant communities and shopping districts are left as ghost towns during the periods when the second-home owners are away.

"Colorado—the entire west," writes long-time resident and long-time critic Joanne Ditmer, "is awash with fast-growing communities; and the money pushes out the less affluent every time. . . . Even more insidious, it's creating modern ghost towns . . . communities are eroded by dozens of large second-home houses occupied by owners only a couple of weeks a year, and by timer lights all other months. It makes for a dead, unappealing town. . . ."

Across the United States, across the Atlantic Ocean to England, Ireland, France, and Italy, similar complaints are being voiced. "Second homes have become the bane of the countryside. Anywhere remotely picturesque is being overrun by city slickers," writes George Monbiot in *The Guardian* (London). "As the rich become richer and the poor become poorer, the ownership of holiday homes is becoming one of the major causes of deprivation in rural areas all over Britain. . . ."

Monbiot continues: "There are cottages in the Lake District, for example, on sale for 500,000 pounds, while the young people who would have once been their residents are living miles away in filthy B&Bs at their local authority's expense. . . . As the young are driven out, rural communities shrivel up and die. Weekenders tend not to use local shops and services; the elderly can only watch their world slipping away from them." Quoting a Colorado housing authority director, the *Christian Science Monitor* reports that "Because [resort] housing prices are not in sync with local wages and salaries, we cannot attract middle-class people to live here. Without that cornerstone of the community, we can hardly recruit police officers, firemen, teachers, and nurses."

Living in the Past?

In a newspaper feature story extolling the virtues of an up-and-coming locale for second homes, the reporter exclaims, "It is the perfect place to buy a peaceful holiday home; and it has all of the ingredients to become the next Tuscany (popularized in the bestseller, *Under the Tuscan Sun*). The only problem, estate agents warn, is that you will be dealing with locals who are living in the past."

The Local Culture

The local culture of an area consists of much more than things to do and places to go. To a large degree, it is shaped by the people: Those who tenaciously cling to local history, local attitudes, local habits, and local customs as well as those people who bring in new attitudes, new lifestyles, and, quite often, new money.

Do the areas that you are comparing display signs of culture clash? Are the recent move-ins and second-home buyers bringing about changes that you favor? Or are they adversely overwhelming the local character and culture. Is the area losing its charm, beauty, and serenity? Or is it becoming more vibrant, interesting, and culturally exciting?

Is Myrtle Beach Losing Its Innocence?

For the past twenty years, Myrtle Beach has promoted itself as family friendly. Ranking second only to Orlando as a summer destination for family vacations, Myrtle Beach has grown in popularity beyond the dreams of its most ardent boosters. Along the way, the area's 60-mile stretch of beach communities known as the Grand Strand has attracted thousands of new residents and second-home owners.

But, unfortunately for many residents, this growth is increasingly drawing in "bad elements" who are transforming Myrtle Beach from "family friendly" to "family fearful." "There's now more sin in Myrtle Beach than in the rest of South Carolina combined," says Charleston state legislator Robert Ford. "That's why businessmen from all over the world go there."

What kind of sin? Gambling, video poker machines, strip clubs, and adult entertainment. "It's become a constant fight to keep out those elements that come in and try to feed around the edges . . . to keep them from invading and becoming the dominant player," says Doug Wendel, head of a local development company. "I can see us being overrun in a hurry," warns radio talk-show host, Liz Gilland. "Our family image is getting tarnished," adds hotel owner Vernon Brake. "It's bad, but that's definitely the way it's going."

The Battle Continues

Of course, not everyone agrees that recent cultural changes in the Myrtle Beach area are bad. Some say that "boys will be boys." So, as Myrtle Beach extends its appeal as a year-round golf resort for businessmen, it must satisfy this market with a nightlife other than country music theaters. "The tourist market is not just families," says one recent arrival, "it's adults, too."

"I would challenge anyone," argues Tyler Greenwell, director of marketing for Casino Ventures, "to look at our customers and tell me they are corrosive people." Well, corrosive or not, the battle continues. In the courts, in zoning board hearings, in the state legislature, and in the hearts and minds of residents and visitors, the opposing forces fight to shape the future of Myrtle Beach.

As you compare resort and vacation areas, keep your eyes and ears open to detect any existing or emerging culture clash. The preceding examples clearly show that a changing population of residents and homebuyers often brings about some combination of "the good, the bad, and the ugly." But beyond these specific types of "people" problems, you can learn a great deal about an area by looking into its total demographics and psychographics.

The Demographics

Demographics refer to "people" characteristics such as age, education, family size, type of household, occupation, ethnicity, religion, income, wealth, geographic origin, and many other personal attributes. By paying attention to demographics, you can answer the questions: Who's living in the area? Who's moving in? Once you learn the "who" of an area, you can decide whether they fit the profile of people with whom you would most like to become neighbors and friends.

Compatibility, Not Bigotry

In an age of hypersensitivity, I should emphasize that I am not advocating racial or religious bigotry. It is a fact of life, however, that most people choose to live in areas (or housing developments) where selected demographic characteristics predominate. For example, in Prince George's County (Washington, D.C., area), many affluent black families choose to live in predominately black subdivisions where housing prices start at $250,000 to $300,000. For the most part, their family incomes top $100,000 per year. Throughout the sunbelt, age-restricted 55-plus communities are growing in popularity. In Miami Beach, many Jewish retirees and second-home owners prefer condominiums occupied by a heavy percentage of Jewish people.

Likewise, South Beach attracts a high percentage of gays. Many South Americans buy second homes in Miami because of its large Hispanic population and the ease with which they can shop and dine without the need to speak English. If you have kids ages 7 and 9, chances are that you will choose an area that caters more to families with children than to the plus-65 set (such as Naples, Florida). It is not bigotry to notice that demographics matter.

Censorship of Real Estate Agents

Although our First Amendment guarantees free speech, courts and government regulators have written real estate agents out of the Constitution. As a result, agents face constant threats of lawsuits, fines, and license revocation if they answer questions that pertain to area demographics. (In fact, agents are even prohibited from using language such as "walk-in closet," "exclusive neighborhood," "walking distance to schools," "master bedroom," and dozens of other everyday words and terms.)

So, if you would like to know the demographic profile of an area (or neighborhood), your realty agent may not be willing to provide you this information. Don't worry, though. In typical government irrationality, various federal, state, and local government agencies (especially the U.S. Census Bureau) publish volumes of demographic data. You can find it at thousands of government-operated public and college libraries. Good real estate agents and reference librarians are able to direct you to relevant reports and publications.

Other Sources of Demographic Data

In addition to government reports, demographic data comprise the stock in trade of marketing research firms. In fact, many firms now post such information on their websites, or they will issue specifically requested reports that you can download for a nominal charge. Of course, nearly all of us use word-of-mouth and observation to draw conclusions. However, try not to rely on merely superficial and casual inquiry.

Instead, walk and talk the areas, neighborhoods, and developments that you are considering. Decide on the demographic characteristics that are important to you (if any). Then ask questions. Keep a sharp eye. Take notice of whether you find the area demographically compatible.

The Psychographics

In addition to demographics, a population can be defined by its psychographics. The compatibility of people depends on more than age, income, education, wealth, ethnicity, and other personal characteristics. It also relates to their attitudes, values, and lifestyles. Within an area, are you more likely to find a bridge group or poker party? Do residents most often think of sports as Monday night football with a six-pack and chips? Or a 10-mile Sunday morning run followed by an outdoor café brunch and the *New York Times*?

Do you see too many people hot-dogging their eardrum-bursting Trans Ams, Firebirds, and Harleys? Can you hear rap music playing six blocks away from its source? Do people leave the beach and parks littered with soda cups and fast-food wrappers? Does the area attract people who demand a good selection of tattoo parlors and body piercing shops? I can think of more than a few resort and vacation areas around the country that display many of the undesirable behavior patterns I've just alluded to. (Out of fear of retribution from their boards of realtors and chambers of commerce, they shall remain unidentified.)

Yet, it's not just downscale areas that can be affected. During a period of time that I lived in Virginia, I maintained a second residence in the upscale area of D.C. known as Georgetown. On Friday and Saturday nights, though, Wisconsin Avenue, the major commercial street, became notorious for "wilding." Hundreds of rude, offensive, and sometimes felonious teenagers would swoop in and disrupt life for all residents, diners, shoppers, and merchants.

In upscale Santa Fe, New Mexico, for a while on Saturday nights, punkers dressed in black would overtake the town square, the prime area of town that is surrounded by art galleries and restaurants. Although I believe the Santa Fe and Georgetown problems now have been remedied, they do illustrate an important point: Don't assume that tranquility reigns. Don't assume that upscale areas and high housing prices cannot or do not attract some people who choose to behave contrary to acceptable community standards.

The Good, the Bad, and the Ugly

If you have been visiting your second-home location for a number of years, you probably know as much as you want to know about the area's population (residents and visitors). On the other hand, if you have "opened your horizons," compare areas with care. Don't rush to buy just because you've fallen in love with a specific property, an area's beauty, or the many things to do.

Before signing on the dotted line, investigate demographics and psychographics. Who are the people? What are they like? Will you be able to find friends and join groups with whom you share interests, activities, and values? Are there elements within the community who generate disharmony? (Within homeowner associations, these disruptive persons are often called "condo commandos"—people who perpetually tell others how they must live.)

I once almost bought a home on a lake that I would have much regretted. During midweek when I first viewed the property, boating activities were relatively limited and tranquil. But on weekends, this public-access lake attracted assorted motorboat speed demons and jet skiers. These rude and offensive people competed among each other as to who could drink the most beer, create the most engine noise, and navigate most recklessly. Somewhat similarly, many people have bought what they thought would be restful vacation homes in serene mountain retreats or the backwoods. Then, they find that both their serenity and their safety are destroyed by snowmobilers.

To some degree, every location includes visitors and residents who reflect the good, the bad, and the ugly. So thoroughly check the areas that you think are appealing to see if you'll find people who are basically compatible—or frightfully annoying.

How Accessible Is the Area?

Most people say that they want to find a second home within a two- or three-hour drive of where they now live. Otherwise, longer travel times might deter many potential weekend trips—"As soon as we get there, it almost seems like we have to turn around and get ready to head back home."

Near and Far

While a maximum two- or three-hour drive might reflect the historical norm, today, many second-home buyers travel across the country and across the world. Greater distances can make sense for a variety of reasons:

- *Reality.* Obviously, if you live in Detroit or Chicago, and want year-round "fun in the sun," you won't find it within a two- or three-hour drive. Do you live in Orlando or Dallas and love mountain hiking and snow skiing? Then you're not going to find it close to home. If the climate, geography, or activities that would most appeal to you are located somewhere distant, then you shouldn't rule them out simply because they seem far away.
- *Cheap air travel.* Over-a-Saturday-night excursion fares and other cheap seats now make flying across the country affordable. For example, even without advance booking, it's often easy to find $200 round-trip fares to Florida from major cities in the north.

Also, with priceline.com and other e-fare websites, you can make last-minute travel plans at fares 50 to 80 percent off unrestricted coach fares.

- *Telecommunications.* Why limit visits to your second home to only weekend trips? Stay longer. Create an office with all of the telecommunications equipment necessary for you to work at home, yet still maintain contact with customers, clients, and coworkers. A friend of mine works full time as an auditor for a St. Paul, Minnesota, hospital. She lives in Florida and averages less than one week per month in St. Paul. A former colleague now works at Harvard, but his primary home remains in Los Angeles where his wife practices medicine.

- *Price appreciation.* If you rank investment returns highly in your list of priorities, you might profit by looking further away from home. As is shown in Chapter 7, some second-home markets offer greater opportunities for price appreciation than others. Also, some markets offer a better chance to buy at a bargain price.

- *Wealth diversification.* As noted before, real estate markets vary geographically in their potential for price swings (up and down). You decrease portfolio risk when you own property in an area other than one close to your primary residence. Consider the early 1990s property recession in New England. If you owned a home in Providence and a nearby second home at Horseneck Beach, you would have lost property value in both locations. However, if your second home had been located in Snowmass, Sugar Mountain, or Casey Key, that property's appreciation may have offset the price decline of your principal home. Portfolio diversification reduces risk by moderating losses.

- *Rental income.* Will you visit your second home only a few weeks a year? Do you plan to generate rental income with your home? Then, if you can employ a good caretaker or property management firm, you might broaden your second-home search to areas outside the three-hour driving limit. While it's usually easier to oversee a property close to home, the rental market might yield higher returns elsewhere. Also, you might consider tax-saving issues as discussed in Chapter 14. By owning a "distant" second home, you may be able to enjoy tax-deductible vacations.

- *Now and later.* Do you plan to shop for a second home with "double vision"? Are you thinking of a getaway now and a retirement home later? If so, close-by weekend trips will not necessarily top your list of screening criteria. In fact, unless concern for friends and family tethers you to a specific area, "double vision" should really encourage you to open your horizons. With so many great areas of the country (and abroad) from which to choose, exploring possibilities can really pay off. You might find nearly everything you're looking for. Plus, you can make the search itself fun and exciting.

As you can see, there's no pat answer to the question of which is better—near or far? Like most questions related to second-home buying, the right distance depends on your priorities and acceptable trade-offs. Just keep this fact in mind as you ponder this issue: By giving up easy access to your second home, you might achieve other very desirable benefits.

Transportation

Of course, ease of access is not limited to the distance you have to travel. Bridges, ferries, traffic congestion, adverse weather, construction projects, two-lane highways, and other impediments can delay (or restrict) access to your second home.

Think Bad Weather

When it snows, do the roads get cleared promptly or does the highway authority frequently close the only route(s) that lead to your property? New snow at Tahoe can mean great skiing, but it also can mean that Interstate 80 access is shut down or limited to four-wheel-drive vehicles equipped with chains. What about rain? Do access roads flood? Does the charming dirt country road that helps guarantee your peace and privacy become one huge mud hole? Will you need a monster truck to navigate the soggy terrain?

Does the area that you're rating suffer any other types of adverse weather that can delay or restrict travel? What about fog, ice storms, or strong winds—or perhaps even rock slides or mud slides? Naturally, every area of the country experiences some weather-related problems. What you need to know is whether these problems occur once in a blue moon, or with enough regularity to keep you from getting to your second home. Or, once there, can bad weather delay or restrict your travel back home?

Peak Travel Periods

Several years ago, I joined friends who live in the San Francisco Bay area for a Memorial Day weekend at their vacation home at Lake Tahoe. Although less than 200 miles (nearly all by interstate highway roads), the drive required five hours. Traffic out of the Bay area was bumper-to-bumper, stop-and-start for the first 60 or 70 miles. It took us nearly an hour just to clear the Caldecott Tunnel—and we had started the trip from their nearby East Bay home in Piedmont.

If you plan to primarily visit your second home during peak travel and vacation periods, take a test drive of the route. What on the map may look like a two- or three-hour drive can turn into four or five hours when everybody else is trying to get to the same place at the same time.

Availability of Alternate Routes

Many resort and vacation areas have just one way in and one way out. In such situations, peak travel periods can generate heavily congested traffic. But just as important, a limited route of access can create delays that arise from highway construction, bridge closures, traffic accidents, and as noted, bad weather. Do these types of delays occur frequently on the route you intend to take to your second home? Can you choose from among more or less equal alternative routes? If not, are you running any significant risk that travel to and from might prove troublesome, difficult, or perhaps practically impossible?

Alternative Common Carriers

Up to now, I have assumed that you can drive to your second home. But many owners of second homes do depend on common carriers such as ferries, trains, and planes. Are you planning to rely on any of these methods of transportation? If so, carefully review schedules and the number of alternative providers.

Some ferries, for example, run irregularly. Or they may run different (and far less convenient) schedules at late hours or during the off-seasons. Is your location served by a half-dozen or more commercial airlines? Can you get flights out every hour, or is the location served by only one carrier that frequently goes on strike or has its planes grounded for safety violations? In other words, if you must (or choose to) use common carriers, do they operate conveniently and dependably? Generally, as with highway routes, the larger the number of alternatives, the better.

Costs of Travel

What if the price of gasoline heads up to, say, $1.50 or $1.75 a gallon? Would you still find your second home affordable? Are there any other costs of driving that concern you such as tolls, parking fees, or ferry rates? Right now, heavy competition on popular airline routes and low fuel prices are making cheap seats widely available. What if these low fares disappear?

What Ifs?

By presenting a series of "what ifs?", I am not trying to worry you. Nor, of course, am I trying to discourage you from buying a second home (near or far). By pointing out the "downside," I want to provide you with a full range of issues to consider. I want to help you accurately compare your possibilities. So, examine those issues that you believe important—some of which may otherwise have escaped your notice or attention. Ignore those issues of little concern. In following this method, you can improve your ability to make a homebuying decision that will yield years of pleasure and profit. As I note throughout this book, far too many second and retirement homebuyers "fall in love" with an area after just one or two visits. But often the love doesn't last. Reality overwhelms first impressions. So, fact finding now guards against later disappointment.

Your Housing Choices

Once you've selected a resort, vacation, or retirement location that's appealing to you, it's time to discover the housing choices that are available, such as:

- Type of property
- Home size, floor plan, and features
- Type of development

Each of these important topics is discussed in later chapters, but introduced briefly here.

Type of Property

Today's second-home buyers frequently can choose from an unprecedented variety of housing types: condominiums, cooperatives, townhouses, patio homes, mobile homes, manufactured housing, and semicustom- and custom-built homes. In addition, there are log homes, kit homes, cabins, and farmhouses. Although not every location offers every type of property, most locations do provide at least four or five types of housing options.

I'm frequently asked "Which is better, a condo or a house?" There is no single answer to this question. In fact, the housing market has expanded so much that it's almost impossible to make any meaningful generalization among the types of properties. Nearly all types now come in a wide variety of sizes, price ranges, and locations. So instead of trying to make false distinctions, I suggest that you ask the following six questions:

1. Is the home secure? After you "lock and leave," will you be free of worry over break-ins and vandalism?
2. How much time and expense will be necessary to maintain the home? Some single-family houses are now built to provide ten years of maintenance-free exteriors. Some co-ops, condos, and townhouses require maintenance fees of thousands of dollars a year.

3. Is the home quiet? As mentioned previously, my Williamsburg townhouse complex and the unit where I lived were wonderfully quiet. In my current heavily treed and landscaped neighborhood of single-family homes, I am frequently annoyed by the racket of leaf blowers, lawn mowers, and chain saws. So, don't arbitrarily assume that a single-family neighborhood offers peace and quiet, nor that a complex of condos or townhouses will prove noisy. You must check the facts.

4. Does the home offer privacy? Even though they share a common wall, some patio homes are designed to provide great privacy from the eyes of neighbors and passersby. In contrast, some single-family houses are designed and sited so poorly that to obtain privacy you would have to keep your blinds closed.

5. How much time and expense will be required to maintain the yard and landscaping? Must you pay monthly fees or employ a yard service? Or, will Mother Nature take care of it herself?

6. What is the price range? Most people believe that mobile homes and condominiums cost less than single-family houses. As a general rule, yes, but that's not always the case. Likewise, manufactured housing can be bought for $25,000 to $100,000 (excluding the lot). But newer, more elaborate models sometimes carry prices approaching $300,000 to $500,000. Of course, lot location, too, counts heavily. The point is that even if you're buying on a tight budget, don't assume, "we can only afford a condo." Ask a Realtor to run a printout of all properties within your price range. Explore the market on your own. You might find a real bargain.

Home Size, Floor Plan, and Features

When you look at various homes, you'll want to compare sizes, floor plans, amenities, and site features for at least three purposes:

1. *To compare relative home values.* This topic is discussed extensively in Chapter 6. For now, keep in mind that before you decide whether a home is bargain priced or overpriced, itemize all of its strengths and weaknesses. Too often, home buyers view a house, get their hot button pressed by certain

features they love, and then buy a home without a detailed value analysis. More often than not, these buyers overpay for their properties.

2. *To examine need over love.* Similarly, if you only focus on the features you love, you may ignore the features you really need. I confess I have made this mistake. In choosing my Berkeley, California home, I was so smitten with its huge den, floor-to-ceiling windows, and magnificent views that I failed to pay attention to the home's totally ill-designed floor plan.

3. *To uncover bonus features and amenities.* When you inspect properties in detail, sometimes you can discover "hidden" or undervalued features or amenities. For example, when friends of mine began stripping paint off the woodwork in their house, they were pleasantly surprised to find beautiful mahogany. When other friends in Vancouver, British Columbia, bought their house, they didn't pay much attention to the fact it was situated on two lots. Several years later when property values shot up, they sold the house to a builder as a teardown for three times the price they had paid.

Type of Development

As a second-home buyer, you not only can choose from among various types of properties, but also from among many types of developments. Would you prefer high-rise, low-rise, or garden style? Do you want a gated community; a community that's limited to owners age 55 or over; a community that includes a full complement of amenities and recreational activities like a clubhouse, golf course(s), tennis courts, polo, pool(s), shuffleboard, and hiking, walking, and biking trails? Would you like a community that tightly restricts everything from parking to pets? Or do you prefer more of a "live and let live" development? Maybe you would like to simply "get away from the madding crowd" and buy a home that stands free of housing developments and those sometimes expensive and controlling homeowner associations.

You also might think about whether you prefer a new community that is still being built out or a more established development. In one sense, the established development gives you less risk because you can see how everything has turned out. Plus, you can determine whether the homeowners' association is operating harmoniously and within budget. With a new community, though, you will probably enjoy the latest amenities and designs. You can buy a newly constructed home that you can finish to fit your tastes and needs. You might, too, enjoy the option of picking out the lot you want. Then you can design, build, and finish your home from the ground up. (More on these topics in Chapter 12.)

For a brief tour through several dozen of the country's best second-home and retirement developments, pick up any Friday copy of the *Wall Street Journal*. As a regular pull-out section, Friday's issue includes the *Weekend Journal* that features a multipage display of ads for "Distinctive Properties and Estates." Some of these featured developments include homes priced in the low hundred-thousand-dollar range, but most fall within the range of $250,000 to $1,000,000. Overall, a quick tour like this will help open your horizons. You surely do face an amazing choice of desirable communities.

CHAPTER 5

Discover Your Best Value

As you move toward actually buying a second home, your concern will shift. Once you have selected the places and properties you find appealing, you need to decide how much you're willing to pay.

Do you want a price so low that you could "flip" the property within ninety days and still come out $25,000 ahead? Or have you set personal use and enjoyment above the goal of making money? Do you want a property that will trade well in national and international vacation exchanges? How about rental income potential? Is that source of gain (or affordability) important to you? Do you want to boost the value of your second home with repairs, renovations, and improvements? What else? You can see that, again, knowing your priorities will be important in determining how much you're willing to pay.

If you're like most buyers of second homes, you will want to accomplish a combination of financial and personal goals. The property that offers the "best value" is the one whose location, features, and amenities best match your reasons for buying. But to realistically determine best value, you must always keep your various reasons for buying in front of your emotions and impulses. Otherwise, it's easy to place too much emphasis on the feature, need, or want of the moment.

Avoid Overpaying

In the past, buyers have often paid too much for their homes because they were blinded by the dazzling home features they fell in love with and forgot to properly weigh other less desirable features. Or they lost sight of the fact that the property failed to meet one or more of their high-priority requirements. In other instances, second-home buyers have overpaid because they didn't really learn the local market. They lacked accurate information about recent sales data for truly comparable properties. Without this information, and without the ability to correctly interpret it, all buyers run the risk of overestimating a home's market value

This risk of overpaying jumps up, too, when emotional highs begin to overwhelm cool calculation. Before making an offer, smart second-home buyers avoid "falling in love" for the wrong reasons. To guard against this tendency, they comprehensively compare and contrast their chief buying motives with the advantages and disadvantages of each home they look at seriously. Then they verify the reasonableness of their bid price according to their needs and the recent selling prices of similar homes.

So, by keeping your emotions and impulses under control, you will not necessarily buy the home that can be bought at the lowest price. But, based on your itemized priorities, you will buy the home that offers you the best value.

The Ins and Outs of Valuing Homes

If you have bought and sold a number of homes in the past, you're probably familiar with property valuation. But to discover a second home that offers the best value, you should go through the appraisal process in detail. This process will help you make sure you don't overlook some property feature that can add (or subtract) value from the home—from either your personal perspective or from the perspective of market prices. In addition, when armed with knowledge of valuation, you boost your power to negotiate effectively and to arrange mortgage financing, especially if you run into appraisal problems.

Market Value versus Prices

You will want to compare the value of the homes you're looking at to the selling prices of other similar homes that have sold recently. But beware—in and of themselves, those selling prices often don't tell you everything you need to know. Sometimes a home's selling price does not equal its market value.

Say that you learn a similar home three doors down from the one you're considering sold last month for $160,000. Does this sales price provide a reliable guide to value? Maybe, maybe not. It all depends on the conditions under which that sale took place. So, before you jump to a conclusion, ask these six questions:

1. *Was the buyer an "informed buyer"?* As noted previously, second-home buyers from out of town frequently overpay because they don't take the time to learn local values.
2. *Was the seller an "informed seller"?* Likewise, on occasion, the sellers live out of state and may not even have visited their property for six months, a year, or sometimes longer. In those cases the sellers may have undervalued their property. They may have priced it according to what they paid, rather than what it's worth today.
3. *Did the sale include furniture or recreational equipment (jet ski, boat, recreational vehicle)?* Often vacation and second homes are sold "turnkey (move right in) furnished." If that's the case, you must clearly separate the value of the home from the value of the extras.
4. *Did the sellers offer favorable terms of financing?* Often older sellers like the flow of income that they receive when they carry back all or part of the buyers' purchase price. However, in a trade-off for granting the buyers favorable terms, owners are frequently able to sell at a premium price.
5. *Were the owners forced to sell quickly because of illness, death, or financial need?* If so, they may have sold at a price less than market value.

6. *Did the sale result from heavy marketing or high-pressure sales tactics?* Some builders and development companies sell vacation homes using tactics that control and coerce buyers into paying excessively inflated prices.

Under certain conditions, then, homes can sell for more (or less) than their market value. So, as a first step to deciding the price to bid for a home, verify that the recent sales prices of similar homes represent an arm's-length (i.e., no insider or special relationship advantage), no unusual pressure transaction. Verify, too, that the sales price wasn't jacked up because the sale included extras such as furniture, recreational equipment, or favorable terms of financing.

True Comparisons

Ideally, for purposes of valuing homes, the best comparable home sale (or "comp") is one that's *exactly* like the property you're looking at: same size, condition, location, amenities, views, and everything else. But, of course, unless we're talking about "peas-in-a-pod" condominium units, such exact comparability is impossible to find. And even "peas-in-a-pod" condo units differ in their building location, owner improvements, and decorating. Relying on comparable prices to guide your offering price isn't quite as simple as it first appears.

When you compare selling prices to estimate the market value of a home, you should focus on the *recent* sales prices of comparable properties. Since real estate prices move up and down—and can do so within relatively short periods of time—the best comp sales are usually those where the sales contracts were signed within the previous three months. Sales that have occurred more than 90 to 180 days in the past may not truly reflect current values. Don't put faith in stale sales data.

Detailed Questions

By guiding you through detailed questions, my goal is to show you how to ask your real estate agent smart questions. Quite often in their efforts to persuade you that you're getting a good deal, sales agents will highlight a home's favorable features, but will downplay or ignore features that compare unfavorably. You can't merely depend on the information that a real estate agent volunteers to give you. To achieve the best value, you must probe with deeper questions than most buyers would think to ask.

Were There Any Sales or Financing Concessions?

The selling price of a comparable home may have been inflated because the sellers gave up unusual concessions in their sales agreement to get a quick closing date, or perhaps they offered favorable terms of financing. Here are some examples of concessions:

- Market interest rates are at 7 percent, but the sellers carried back financing at 6 percent.
- The typical down payment required by most lenders was 25 percent, but the sellers were willing to accept 10 percent down.
- The typical down payment required by lenders was 25 percent of the purchase price, but the sellers carried back a second mortgage for 15 percent, which lowered the buyers' actual out-of-pocket cash down payment to 10 percent.
- The sellers included custom-made blinds, premium-grade appliances, and a $5,000 buyer allowance for repairs and renovations.
- At the time of sale, typical seller contribution to points and closing costs equaled 1 percent of the purchase price. In this transaction, the sellers agreed to pay five points to buy down the purchasers' mortgage interest rate.

Whenever a sales contract for a comp home has included a substantial sales or financing concession similar to those listed, you must discount its sales price accordingly. In other words, a home that sold for $160,000 with concessions or "extras thrown in" might really have a market value of only $150,000.

Ask your agent to get the specific terms of sale. Otherwise, you might erroneously conclude from the comp sales price that the house you're bidding on is worth more than it really is. By relying on misleading sales data, you could be tempted to offer too high a price for the home you're interested in.

What Was the Date of Sale?

You want to look at the *recent* sales prices of similar properties, but what is "recent"? Sometimes, sixty to ninety days or more may elapse between the date the sales contract was signed and the date the sale actually closes. Therefore, a "recent" sale may not prove to be as recent as it appears. Say the buyers and sellers of a comparable property signed their purchase contract on July 31. Then, due to various delays caused by mortgage problems and erroneous credit blemishes, the sale didn't close until November 1. If you're looking at properties in the following January or February, the sales price for that comp sale was really agreed to six or seven months ago, not the three or four months ago that the closing date seems to imply.

If during that six- or seven-month period home prices have remained stable, the longer elapsed time wouldn't matter much. On the other hand, if the market is heading up (or down), then the sales price of that comp could mislead you. So, check both the date the sales contract was signed as well as the date of closing.

How Do the Locations Differ?

You have probably heard the cliché: "What are the three most important words in real estate? Location, location, location." Unfortunately, this cliché begs the real question. Since no two homes can occupy the same space, the real question is, "How do the locations of the homes differ?" And the answer to that question requires a little more thought because the concept of location encompasses a great variety of factors—many of which aren't immediately obvious.

Where Is This House Located?

The postal address for one of my previous homes was 73 Roble Road, Berkeley, California. Now, you might think that this house is located in Berkeley, but it isn't. Because it sits well back from the street, the house is actually located in Oakland. As a result, the house does not fall under the onerous property regulations imposed by the City of Berkeley (sometimes known as the People's Republic of Berkeley). In other words, this house enjoyed a locational advantage over neighboring houses that only a careful inquiry would have revealed. You might think that such subtle differences would rarely amount to much, but they often do.

Too often in everyday speech, real estate sales agents, homebuyers, and even real estate appraisers talk about homes with a "great" location or a "poor" location. But the term "location" is a word of many meanings. It includes accessibility, demographics, government regulations, esthetics, and security. Any detail within these categories can drive a home's value up or down. Any detail can affect your ability to use and enjoy your home as you please.

Do you want your eight- and twelve-year-old grandkids to stay with you for two weeks during their Christmas vacation? Do you want to create an accessory apartment? Would you like to grab a taxi or limousine to travel to and from the airport? Do you want to avoid high property insurance rates? Do you want compatible neighbors with whom you can play cards, get together for outdoor cookouts, or go fishing? Do you want to lock up and leave your home with peace of mind? Do you want your home to appreciate? Do you want to park your recreational vehicle or boat in your driveway? Do you want to rent out your home? Would you like to participate in an international vacation exchange program?

If you answer yes to any of these questions, get the facts on the neighborhoods and developments that you are evaluating. The answers to these and a dozen other similar questions will depend on where your home is located.

What Is the Egress and Ingress Like?

Can you easily get in and out of the property? Have you ever tried to back out of a driveway onto a busy four-lane highway? Have you ever wanted to turn left into a property, but were blocked by a median? Or, perhaps, the roads leading in and out of a property may be closed or impeded during periods of bad weather or for other reasons. Or, might traffic congestion leave you blocked in the driveway for ten or fifteen minutes until some kind soul lets you out?

When a home is located on a waterway, ask what size boats can be accommodated. What is the distance and how much time does it take to get to open water? Is it relatively easy to maneuver a boat in and out of the docking space? Must the boat pass under any low bridges? If so, what's the maximum height of the rigging that will clear the bridges safely?

Is the Property Served by Various Means of Transportation?

On North Captiva Island, the vehicular traffic of residents is limited to golf carts and bicycles. No buses, no taxis, and no personal autos are permitted. (Of course, that rule applies to everyone who owns a home on the island. It doesn't matter where the home is located.) In less restrictive areas, some homes are located more conveniently than others. Is the bus stop just a few steps down to the corner? Is there a bike path that leads to the beach and the village? Is the property served by a taxi service? Are airport limousines available? Do rental car companies offer door-to-door pickup? In a few instances, homes may even provide property access to a private landing strip or helicopter pad. (Arnold Schwarzenegger turned down a second home he had wanted to buy in Santa Barbara. His neighbors-to-be raised a ruckus over his plans to travel to and from the home by helicopter.)

How Conveniently Located Is the Home?

Is the home within walking distance of parks, shopping, entertainment, recreational areas, or restaurants? If not, are these and other attractions within a few minutes drive? Or will you face the bother of winding up and down 8 miles of curvy two-lane road just to buy a gallon of milk? Sometimes isolation seems great only until you have to go somewhere. Then it becomes a chore.

What Are the Esthetics of the Neighborhood?

Before you make an offer to buy a second home, slowly drive through—or, even better, walk through—the neighborhood where you plan to buy. Are the homes well kept? Is the landscaping attractive, or at least a cut above average? Is the area perfectly quiet, or do you hear traffic noise, kids at play, televisions, radios, stereos, or other sounds? Is the neighborhood crowded with too many cars and not enough parking? Are there unsightly boats and RVs seemingly stored anywhere and everywhere?

Go through this same exercise in the neighborhoods where the comp sales have occurred. Walk the streets where these homes are located. How do they compare? Are they more (or less) attractive? More (or less) quiet? More (or less) congested? Do the neighborhoods appear equally pleasant? Or does one stand above the others?

Who Lives in the Neighborhood?

Chapter 4 presents information about the demographics (ages, family size, income, wealth, sex, ethnicity, religion) and psychographics (lifestyles, attitudes, culture, habits, activities) of general areas. Now, you may want to apply that same type of investigation to the specific neighborhoods and developments in which you're looking at homes. Are the people friendly, neighborly, and open? Or do they tend toward the private or, perhaps, even the contentious?

Are there a few people who create problems for everyone, or do the property owners all work together to enhance the attractiveness and desirability of the neighborhood (or development)? How does this development compare to others? Would your family fit in? Does it matter to you? Do the differing demographics and psychographics of various neighborhoods and developments seem to affect their respective property values?

What About Property Taxes and Government Services?

If you are moving to the countryside to escape the high property taxes of urban or resort areas, don't forget to check the availability of government and other types of services. Low taxes and outlying areas often mean limited (or nonexistent) water lines, natural gas lines, sewers, trash pickup, schools, cable TV, libraries, police, firefighting, snow clearance, home security, and other everyday services that you may have come to expect without question.

Likewise, even within urban, suburban, and resort areas, the availability of these services and the corresponding taxes or fees may differ among developments and neighborhoods. In California, for example, some new home developments are subject to Mellos Roos bond payments for infrastructure, whereas homeowners in other developments located perhaps less than a mile away may be exempt from such levies.

You're probably quite aware that school-district quality can affect home values, but the same is true for other types of services. Naturally, the worst combination of all is high property tax rates and low (or no) quality services. Before you decide on the price to pay for a property, ask how that home compares to others on the basis of the amount of tax levies and the corresponding quality and quantity of benefits to which you will be entitled.

What Government Regulations Apply to the Home?

Because of its importance in a variety of specific situations (repairs, renovations, new construction, rental agreements, insurance), this topic also appears in several later chapters. For now just remember that, depending on where it's located, a home may be subject to a myriad of government property, land, air, and water regulations. Here are just a few examples:

- *Environmental laws.* These regulations might apply to wetlands, endangered species, underground heating-oil tanks, the building or replacing of boat docks, asbestos, radon, lead paint, beach erosion and replenishment, tree removal, and leaf burning. In the hills of Los Angeles, homeowners wanted to clear dead brush from their properties because it created a fire hazard. The Environmental Protection Agency said no. The brush provided comfort to the kangaroo rat. (Fires did break out. No more homes, no more kangaroo rats.)
- *Zoning laws.* These laws primarily designate areas as agricultural, commercial, industrial, or residential. Within residential areas, the laws may set minimum lot sizes; minimum and maximum house sizes; maximum occupancy (e.g., no more than three unrelated adults); number of units per site (e.g., whether you can add a guest suite or accessory apartment); street setback, sideyard, and height restrictions; and parking regulations (e.g., no recreational vehicles on the street overnight).

- *Rent laws.* If you plan to rent out your second home, you especially want to pay attention to various state, local, and federal landlord and tenant laws. These may apply to everything from rent levels to civil rights to smoke alarms to eviction processes.
- *Building codes.* State and local building codes usually tell you what building materials you may or may not use (plumbing; electrical; heating, ventilation, and air conditioning; roofing); construction techniques; permissible types of repairs, renovations, and improvements; and standards for safety. (For example, friends of mine built a deck on their house with a wide stairway leading down to the backyard. The building code required them to install a middle handrail on the stairway that they didn't want. So, their contractor first built the steps according to code. The building inspector approved the job. Then the contractor returned and removed the handrail.)
- *Historical commissions.* From San Francisco to Annapolis, various types of federal, state, and local historical commissions have gained increasing power over an increasing number of properties and designated historical districts. If you buy a home that is subject to historical "purity" laws, beware! You may find that you can't even replace a doorknob or change the color of paint in your bedroom without permission from the historians.
- *Private government.* If you now live in a condominium, co-op, or development that's governed by a homeowners' association, you realize that this essentially private government typically has the legal authority to levy taxes, assess fines, and issue enforceable rules and regulations. These rules, restrictions, and permissions may apply to nearly everything, from parking to architectural review boards, from basketball hoops to lawn care.

How Secure Is the Neighborhood?

You will want to determine the level of safety of persons and properties in the neighborhood. Is it plagued by break-ins, robberies, or other more serious crimes? Don't assume that a gated community or guarded building eliminates your need for concern over security. Talk with neighbors-to-be. Possibly consult police reports. It's better to be safe than sorry.

What Is the Relative Danger of Natural Disaster?

Especially in many vacation and resort areas, a home's location definitely affects its exposure to dangers such as flood, hurricane, mud slide, fire, avalanche, and sinkholes. Not only can these natural disasters destroy life and property, their relative potential for damage will increase (or decrease) your property insurance rates.

Will You Own the Land?

Many mobile home parks, condominium complexes, co-ops, time-shares, townhouses, and even single-family houses are sitting on land that the homeowners themselves (either individually or collectively as a homeowners' association) do not own. Instead, the homeowners lease the land from the developer or an investor.

If you are considering a home that's built on leased land, look at the land lease very carefully: How many years remain on the lease? Does the lease grant the homeowners an option to buy the land at (or before) the end of the lease period? If so, at what price? What amount of lease payments are due annually? When and by how much can the landowner increase the rents? If you or the homeowners' association fails to make the scheduled lease payments, what legal remedies are available to the landowner?

Land leases to homeowners and homeowners' associations have spurred thousands of complaints of abuse and subsequent lawsuits. In response, many state legislatures (e.g., Hawaii, Florida, California) have enacted laws that limit rent increases and force (under certain conditions) landowners to sell the leased land to the homeowners. Nonetheless, as a rule, I would advise against buying a home that sits on leased land. Over the long run, those homes will not increase in value. In fact, as the end of the lease period begins to come into view, homes on leased land typically go down in value. In addition, leased land creates numerous other complications such as what legal liabilities for rent payments remain if the homes are destroyed by fire or other disaster.

If you do decide to buy a home that sits on leased land, make sure you fully understand the terms of the lease, your personal liabilities and restrictions, and any state and local laws that govern rent increases and purchase options. Moreover, if you buy based on government protection, first hold your finger up to the political winds. Political power usually tips toward homeowners, but that's not always the case (as mobile homeowners in California learned several years ago). Plus, few laws have ever been written that scheming lawyers couldn't find a way around, over, or under. Buying on leased land? Before you sign your name, think twice.

What Is the Size and Quality of the Site?

When comparing homes, don't forget to determine size, shape, and quality of the site. How many square feet? How much shoreline? How much golf course frontage? Does the site steeply slope up or down? Will rainwater run toward or away from the house? After a snow and ice storm will you be able to get your car safely up and down the driveway?

Is the site well landscaped? How much time and expense will the yard and landscaping require? Does the site size and landscaping provide a desirable level of privacy? Do you plan to garden or plant flowers? What is the soil composition and fertility? Does the site present any potential environmental hazards such as buried heating-oil tanks or radon?

Are You Paying for the House or the Site?

Keep in mind that when you buy a home, the lot value may typically account for 10 to 30 percent of your purchase price. Often, though, if you're buying a lot with frontage on water or a golf course, the lot value might account for 50 percent to as much as 100 percent (in the case of teardowns) of the purchase price. Likewise for neighborhoods or areas where home prices have skyrocketed. It's the lot, not the house, that accounts for the largest percentage of the property's total value.

Some years ago, I was offered the chance to buy a house that I was renting in the West Point Grey area of Vancouver, British Columbia. The offering price was $90,000. I focused on the small, one-bedroom house and concluded that the price was ridiculous. No way was this house worth $90,000. And, I was right. The *house* wasn't worth $90,000.

But the lot was worth much more. Today, it would sell for at least $500,000. This hilltop site offered spectacular views of English Bay, Grouse Mountain, and the city lights of downtown Vancouver. From that site you could walk to parks, beaches, shopping, and the University of British Columbia. The central business district and the magnificent Stanley Park could be reached within ten minutes by bus or car.

It was an absolutely world-class location. Unfortunately, at the time, I wasn't long out of a small-town, midwest college and completely inexperienced in world-class cities. I didn't comprehend that I was being asked to pay for the *site*, not the house. Don't make this same mistake. Don't pass up a well-priced property because you focus on an inferior house, rather than on a fantastic lot.

Does the Site Give You an Extra Buildable Lot?

When desirable resort, vacation, and other second-home locations get "discovered," more people with more money push lot and land prices up beyond anyone's expectation. As a result, you can sometimes profit big when you find a home that sits on buildable lots.

"Where else but in Santa Fe," Realtor Dee Treadwell asks, "could you buy a home for $285,000, later subdivide the property, sell the house for $550,000, and still have a lot to sell?" Although Dee may not realize it, you can find similar hidden values in many areas throughout North America. Sure, Santa Fe's prices rank at the high end. But whenever a house sits on two lots, you may be able to split one lot from the site and then sell the house or extra lot separately. Or, if an existing house sits across two or more lots, you can tear the house down and sell the vacant lots individually. If you buy a house that sits on several *buildable* lots, you might be looking at big *future* profits.

One key word here, though, is "buildable." Just because a house sits on a lot that's large enough to accommodate two or more newly constructed houses doesn't mean you can actually realize the site's profit potential. To reap the rewards, government zoning regulations must permit additional development. If zoning or other regulations restrict new construction, then all you've got is a house with a large lot.

The other key word is "future." As a rule—although every rule has its exceptions—you will find it tough to buy, split, and profit all within a short time frame. Usually, the extra lot provides hidden value only because a majority of home buyers and investors don't yet recognize its potential. After buying, you often must wait until the next "hot" market.

On occasion, though, sellers (usually for-sale-by-owners or owners who list with inexperienced realty agents) will underprice their homes because they fail to see the significance of two buildable lots. These types of sellers often live out of town and have not taken a recent, active interest in their property or the local market. Obviously, such underpriced homes sell quickly. You must prepare yourself to act fast. Learn to recognize value, and then, when you discover it, get your offer in without delay.

What about Sidewalks, Driveways, Fences, and Other Site Improvements?

To further evaluate the features of a site, list all of the improvements such as the driveway, fences, sidewalks, paddleball court, swimming pool, landscape timbers, and any other add-ons that enhance the site's appeal. A concrete, double-width driveway, for example, could be worth $3,000 to $6,000 more than a single-car driveway of crushed rock. Fences can cost anywhere from $500 to $5,000 or more, depending on size, quality, and condition. Sometimes, a swimming pool might add $5,000 to $25,000 to a home's value, but it can also reduce a home's value because the cost of upkeep overwhelms the benefits it provides.

No absolutes apply. You have to consider local market data and the advice of your Realtor. Like other features of a home, you want to pay attention to site improvements so you know exactly what you're getting; how these site features compare to those of other houses; and how much extra these features are worth to you.

What Is the Quality of the Views?

Some years ago, when I was looking to buy a lakefront home in Winter Park, Florida, I was amazed (and disappointed) to find that so few houses offered quality views from throughout the home. In fact, more often than not, the ill-conceived designs of the houses placed the master bedroom facing streetside. Since that time, I have looked through hundreds of so-called view houses throughout North America. Again and again, I have walked away bewildered. I have asked (yet never received a sensible answer): How could so many home builders (or architects) have started with lots that offered such wonderful potential, yet ended up with (at best) quite ordinary houses?

When you compare the asking price of a view home you're interested in with the sales prices of view homes that recently have sold, make sure you get accurate information about the true quality of their respective views. Some homes provide a drop-dead gorgeous panorama from every room. (In the San Francisco East Bay the ultimate panorama encompasses a four-bridge bay view that ranges from the San Mateo, to the Bay Bridge, to the Golden Gate, to the San Rafael. In Casey Key, Florida, some homes give a bay-to-gulf panorama. In mountain areas, panoramas are named by the noted peaks that are brought into view.) In contrast, some view homes give nothing more than a peek-a-boo glimpse of scenery from the upstairs bathroom window. Other homes may permit gorgeous views, but only from one or two rooms.

If you aren't familiar with view homes, you may not realize that view properties can command price premiums ranging from, say, $50,000 up to $500,000 or more. Given the size of those price tags, it can certainly pay to ferret out truly accurate and descriptive market information. In addition, with a persistent search, you can probably find a home with an "underpriced" view (or view potential). My persistent search for a spectacular lakefront home in Winter Park eventually turned up a house that (after some remodeling) provided picture-window lake views from eight of nine rooms. The home even displayed a western exposure for viewing beautiful sunsets.

Is the View Protected?

During a six-month stay in Chicago, I rented a 39th-floor apartment at Columbus Plaza (right next to the Hyatt Hotel at Wacker Drive and North Michigan). One great attraction of the apartment was a southeast view looking out over Grant Park and Lake Michigan. Unfortunately, three months after I had moved in, I had lost approximately 70 percent of my view. Instead, I looked out at a fast-rising 55-story office tower. Fortunately, my stay was short and I had not bought the unit.

A former colleague bought a townhouse with great views of a wooded tract of land. Within two years, the developer had clear-cut the woods and built a shopping center in their place. When my parents bought their house, the picture window framed open fields of corn (not a bad view by midwest standards). Now, they look out at a 2,000 student high school and huge, unlandscaped asphalt parking lots.

It's great to buy a home with a view, but unless that view is protected by law, deed restrictions, geography, or topography, you could lose it. Before you pay a fancy premium for a view home (or lot), verify whether it might be here today, but gone tomorrow. For one fact is certain, a home that loses its view also loses much of its appeal and its value. (When Tiger Woods bought a one-million-dollar second home in Huntington Beach, the *Los Angeles Times* made a point of emphasizing that Tiger's townhouse had "an *unblockable* ocean view.")

CHAPTER 6

Choosing Your Second Home

When you're ready to focus on the home itself, carefully inspect the outside and inside. See how the home's features match up against the features of other homes that recently have sold. Does the home that you're considering seem to offer better or worse value?

The Big Differences Between First and Second Homes

Inspecting a home that you plan to use for vacations or retirement may not seem much different from the inspection process you went through when you bought your primary home. However, there are several big differences that you should keep in mind.

Multiple Needs and Objectives

When you bought your principal home, you probably focused heavily on the personal needs of your family. In looking for a second home, you are combining objectives such as personal use, rental income, vacation exchange, property appreciation, business purposes, future retirement, or fix-up (value creation) potential. Consequently, multiple objectives require multiple viewpoints. Features that might not matter to you, might matter greatly to the rental market. Likewise, if you plan to create value through repairs, renovations, or improvements, you are wise to shift from a personal perspective to a market perspective. You may love black lacquer kitchen cabinets. You may not mind walking up two flights of stairs. But if typical homebuyers or vacationers object to such features, then you, too, should avoid them.

Unfamiliarity Breeds Mistakes

Most buyers of second homes can't estimate real estate values in their second-home market area nearly so well as they can in the neighborhoods where they now live. Don't assume that buyers in a resort, rural, or vacation market place value on housing features in the same way that similar features are valued back home. Often, second-home buyers make mistakes when they apply the "buying rules" of their previous experiences to new and different second-home buying situations.

Even if you have bought many homes, you'll profit by adopting a more diligent approach to inspecting your potential second homes. I have bought and sold many houses throughout the United States and have learned (at least) two important lessons:

1. Every market differs from all others.
2. The more you know about a home, and the more you know about the features and sales prices of other properties, the more likely you can discover the best value available (for your needs).

With those lessons in mind, the rest of this chapter provides a guide to a systematic and thorough home inspection. (Although I write as if you are evaluating a single-family house, you can apply the same basic steps to the inspection of condominiums, co-ops, townhouses, mobile homes, and other types of housing.)

What Is the Home's Exterior Like?

After completing your lot valuation, examine the exterior of the house for appearance, condition, building materials, and expense of maintenance. In addition, take note of site placement (how the house is situated on the site) and the availability of parking and exterior storage.

The Appearance

As you inspect the exterior of a home, stand back at least 50 to 100 feet. Place the home in perspective with its site and with other homes in the neighborhood. Does it fit in? Is it too large or too small? Does the architectural style give the home an appealing uniqueness, or is it a simple box design with no windows on either side? Have a half-dozen other homes in the neighborhood been built with the same design?

Can you imagine ways to enhance the home with shutters, flower boxes, a dramatic front door and entryway, new or additional windows, fresh paint, a contrasting color for trim, or accenting the design with architectural details? How well does (or could) the home's exterior distinguish it from other comparably priced homes? Do you rate its appeal as great, so-so, or awful? Start listing your possibilities for profitable improvements. (See "Can You Profitably Improve the Home?" later in this chapter.)

The Condition

To accurately evaluate the condition of a home's exterior (as well as its interior and major systems such as plumbing, electrical, heating, cooling), hire a professional home inspector. Before you make an offer, though, develop a general idea of about how much fix-up work the home might require. Be careful, too, because a home's state of disrepair may make it look much worse than it really is. Careful inspection gives you an opportunity to find a diamond in the rough that other potential buyers have rejected too quickly.

Perhaps more than any other common problem, dirt turns buyers off. Dirty windows, accumulated dirt and debris on porches, patios, and entryways, and even old and dirty doormats seem to build a wall of emotional resistance. Dirt signals that a home has not been well cared for. If you're like most second-home buyers, you'll steer clear of dirty houses.

But that decision could prove to be a costly mistake. Instead, imagine the home's appeal if it were given a top-to-bottom cleaning. Since houses with dirty exteriors frequently have unkempt yards, you may have to picture the home as if the grass were neatly cut, shrubs trimmed, and flowers blooming. Close your eyes. Now what does the house look like? If you could buy this house at a discount, would you be interested? Smart buyers view a home not just as it looks today, but as they could make it look tomorrow.

Materials and Maintenance

Each area of the country has its own types of construction materials that are popular and effective for that locale. Wood, brick, brick veneer, adobe, concrete block, stucco, and steel are possibilities. In addition, some houses are built on a pier and beam foundation; others sit on concrete slabs. Windows and roofs, too, differ. Crank-style aluminum awning windows are popular in some warmer climates, but seldom found up north. In California, you see tile roofs; in the mountains of North Carolina, that type of roof is rare.

Evaluate the Quality of Construction and Building Materials

Regardless of the specific types of construction materials used in the area, you can bet that they vary widely in costs, function, and desirability. Before shopping for your second home, talk to knowledgeable real estate agents, builders, contractors, or building supply companies to learn the differences between high-end, mid-range, and low-cost building materials. Talk with someone in the area who has recently built a new house. They've probably spent months shopping for materials. To compare homes effectively, move beyond superficial appearance. Just as you can't tell a book by its cover, you can't judge the quality of a house by its paint job.

Consider Maintenance Time, Effort, and Costs

Apart from the quality of construction materials, consider how much time, effort, and money it's going to cost to maintain the home. Growing up, I recall that every three or four years we had to scrape peeling paint with a wire brush to prepare our home for its next coat of paint. With many of today's durable paints, stains, and materials, the time between major exterior maintenance work could be ten years or more. This is certainly a feature to look for. If you are thinking about buying a condominium because you think owning a house will require too much work, that need not be the case. For people who prefer to bike, fish, or golf, rather than scrape paint or clean leaves out of gutters, a low-maintenance single-family house is one other way to go.

Site Placement

In looking at a home from the outside, note how the building is situated on the site. Are the windows positioned to bring in 10,000 watts of natural light? How about privacy from neighbors? Can you sunbathe au naturale in the backyard without prying eyes upon you? Are the sleeping areas of the house protected from street noise? How will prevailing winter winds (or summer breezes) strike the home? How will these affect your comfort and your energy bills? Does the site placement meet the standards of Feng Shui, which is important to many Chinese buyers?

Parking and Exterior Storage

Does the home offer enough storage for cars, a boat, recreational vehicle, other recreational equipment, and sporting gear? How about a carport or garage? How large? How many cars? How much extra storage space? Is there room in a crawl space under the house for safe and clean storage? Are there exterior closets? Are there any storage sheds or other outbuildings that can be used?

If the home is a condo or co-op, does the complex offer storage lockers? Does it provide a special storage or parking area for recreational vehicles and boats? Are these areas safe and adequate in size? How convenient are they to the specific unit you are evaluating? Does the complex limit the time you can park or store vehicles in common areas? What about dinner guests and overnight visitors—is there enough parking for their cars?

What Is the Interior of the Home Like?

For most homebuyers, the interior of a home is the main concern. Especially if you're thinking rest and recovery, or "cocooning," make sure your second home will live as well as it looks. In my last house, I was so taken with its wooded views, expansive windows, beamed ceilings, hardwood floors, skylights, and Jacuzzi in the master bedroom, I didn't think carefully about floor plan, internal traffic patterns, and functional efficiency. After moving in, though, I came to recognize many serious flaws in the home's design and function. The master bedroom was located directly above the den and sounds from the television came right up; the hot water heater didn't have enough capacity to fill the Jacuzzi; and access to the kitchen from the garage was quite cumbersome when carrying bags of groceries. (I might add that this house was only three years old!) Don't just fall in love with the home's appearance. Get to know how well it will serve functionally for your household.

Square Footages and Home Values

"In my building, a vintage co-op built in the 1920s," says Janice Delozier, "I've seen units just like ours listed as low as 1,700 square feet to a high of 2,300 square feet. Six hundred square feet is an entire apartment in New York." Janice is making the point that although the size of a home directly affects its value, you must interpret square-footage figures with caution. To avoid mistakes, use these three guidelines to check the figures:

1. *Watch out for measurement errors.* One of my previous homes was listed on the property tax rolls as 2,460 square feet. In fact, its size was closer to 3,200 square feet. Errors happen.

2. *Take note of inferior quality space.* The square footage of an attic that's been converted into a spare bedroom isn't worth as much as the square footage of the main house. A finished basement of 800 square feet doesn't equal an 800-square-foot second story that's fully integrated into the home. Don't just compare houses in size, but also compare the quality and livability of the finished space.

3. *Be wary of inconsistent size comparisons.* The sellers of one house may describe it as 1,980 square feet and include a converted garage that's now a den in that square-footage figure. Another owner of a similar home may describe it as 1,600 square feet and simply footnote the makeshift den as an extra, but not include its size in the quoted square footage of the house.

Used intelligently, square footage comparisons can point you toward the best values in a neighborhood. It's good to know that one home is priced at $175 per square foot (p.s.f.) and another at $145 p.s.f., but be careful. Used naively, p.s.f. can mislead you into believing you're getting a bargain when you're actually overpaying. Watch out for measurement errors. Watch out for those converted garages, finished attics, enclosed porches, and basement dens. Figure them as nice extras, but keep in mind they're often not worth as much as many sellers think they are.

Esthetics: How the House Looks, Feels, and Sounds

"I was once in a house," recalls real estate appraiser Dodge Woodson, "that made me feel as if there should have been a coffin sitting in the living room. The drapes were dark and heavy—ghastly green that gave me an eerie feeling. I don't spook easily, and I'm used to seeing a lot of houses in a lot of different conditions, but this house made me uncomfortable. If I had been a prospective buyer, I would not have been able to focus on anything but the drapes."

Dodge Woodson's reaction to this house with the "eerie dark green drapes," wouldn't have surprised Professor Mary Jasmosli of George Washington University. Mary has developed a specialty area of study she calls "environmental sensitivity." Through her research she has found that people react emotionally to the interiors (and exteriors) of homes in ways that they themselves can neither explain nor understand.

Using her knowledge, this professor has developed a side business of counseling potential homebuyers. She wants to help them choose the best possible house for their emotional makeup. Through her counseling, Mary encourages clients to describe the different kinds of surroundings where they're likely to feel happy, secure, comfortable, sad, or depressed. "Home features such as number of windows, window treatments, color schemes, views, placement of walls and doorways, room size, ceiling height, and amount of light, all hold special meaning," says Mary.

Second-Home Highs

Can you identify the features of homes that bring you up emotionally or pull you down? Do you need quiet? Do you need bright colors, a feeling of spaciousness, views of mountains, woods, or the bay? To the best of your ability, try to recall how the homes you have looked at have triggered your emotional responses—either positive or negative. Like John Denver's "rocky mountain high," you probably want your second home to lift your spirits and boost your mental well-being. So, fine-tune your awareness of these features to help you find it easier to describe homes that will give the look, feel, and emotional lift you need. When you learn to recognize the features that bring you down, isolate those features from the houses you're evaluating. Ask, "How would this house look, feel, or live if we got rid of those eerie dark green drapes or opened up a wall to eliminate a closed-in feeling?"

Getting Rid of the "Eerie Dark Green Drapes"

Let's again listen to Dodge Woodson. "The next time I entered that house, I couldn't believe the difference," he remarks. "The owners had replaced the dark green drapes with flowing white window treatments. . . . Not only was the house pretty, it appeared much larger. . . . I noticed features that I had never seen before. The house was alive with light. This experience convinced me of the power that window treatments have."

It's not just window treatments that can change the emotional appeal of a home. You can dramatically improve the look and feel of any home by changing, replacing, or removing any of its negatives. If a house you are looking at doesn't generate the warmth, brightness, or romance you want, don't hurry out of it and get back into your car. Linger a while. Isolate the source of your discomfort. Mull over ideas. Imagine how the house would look, feel, sound, or smell if you were to do any of the following:

- Put in skylights
- Remove a wall
- Eliminate the litter-box and pet odors
- Replace the worn, ugly carpeting
- Increase the size or number of windows, or add brighter, more modern window treatments
- Paint and wallpaper with different colors or textures
- Install new cabinets or appliances
- Pull out that dropped ceiling acoustical tile and create a vaulted ceiling
- Soundproof with insulated windows, shrubs, or an earth berm

Remember, little things can mean a lot. Put your imagination to work. With good ideas you can transform any home to make it more comfortable, appealing, and valuable.

Floor Plan: How the Layout of the House Works for You

Once you have moved beyond the esthetics of a house, evaluate its floor plan. Does the layout of the house offer convenience, privacy, and work efficiency?

When you first approach the main entry of the house, do you have to climb steep steps? Is there a covered area so visitors can avoid standing in the rain or snow while waiting for someone in the house to answer to their knock? If the main entrance lies below grade, does it appear that water may build up in the entrance area? As you walk in the front door, notice whether you enter immediately into a living area or if the house has a foyer. Is there an adequate-size coat closet nearby? Relative to the main entrance, where is the kitchen located? Can you walk from the entry door to other rooms of the house without passing through a third room? What about the location and size of bedrooms, baths, and closets?

Is It an Easily Livable Floor Plan?

Imagine yourself spending days and nights in the house. Where will your kids (or grandkids) play: both indoors and outdoors? Will you be able to keep an eye on them if you want to? Does the house have a "Grand Central" living room? Or is it pleasantly isolated from other home action areas?

Go into the kitchen. How long does it take the faucet to draw hot water? For purposes of work efficiency, can you step conveniently between the refrigerator, oven, stove top, and sink? Do you see adequate counter and cabinet space? How much natural and artificial light? Is there an eat-in kitchen area that separates the family members who are eating from those who are working (preparing meals, cleaning up)? Is there easy access to the kitchen from the garage or carport? Can you conveniently enter the kitchen from the parking area while carrying several bags of groceries?

On this tour to evaluate floor plan, make trips "to and fro" throughout the house as you would if you were living there. Perhaps the long walk from the kitchen to the master bedroom won't faze you on a quick walk-through. But how would you like to make that trip a dozen times a day or more? Would it then get tiresome? If you're looking at the home for retirement, are there stairs or other features that you will find troubling as you get older?

Will You Enjoy Peace and Quiet?

Noise is a potential problem within households. Will sound from your television or stereo carry into other rooms? You might even bring along a portable radio on your house inspections. Place it in various rooms. Turn up the volume. Do the walls give you enough soundproofing? Just as important, will you be able to hear neighbors or neighborhood noise from inside the house?

Although potential neighbor and neighborhood noise are especially important to note in townhouses and condominiums, single-family developments are no strangers to loud stereos, barking dogs, and engine revving. Don't assume that a neighborhood offers peace and quiet. Check it out with the sellers and talk to other people who live in the neighborhood. If you want second-home rest and relaxation, watch and listen closely for sources of potentially disturbing noise.

Condition: How Much Time, Effort, and Money the Home Will Require

Before buying a house, plan to hire a professional to inspect it. Place an inspection contingency in your written offer. Then, depending on what the inspector turns up, you can either go ahead with your purchase, renegotiate price and repair credits, or withdraw from the agreement. However, before you hire a professional inspector, closely check the physical condition of the house yourself.

For one thing, you'll need to get a general idea about the home's condition so that you can accurately compare the home to other houses that have sold recently. For another, you can use any shortcomings you initially discover to start to persuade the sellers to accept a lower price, better terms, or an escrow credit for repairs. Finally, you'll want to rule out some houses because they clearly don't fit your goals. Too many repairs could mean risk and work. Maybe you would rather avoid spending "vacation getaway time" on home improvement projects.

As you go through your preprofessional inspection, here are six items to look at: (1) plumbing, (2) heating, ventilating, and air conditioning (HVAC), (3) electrical, (4) ceilings, walls, and floor, (5) cosmetics and floor plan, and (6) quality of materials.

Plumbing

To check the working condition of the plumbing in a house, test the water pressure. Turn on a couple of baths or showers, flush the toilets, and see what happens. Is the water pressure enough to maintain the water flows? Check all the water faucets for drips. Ask whether the water heater is large enough to keep your family from taking cold showers when everybody is trying to get ready at the same time. Inspect all the pipes and shut-off valves under sinks and cabinets for any signs of leaking, rust, or corrosion. If the house has a basement or accessible crawl space, inspect the plumbing from that vantage point. What type of piping has been used (plastic, copper, galvanized steel, lead, or other)? Each of these materials has its own advantages and disadvantages, installation procedures, and building code standards. Discuss these points with your professional inspector.

Heating, Ventilating, and Air Conditioning

Depending on the season of the year you're looking at houses, you may not be able to adequately test the heating, ventilating, and air conditioning (HVAC) system of a house, but at least note the location and size of the vents. Do any rooms lack outlets? Are the vents positioned to evenly and efficiently distribute heat throughout the house? If the house (or specific rooms) lacks central heat or air conditioning (having instead floor furnaces, wall furnaces, window heat and air units), you may experience hot spots and cool areas throughout the house. Since most HVAC equipment has a limited life, ask the age of various components. An age of more than eight or ten years may point to coming problems. Check with your expert.

Electrical

As with plumbing and HVAC systems, judge the condition of an electrical system by how well it serves your needs and whether it meets modern standards of performance and safety (a judgment best made by experts). You can evaluate the home's amperage (60/100/200), voltage (115/230), whether it has circuit breakers or an old-fashioned fuse box, and the number, location, and convenience of electrical outlets, switches, and built-in light fixtures. Many older vacation homes need to be upgraded. How much will you have to spend?

Ceilings, Walls, and Floors

As you walk through a house, examine its ceilings, walls, floors and floor coverings. Note their condition, but also note any related problems. Water stains may indicate roof or plumbing leaks. Cracks may point to foundation problems. Check floors to see whether they are level. Would a marble placed in the center of the room roll swiftly to one side or the other? Don't feel as if you're out of line to pull back rugs, peek behind pictures, and look under furniture. More than a few sellers have been known to selectively place wall hangings, rugs, and furniture to hide stains, cracks, or other defects. I once pulled back a room-sized oriental rug and discovered the underlying floor was particleboard.

Cosmetics and Floor Plan

A home may not *require* redecorating, repairs, or remodeling, but it still may not look the way you want it to look. If you can't stand earth-tone carpeting or a closed-in kitchen, you're going to have to spend some time and money to bring the house within your comfort zone. But if you redecorate or remodel simply to suit your own preferences (as opposed to that of typical vacationers or homebuyers), you may not be able to make money from your improvements. On the other hand, if you plan to own the house for a number of years or rank personal goals above rental income or appreciation and profit, then you still may want to change the home to match your tastes. Just keep in mind the difference between "market appeal" and "personal" improvements. (Again, I will remark that I have probably been through hundreds of homes. My guess is that at least half of their owners have spent their improvement money unwisely.)

Quality of Materials

Check the quality of the materials used throughout a home's interior. The cost of carpeting may range from $10 per square yard up to $80 or more. Some interior flat-paneled, hollow-core doors can be bought for $10 to $15 each. Other doors that are solid wood, stained, and decoratively paneled, can cost upwards of $200 each. You can buy a set of kitchen cabinets for $1,500 or $25,000. Low-grade vinyl floor coverings run $4 per square yard; top of the line can cost $50 or more.

You can find similar large differences in quality and costs for light fixtures, wood paneling, paints, wallpapers, sinks, bathtubs, faucets, and nearly all other interior building materials. Of course, the real question is, what price should you be willing to pay for added quality?

No hard-and-fast rules apply. You must compare and contrast the advantages of higher quality with your own tastes and patterns of usage. Also consider whether you plan to rent out the home (or make it available to friends and family). What quality levels do paying vacationers expect? What is the risk of damage? Do the higher quality furnishings require more (or less) care? Does the higher quality look excessive for the price range of the home? If so, consider it a nice extra. Avoid paying an arm and a leg for overimprovements—no matter how hard the sellers or their realty agent tries to convince you otherwise. Typically, Sub-Zero appliances or top-of-the-line Wood-Mode kitchen cabinets do not add much *market value* to an $85,000 condominium unit.

Can You Profitably Improve the Home?

One day I visited twelve open houses on Siesta Key, Florida. At least six of those homes were great candidates for profitable repairs, redecorating, remodeling, or renovation. And what is true for Siesta also proves true for many other resort and vacation areas around the country and around the world.

At least two of three factors combine to create value-increasing opportunities in these popular second-home locations:

1. Such areas include a substantial percentage of second homes that are owned by older people who often live out of state or out of the country.
2. Demographically, such areas are moving upscale. They are attracting buyers who enjoy more wealth and higher incomes than many existing homeowners.
3. Since the early 1990s, the price levels for homes in these areas have climbed by 50 to 100 percent or more.

A Typical Example

As homeowners advance in age (especially owners of second homes who live primarily outside the area), they may not only lose interest in keeping their homes up-to-date, they may also lose touch with modern tastes in decorating and design. Failing health and limited finances also may help explain why the homes of these owners offer opportunities for value-creating improvements.

For example, one small Siesta Key home I looked at was priced at $189,000—absolute rock bottom for canal waterfront. If this home were redecorated, renovated, and enlarged, in today's market it could command a price of up to possibly $300,000 or more. It offered walking distance to the beach and the village, as well as easy boat access to the Gulf of Mexico.

The 80-year-old sellers lived in Winnepeg and had owned the property since the late 1970s. They had paid $55,000. Contributing to their desire to sell was the recent falling value of the Canadian dollar against the U.S. dollar. When this couple weighed their rising costs of ownership and decreasing usage against their large "windfall" gains, an immediate sale looked like their best decision. As to fixing up the home prior to putting it on the market—not realistic. The couple lacked the time, health, knowledge, and resources to take on a major home improvement project.

What's Your Preference?

Many (perhaps even most) second-home buyers don't want to buy homes that need work; they prefer move-in condition. They want their second homes to provide refuge, relaxation, and recreation. They don't want to fool around with do-it-yourself projects. They don't want to deal with surly contractors who seldom do what they're supposed to do when they are supposed to do it.

If that, too, is your preference, then skip the rest of this chapter. But, wait. Before you decide, recall the experience of Ray and Annie B. from the Introduction. "We bought our Sonoma retreat," reports Ray, "just as home prices were peaking in the area, and we sold five years later, two months before prices hit bottom. Yet, we made a $100,000 profit. Our secret? Woodpecker Haven was a fixer we renovated inside and out."

Could you use an extra $10,000, $50,000, $100,000 or more? Do you enjoy putting your creativity and imagination into high gear? Then, maybe you should consider buying a "fixer."

What Is a "Fixer"?

As the experience of the Browns shows, a fixer is any home that could look better, live better, or feel better than it does. (Remember, at the time they bought, Woodpecker Haven was only five years old.) The name of the home improvement game is profitable creativity. At the worst, to fix up a home may require you to scrape encrusted bubble-gum off floors and counters, patch holes in the roof, fight a gnarled mass of weeds and debris in the backyard, or pull out and replace rusted and obsolete kitchen and bathroom plumbing fixtures. But fixing up a home also can mean redecorating, redesigning, remodeling, expanding, or romancing the home.

To profit from fixing up a home, you don't have to get your hands dirty. Yes, "sweat equity" can pay big dividends, but so can creativity, imagination, and market research. To create value you can (1) look for houses that obviously need work; (2) focus on properties that might have hidden possibilities overlooked by most buyers; or (3) find a home that, to a certain extent, fits both descriptions. Overall, the better you can envision opportunities that other potential buyers are likely to pass up, the greater your potential for profits.

When Jeff and Nancy Mauler first saw their country home, Nancy recalls, "I wouldn't even go into it. I thought it was hideous." Eventually, though, husband Jeff prevailed. "Jeff was the one who could visualize all of this," Nancy says as she proudly displays their beautifully renovated 2,700-square-foot 1920s farm house in Reisterstown, Maryland.

How Can You Create Value?

To create value, no rules or suggestions apply to all areas, all types of homes, or all kinds of buyers. Features that one person loves, another may hate. What's popular in Santa Barbara may look odd in Key West. Today's most faddish options may become outdated tomorrow. What suits you may not appeal to the tastes and lifestyles of most people. Money spent for a remodeled bath in Bellingham may pay back $3.00 for each $1.00 invested. In Branson, returns for the same improvements may fall to 50¢ per dollar spent.

The Need to Research Your Market before Planning Improvements

With so many variables entering the value equation, profits dictate that you learn what features your future buyers or renters will pay for before you plan your improvements. When you plan to create value, don't let personal tastes or preconceived notions stand unchallenged. Instead, like smart home builders who want their homes to sell, you've got to research your market. You must develop a market-based improvement strategy.

Ask local Realtors to tell you the "turn-ons" and "turn-offs" for home shoppers. Try to identify unique niches for uncommon, yet highly desired features. Tour new home developments. Notice colors, decorating themes, floor coverings and floor plans. Discover the models, features, and amenities that are selling best. Which ones are rarely chosen? Which features are functional, rather than merely glitzy?

Visit open houses to excite your creative impulses. Look for ways that other homeowners have remodeled, redecorated, or redesigned their homes to make them more livable or more appealing. Talk to friends, relatives, or acquaintances who have previously improved their homes. Buy a boxful of those supermarket and bookstore guides with titles like *1001 Ideas To Improve Your Home*. The more creative ideas you can come up with, the better you can design a profit-generating improvement strategy.

Improvements to Consider

When shopping for a home with an eye toward creating value, corral your enthusiasms as well as your negative reactions. Don't dwell on whether you "like" or "dislike" a home. Ask yourself questions like: "Based on what we've learned from market research, can we spend $5,000 to reap a return of $15,000?" In other words, don't only judge by how well the home suits your personal tastes, judge its potential profitability. Take measure of your "can do's" such as:

- *Can you add living space by finishing off a basement, attic, patio, or porch?* Can you easily build up or out from the current house? Can you convert the garage to a den and add a carport?
- *Can you create extra storage space?* Can you bring life to dead spaces under stairways, at the end of halls, in the kitchen cabinets, under windows, or around doorways? Can you reshape or redesign existing spaces to multiply their usability or storage capacity? (The California Closet Company, whose striking ads you may have seen, built a multimillion dollar corporation simply

by redesigning existing space in closets to serve more functions.) Space costs money. Make it work more effectively and you've created value.

- *Can you redecorate to give the home a better look and feel?* Color schemes, borders, trim, window treatments, chair railings, new wallpaper, new cabinet facings, new hardware, as well as resurfacing appliances, bathtubs, and countertops can completely change the character and appeal of a house.

- *Can you bring more natural light into the house?* "The previous owners had brick all across the inside wall, so it was very dark and dreary," says John Phelps. To solve this problem Phelps spent $2,620 to tear out much of the brick and add windows on each side of the fireplace. The result was dramatic. When John and his wife put their home up for sale, "We had two offers and a backup buyer the first weekend. First impressions really sell," advises John.

  The Phelps not only got the price they wanted, but another nearby home with the exact old design sat on the market unsold for months. People will pay a premium for a bright, cheery home. Can you add windows, skylights, different window treatments (get rid of those heavy dark drapes)? Can you rip out those low ceilings? With more height, you can bring in more light as well as eliminate that closed-in feeling created by low ceilings.

- *Can you reduce noise levels within the home?* People will pay for quiet and discount heavily for noise. More home insulation, trees and shrubs, soundproof windows, caulking, and earth berms are all possible solutions.

  I recently attended a home improvements fair where one exhibitor had a boom box blasting hard rock music. But this offensive noise machine sat behind the exhibitor's product: sound-insulating windows. As people approached, the man at the exhibit closed the window. The noise disappeared. Quite an effective demonstration of how soundproof windows can muffle or eliminate outside noise.

- *Can you improve the views from the home?* Landscaping, wood fences, chainlink fences with a heavy growth of ivy, a changed window location, or an enclosed courtyard and flower garden can all serve to eliminate an unpleasant view or enhance existing views. Remember, beautiful views typically command fancy price premiums. But you don't necessarily have to have natural scenery. You can create your own.

Most people inspect and evaluate a home to discover its flaws and shortcomings. Then, they quickly reject it and move on. That's good. It leaves more opportunity for buyers who are willing to linger and think. If you would like to turn this fact to your advantage, don't complain about a home's faults. Instead, turn problems into possibilities. Generate ideas that will profitably convert negatives into positives.

Estimating Costs to Repair, Redecorate, or Remodel

When you decide to invest some time and money to repair, redecorate, or remodel the house you choose, here are three tips to keep in mind: (1) little things can mean a lot; (2) beware of hidden costs; and (3) know who will perform the work.

Little Things Can Mean a Lot

Each time you note something in or around a home that you would like to change, write it down. "When we were buying our home," recalls Shannon Grime, "we never made a list of everything we wanted to do. We just made mental notes like, 'We can repaint those rooms, retile the bath and kitchen, add a window, buy new blinds, recarpet the living room.' Since we didn't write out a complete list and then figure all the costs, we underestimated expenses by around $4,800. I guess it's true what they say, 'little things can mean a lot.'" To avoid Shannon's oversight, list each change you would like to make to a house. Go into your purchase negotiations with a good idea of your proposed repair, redecorating, and remodeling costs. Otherwise, you risk paying more than you should.

Beware of Hidden Costs

I was recently looking at a house that needed a new roof. "That's not a problem," the seller said. "You'll spend about $2,800 to replace it with a new one and we're willing to give you an escrow credit to cover it." Now the question is, "Could a buyer replace that roof for $2,800?"

Maybe, maybe not. The potential problem is that even if the roof costs $2,800 to replace, total repairs could run much more. If the sellers had played the "notice a leak, patch it, notice another leak, patch it" game for a long time, that house could require repairs for wood rot and plaster damage. But you may not be able to tell for sure until after the old roof has been removed.

To address this potential problem first anticipate whether your repairs or remodeling plans may discover hidden damages. If you decide more extensive damage is likely, then either ask the sellers to satisfactorily repair all damage or that they set up an escrow credit that will pay for contingent damages as well as basic repairs. Alternatively, ask the sellers to drop their price. If you can't pin down how much you must pay for repairs or improvements before you buy, it's not unreasonable to ask the sellers to price their house to offset these uncertainties.

Know Who Will Perform the Work

Some years ago, I gutted the kitchen in one of my homes and spent $8,000 to renovate it. I did the design, shopped for the materials, and scheduled work for all of the manual and skilled labor (electrical, cabinetry, appliance installation, and roof cuts for skylights). If, instead, I had performed the labor myself, I could have spent as little as $5,000. On the other hand, had I employed a kitchen design firm to do the full job from start to finish, the same remodeled kitchen would have cost more than $12,000.

This example illustrates the difference between do-it-yourself, self-contracting, and full-service retail cost figures. When you're talking cost estimates, keep in mind which type of figure you're referring to. Will you perform all of the labor yourself? Will you serve as general contractor? Will you delegate responsibility for the entire job to someone else? There are large differences in cost among these choices.

Caution: Before You Buy to Improve, Check the Laws and Regulations

Just because you own it, you are not free to improve your property in any way that you might like. Your right to use, occupy, repair, redecorate, remodel, renovate or even rent out your home is restricted by a tangle of federal, state, and local laws. Then, piled on top of these are private deed restrictions and homeowner association bylaws, rules, and regulations. So, don't *assume* that you can build a second story, create an accessory apartment, add a fireplace, put in an asphalt circular driveway, or lengthen your boat dock. You need to check all the applicable restrictions before you take any action.

Allan Funt's Surprise

Consider what happened to Allan Funt, popularly known for his *Candid Camera* television shows. Allan bought 1,200 acres of land near Monterey, California. He intended to construct four buildings on the site: a house, a visitor's guest house, a barn, and a stable. The California Coastal Commission (the "zoning" authority over the 1,200 acres) refused permission. Instead, the commission allowed Mr. Funt to build just two structures and ordered him to grant the public a 300-acre scenic easement through the site. To top that, the commission further specified that Funt position and landscape his home such that after dark, no passersby along the Pacific Coast highway would be able to see the home's lights.

Many Types of Regulations

Let's hope government won't regulate you to the same degree that the California Coastal Commission has regulated millions of Californians. Yet, here are some of the types of restrictions you might face concerning your second home:

- *Height restrictions*. Most homes must fit within a specified height. You may not be able to add a second or third story. In addition, even though you don't exceed the maximum height, your plans could be curtailed. Your neighbors might complain that your proposed second story will block their view, or maybe even their sunlight.
- *Side yard, front yard, and backyard setbacks*. Land-use laws typically require a home to be set back a certain distance from each

of the site's boundaries. You may not be able to extend the house, garage, or outbuildings.

- *Floor area ratios (FARs)*. These regulations limit the maximum square footage of your home. For example, say the FAR maximum is 1:3. If your lot size equals 7,500 square feet, then your house and garage could not exceed 2,500 square feet.

- *Energy conservation*. These laws may apply to anything from window size and placement to retrofitting your toilets with water-saving devices. Such restrictions might even exclude certain types of grass or landscaping that require sprinklers.

- *Architectural review boards*. These boards may regulate everything and anything that involves how your home will look to passersby; for example, roof color and composition; curtain and drapery liners; home color and building materials; driveway size, placement, and composition; and, of course, overall home design.

- *Environmental controls*. Will your plans to add on a room require you to cut down a tree? Better check the environmental restrictions. Want to add a wood-burning fireplace? It may be prohibited under a clean air restriction. Want to build a boat dock or fill in some "wetlands"? Be prepared to hire an experienced environmental lawyer. (I place "wetlands" in quotation marks because state and federal Environmental Protection Agency officials define wetland far more broadly than most property owners find reasonable. That's certainly true for the megamillionaire commodities trader Paul Tudor Jones. He served six months in jail for "wetland" offenses he allegedly committed on *his* Virginia farm.)

Forget the Rule of Law (Almost)

Throughout the Clinton impeachment hearings and trial, many who favored prosecution championed "the rule of law." More than likely, though, up to the time of this debate, few Americans knew the significance of this concept that mandates that laws shall be clearly written and applied to everyone equally and without favoritism or special treatment.

However, if your plans to renovate (or build) end up in a maze of permitting rituals and public hearings (as is often the case in resort areas), you will soon wish you could claim refuge under the rule of law. Alas, those wishes probably will not be granted.

Permissible, Prohibited, or "Let's Argue About It"

When it comes to government land-use restrictions governing things you may want to do, the general categories are: (1) permissible ("Yes, you can paint your bedroom green, as long as you're not covered by historical 'purity' regulations."); (2) prohibited ("No, you can't dump your used motor oil down the storm sewer."); and (3) maybe yes, maybe no ("Let's argue about it.").

Unfortunately, far too many property rules and regulations fall into the "let's argue about it" category. As a result, the rule of law is violated time and time again. You never know for sure how you might proceed until an assortment of disgruntled neighbors, planning agencies, development boards, review commissions, county councils, and, all too frequently, judges have had their say.

Putting Up the Ritz (Maybe)

"It's official—Sarasota's a 'Ritzy' Town—Buford Watches as His Project Gets Its Final OK," reads the headline in the *Pelican Press* on January 7, 1999. After four years of public hearings and bare-knuckle legal brawls, the Ritz-Carlton hotel was at last ready to start construction. Or was it?

Two months later (March 11, 1999), the *Pelican Press* reported another glitch for the Ritz. "Ritz-Carlton Awaits Commission Rescue—Dreams of a Ritz-Carlton hotel in downtown Sarasota were left twisting in the wind Tuesday by the city's historic preservation board."

Another article in the same issue of the *Pelican* reports the difficulties that homeowners on Phillipi Creek have faced in trying to get the creek dredged to reduce pollution and allow easier navigation. "State environmental officials have proved to be formidable obstacles in recent years," the article tells us, "often either killing projects or tying them up in endless red tape."

Home Improvements: America's Favorite Pastime

Lest you think the situation impossible, it's encouraging to note that every year millions of homeowners, building contractors, and housing developers do successfully complete building projects. The Home Depot has created a multibillion dollar business catering to do-it-yourselfers and small contractors. Home improvement has become America's favorite pastime. Through redecorating, remodeling, renovating, and restoration, homeowners are making their properties more useful, enjoyable, and valuable. In fact, you may have already joined this group in connection with your principal home.

Today, however, land-use laws and property restrictions can regulate everything from fireplaces to clotheslines, from septic systems to roofing, from landscaping and yard care to window shutters and flower boxes. Nearly everyone agrees that these rules and restrictions often boost property values. They can assure clean air and water, preservation of natural habitat, esthetic attractiveness, and safer buildings. But here's the rub: Too often, the rules trivialize their true purpose. They entangle unwilling victims in a labyrinth of meetings, bureaucracies, and public hearings. In contrast to the rule of law, outcomes sometimes depend as much on who you are, the amount of your political power (compared to your opposition), and the cleverness of your lawyer(s).

Lawyering: America's Most Costly Pastime

Before you offer to buy a second home that you plan to improve, don't just look at whether your plans are "permissible." Look at the legal process that you will have to navigate to obtain your permits. Is it simple and quick? Or, will the process weave you through an arbitrary and endless maze: A process where the outcome can be held hostage by neighbors, your homeowners' association, government agencies, or some so-called citizens group?

Although home improvement has become America's favorite pastime, lawyering and litigation have become our most costly pastime. So, don't gloss over this fact: On occasion (especially in resort and vacation areas), permitting for property improvements can prove complex, cumbersome, and costly. To assure a happy second-home experience, estimate the time and money costs for lawyering, just as you must estimate the time and money costs for the improvements themselves. Otherwise, you may end up paying for a new wing on your lawyer's house—rather than your own.

Other Regulatory Concerns

Even if you don't plan to renovate or remodel, as a precaution, verify whether the home you're buying meets all current building codes, ordinances, and restrictions. Otherwise, you unknowingly run the risk of noncompliance, and then later, if for some reason the authorities discover a violation, you could be forced to remedy it.

I once owned a rental house that had an old-fashioned 60-amp electrical system. Then current building codes specified a minimum of 100-amp service. Unfortunately, the home suffered a small fire and some of the wiring was damaged, but the building inspector wouldn't allow simply a small repair. Instead, he required me to completely rewire the house to comply with lawful standards. A $200 fire cost $2,000 to repair.

Throughout the United States, as many as 50 percent of houses and small apartment buildings may violate some neighborhood zoning ordinance, building regulation, or environmental restriction. Especially if you're buying an older home, you may not be able to avoid these kinds of properties. Just don't buy blind. And if you do discover the violations, think through the risks they might present. As the risks grow larger, your offering price should drop. If you're expected to bear the risk of noncompliance, then the sellers should discount their price to make up for it.

Never merely accept the glib response, "Oh, those regulations are never enforced." Even if that claim is true, who's to say what the future holds? A shift in the political winds can easily bring about stricter enforcement practices, or a small necessary repair might trigger a far more costly compliance remedy.

Summing Up

Chapters 5 and 6 provide a comprehensive and systematic way to inspect, compare, and evaluate properties. They can help you discover the home that offers the best value by being:

- A home that comes closest to matching your personal and financial goals.

- A home that is well priced relative to the features and recent selling prices of comparable properties.
- A home that will give you years of enjoyable use without the risk of major unpleasant surprises.

I have bought many properties throughout various parts of the country. I have worked as a market and financial consultant for developers of vacation condominiums, golf course communities, and resort hotels. Years of experience have taught me that success in real estate (home buying, home improvement, and home investment) cannot be taken for granted. Such success continually requires planning, research, and, often, creative thinking.

This point becomes even more important when you step outside the areas or types of properties where you have everyday experience. When buying a second home, walk cautiously. Push your real estate agent to really earn his or her sales commission. The more questions you ask, the better the answers you receive, the more likely your second home will make you happy as well as eventually make money for you.

CHAPTER 7

Fun Now, Profits Later

Many so-called experts claim that you should own a second home only for the enjoyment that it brings to your family and friends. However, this mistaken view contradicts the lessons of history. Through smart buying, your second home will not only provide you with years of fun, happiness, and memories of good times, it also will boost your net worth. Smart buying rewards you with fun now and profits later.

Lessons of History

No matter what your chief purpose (vacation, retirement, rental income, business use, personal enjoyment), home ownership has and will continue to offer excellent investment returns. Here's what a recent study has shown: "The latest national data on home-value appreciation in the 140 largest real estate markets confirms what may be the least-heralded financial story of the decade: For home owners the combination of the low national inflation rate, federal tax policy, and the growth of home resale values has produced real after-tax returns that are unprecedented in the post World War II era," reports the Washington-based, syndicated columnist Kenneth Harney (*Sarasota Herald-Tribune*, March 14, 1999).

View Home Ownership as an Investment

Harney is right. As the stock market has continued to make headline advancements, housing (as an investment) has not received the attention that it deserves. Rather than acknowledge the strong capital gains (possibly tax-free, see Chapter 14) that most homeowners have consistently achieved during the past ten to fifty years, many media commentators still continue to say things like, "Buy a home as a comfortable place to live, but don't think of it as a bank account with a white picket fence." Especially with respect to second homes and vacation homes, here's just a small sampling of the nay-saying advice found in the media:

- "Second homes are rarely a good way to make money." (*Financial Times*, March 1998)
- "Buy it [a vacation home] for recreation and relaxation, rather than as a profit making venture. . . ." (*Pittsburgh Post-Gazette,* September 1, 1998)
- "You can't expect most vacation homes to be moneymakers. . . . A vacation home only makes sense if it's a place you want to be." (*Milwaukee Journal Sentinel*, June 7, 1998)
- "Experts warn against buying second homes as investments." (*U.S. News & World Report*, September 28, 1998)
- "When clients ask, I always urge them not to view a second home as an investment. . . . It should be like a painting—you buy it because you want to hang it on a wall and enjoy it." (*Fortune*, December 29, 1998)

But my favorite examples of off-the-mark vacation-home quotations were published December 20, 1987, by the *New York Times*:

- "The future of the resort market lies in ownership for its own sake and its own enjoyment. . . ."

- "People are now buying as users instead of investors. . . ."
- "The market is not going to go down much more, but it's not going to go up much either."
- "Buyers should regard their [vacation] home as a 'wonderful toy,' not as a ticket to fun now and profits later."
- "This is not a good place to expect to make a lot of money."

Where was that "place" where no one should expect to make money? That place where homes were only a "wonderful toy"? The answer: Colorado resort areas such as Aspen, Vail, Beaver Creek, and other lesser-known spots. Since those dark days in 1987, home prices in those resorts have multiplied (depending on specific resort and property) somewhere between two- and tenfold.

Forget the Naysayers, Home Prices Are Going Up

If you really want to know where home prices are going, look to history as a guide. Too often we look only at today's prices and think, "Boy, we missed our chance. We should have bought when prices were lower. They can't go much higher now." With history as a guide, though, you will see that since the end of World War II, the warning, "prices can't go any higher," has been wrongly voiced time and time again. Look at these erring naysayers from years gone by:

- "The prices of houses seem to have reached a plateau, and there is reasonable expectancy that prices will decline." (*Time*, December 1, 1947)
- "Houses cost too much for the mass market. Today's average price is around $8,000—out of reach for two-thirds of all buyers." (*Science Digest*, April 1948)
- "If you have bought your house since the War . . . you have made your deal at the top of the market. . . . The days when you couldn't lose on a house purchase are no longer with us." (*House Beautiful*, November 1948)
- "The goal of owning a home seems to be getting beyond the reach of more and more Americans. The typical new house today costs about $28,000." (*Business Week*, September 4, 1969)

- "You might well be suspicious of a 'common wisdom' that tells you, 'Don't wait, buy now. . . .' Continuing inflation will force home prices and rents higher and higher." (*NEA Journal*, December 1970)
- "The median price of a home today is approaching $5,000. . . . Housing experts predict price rises in the future won't be that great." (*Nations Business*, June 1977)
- "The era of easy profits in real estate may be drawing to a close." (*Money*, January 1981)
- "In California . . . for example, it is not unusual to find families of average means buying $100,000 houses. . . . I'm confident prices have passed their peak." (John Wesley English and Gray Emerson Cardiff, *The Coming Real Estate Crash*, 1980)
- "The golden-age of risk-free run ups in home prices is gone." (*Money*, March 1985)
- "If you're looking to buy, be careful. Rising home values are not a sure thing anymore." (*Miami Herald*, October 25, 1985)
- "Most economists agree . . . [a home] will become little more than a roof and a tax deduction, certainly not the lucrative investment it was through much of the 1980s." (*Money*, April 1986)
- "We're starting to go back to the time when you bought a home not for its potential money-making abilities, but rather as a nesting spot." (*Los Angeles Times*, January 31, 1993)
- "Financial planners agree that houses will continue to be a poor investment." (*Kiplinger's Personal Financial Magazine*, November 1993)
- "A home is where the bad investment is." (*San Francisco Examiner*, November 17, 1996)

I especially smile when I read that last quotation from the *Examiner*. Like the supposed experts writing about the Aspen and Vail of 1987, this well-known Oakland, California real estate writer was staring blind at one of the best home-buying opportunities of the past thirty years. In the few years since he wrote those words, San Francisco Bay Area home prices have jumped 30 percent and rental housing is almost impossible to find—and if found, almost impossible to pay for.

It's Your Choice

There's absolutely no doubt that your second home can yield excellent returns through appreciation. The question is, Do you want to shop for a home with capital gains in mind? For some buyers, the purchase of a second home comes as a reward for years of work, saving, and investing. Their second home does serve primarily as a "wonderful toy." Although they don't want the home to lose value, if it does, it's no big deal to them. Neither their livelihood, their overall wealth, nor the quality of their life would change in any big way.

On the other hand, many second-home buyers (especially those under the age of 50 or 55) certainly want a second home where they can enjoy the three Rs (relaxation, recuperation, and recreation), but they also realize the important financial role that a second home can play in their portfolio planning. They realize that stock price volatility can threaten their peace of mind and their financial well-being. These buyers understand that holding wealth in the form of a tangible asset such as a second home offers more security than paper (digital) assets. In contrast to stocks, you can enjoy the use of a second home. You can collect rental income. You can combine the two in various proportions. You can sell the home to someone else who will enjoy it or rent it out. Whether to you or to someone else, real estate represents real wealth.

So, the choice is yours. Do you want only a wonderful toy, a reward for past achievement? Or, do you want a "ticket to fun now and profits later"?

Buy Smart, Not Blind

If you answer yes to the fun *and* profit motive, then don't focus on the advice of naysayers who ignore the lessons of history—those who display no fundamental knowledge of longer-term house price trends. Don't pass up profit opportunities because of the advice given by people (chiefly journalists, lawyers, accountants, and financial planners) who don't seem to understand that smart buying can dramatically enlarge the second-home investment results that you actually experience.

By "smart buying" I mean following the detailed location and home inspection process described in chapters 5 and 6. But smart buying also means shopping for bargains, ferreting out underpriced locations, and paying attention to market traffic lights that flash green, yellow, or red (all of which is covered in detail in Part II). The naysayers write as if mid- to long-term appreciation were simply a matter of happenstance. If you get it, count yourself blessed; if not, well, that's the way the ball bounces. "We told you not to count on making any profits," they respond. But smart buying can ensure that the purchase you make will be one that increases in value.

Buffettology: A Lesson for Home Buyers

As you may know, Warren Buffett has practically made the concept of "value investing" a household word. Beginning with just $105,000, Buffett built a personal fortune that now tops $20 billion. His secret: buy into companies whose current stock prices don't reflect their true value.

How did he see what others did not? By keeping his eyes and mind open. When most stock market "experts" were claiming, "The stock market is too efficient. You can't consistently beat market averages," Buffett just laughed all the way to the bank (several of which he has bought, including a major interest in the investment banking firm, Salomon Brothers). Buffett says, "Investing in a market where people believe in efficiency is like playing bridge with someone who has been told it doesn't do any good to look at the cards. It has been helpful to me to have tens of thousands of students turned out of business schools who were taught that it didn't do any good to think."

The same circumstances hold true for buyers of second homes for vacations, weekend getaways, and retirement. Since so many "pleasure" buyers have been told not to think profit, they don't look for ways to beat the market. They just buy what they like and then hope for the best. But smart buyers use "Buffettology" when shopping for a second home. Of course, Buffettology requires effort. It takes time to study property prices in a variety of areas; look at many possible choices (houses, townhouses, condominiums, and mobile homes); and systematically compare what you're getting with what you're being asked to pay. In addition, if you find a bargain-priced "fixer," you may (but not always) need to invest more time, effort, and money before you see your home gain value.

Nevertheless, for many second-home buyers, this extra thought and effort will pay off generously. Over a period of years, the rewards can total $50,000, $100,000, $250,000, or more. If capital gains of these amounts appeal to you, then you will benefit by applying the buying and investment guidelines spelled out later. Through smart buying, second homes can bring both fun *and* profit. The choice is yours.

The Profit–Inflation Connection

In recent years, many of the "don't count on big profits" crowd point to low rates of inflation to support their advice. This conventional wisdom alleges that strong appreciation in home prices depends on a high rate of inflation. The logic of this argument seems straightforward. It goes like this: As prices of labor and materials go up, home builders cut back on new construction and raise their prices. With higher prices for new homes, many homebuyers switch to the resale market. As more buyers bid for existing homes, those home prices go up.

High Inflation, High Interest Rates

Although this argument is partially true, it doesn't reveal the full picture. Ask any Realtor or home builder who lived through the double-digit rates of inflation of the early 1980s. Contrary to today's recollections, those were not good times for real estate. Reporting on the Southern California market of 1982, a leading national newspaper wrote, "Not only are asking prices falling, but in some cases people who have bought homes in the last few years are selling them for less than they paid. . . . Now people are buying shelter. . . ." And recall the *Money* magazine quotation of January 1981, "The era of easy profits in real estate may be drawing to a close."

Although over time higher rates of inflation will increase building costs, higher inflation also causes interest rates to rise. As interest rates go up, home affordability goes down. People who might like to buy are blocked from the market. Sooner or later, demand for homes falls because higher interest rates mean that homebuyers can't qualify for financing. Fewer buyers bring price increases to a halt.

Low Inflation, Higher Home Prices

On the other hand, a low rate of inflation creates low interest rates. More people can afford to buy. If current predictions of low inflation hold true, millions of Americans who would have been shut out of the mortgage market if interest rates were at 10 to 14 percent—the rates that prevailed throughout most of the 1980s—will continue to flood into the housing market for first, second, and even third homes. More buyers will push prices higher.

If we look back to the 1980s, it wasn't the high inflation years that brought the steepest home price increases. The greatest rates of appreciation (except for the oil belt), occurred between 1985 and 1988. Then, in 1989, inflation climbed up close to 5 percent. It was the largest increase in the consumer price index (CPI) since 1982. Mortgage interest rates again went above 10 percent. Home prices stalled (and even retreated) in many cities. Construction of new homes fell. Defense-related industries suffered cutbacks and layoffs. Downsizing became a corporate buzzword.

To become more competitive, firms with bureaucracies, such as General Motors and IBM, shed employees. The country experienced its seventh post-World War II recession and a slowdown in economic growth. In 1992 at the urging of the "ragin' Cajun," James Carville, William J. Clinton campaigned with the slogan "It's the economy, stupid!"

Low Inflation, Low Interest Rates, Great Economy

Regardless of whether you credit Bill Clinton, Alan Greenspan (Chairman of the Federal Reserve), or the Republican Congress, the mid- to late 1990s brought the best economy our country experienced since at least the early 1960s. Low interest rates stimulated business investment, low unemployment, record levels of homebuying and homeownership, strong housing appreciation rates, and historically high stock prices. Do not misread history and conclude that a high rate of inflation is good for home prices. Between 1950 and 1970 average home prices tripled ($10,000 to nearly $30,000). Yet, during this twenty-year period, increases in the CPI typically ranged between 1 percent and 3 percent per year.

The Rise of Home Prices in the 1970s

Throughout the high inflation 1970s, home prices in most major metropolitan markets did jump substantially, but the primary reason wasn't inflation. It was job growth. It was all those recently graduated baby boomers who were going off to work in those newly constructed downtown (and suburban) high-rise offices.

A complex of office buildings that sits on less than a city block of land might employ 5,000 people. Most people want to live within a convenient commute to work. Each time a new office tower went up, thousands of people looked to live nearby. Of course, the number of conveniently located homes was far too few to accommodate all of those potential buyers. "Bidding wars" broke out. Homes were sold to the buyers who were willing and able to pay the highest prices. And by the standards of the day, those prices became very high indeed.

Price Increases Have Varied across the Country

Generally, during the 1970s and 1980s, huge increases in home prices resulted only in those metro areas where rapid job growth outran the available supply of close-in land and housing. San Francisco, Washington, D.C., New York City, Boston, Los Angeles, and San Diego represent prime examples. Outside the United States, Vancouver, London, and especially low-inflation Tokyo, Hong Kong, and Singapore illustrate the same principle.

In Orlando, home prices didn't jump up (except for close-in lakefront). For there were always more orange groves to bulldoze and burn to make way for hundreds of new subdivisions. In Champaign-Urbana, surrounding cornfields provided plenty of land on which to build new houses. In Las Vegas, hundreds of square miles of desert continue to make rapid population and job growth possible while maintaining home prices at one-fourth (or less) the price levels of Manhattan or San Francisco.

The Potential for Profit

Once you recognize the real story of rapid home prices increases, two overriding facts become obvious:

1. You don't need inflation to propel home prices to higher and higher levels.
2. Rapid price increases result when too many willing and able buyers chase after too few homes.

In looking at the future demand for and the supply of second homes for getaways, vacations, and retirement, we see a blend of circumstances that favor the profit-making potential of owning a second home. We see the same kinds of economic conditions that led to a tripling of home prices between 1950 and 1970: low interest rates, low inflation, technological advances, strong job growth, and large increases in household incomes. In addition, we see several of the same critical factors at work that pushed up home prices in major metro areas during the mid- to late 1970s (and mid- to late 1980s), namely, favorable baby boom demographics; favorable psychographics; and in the most desirable locations, a highly limited (or nonexistent) supply of low-cost or even buildable land. Without low-cost land to accommodate the construction of new homes, growing demand must push home prices to new heights.

Boomer Demographics

In the field of market analysis we often say "Demographics is destiny." Boomer demographic trends strongly signal a soaring market for vacation, retirement, and getaway properties. The boomer generation measures *twice the size* of the generation that preceded it, but, more important, during the next ten years the total number of people who "fit the income and lifestyle profile" of second-home buyers will jump fourfold. (If you want to reserve your place in the sun, start planning now. Prices are heading up and supply is heading down.)

In reviewing baby boom demographics, four demand-inducing characteristics stand out: (1) sheer numbers, (2) stage of life, (3) dual incomes, and (4) accumulated wealth.

Boomer Numbers

By now (even if you're a member of this generation), you may be sick of hearing about the 76 million boomers whose huge numbers in successive waves flooded schools, colleges, the job market, the housing market, and now the stock market. Nevertheless, in projecting demand for second homes, boomer numbers cannot be ignored.

To give you some sense of the magnitude of change we are about to witness, consider these birth figures: During the eighteen years (1928 to 1945) preceding the baby-boom years, American families brought approximately 42 million babies into the world. Unfortunately, because of major wars (World War II and Korea) and higher death rates (accident, disease, and illness) perhaps only 28 to 30 million of these babies reached age 55. In contrast, among the 76 million babies born during the years 1946 to 1964, approximately 65 million will live to celebrate their fifty-fifth birthdays.

To put it starkly, the number of people who will be entering middle-age and, subsequently, their retirement years, is about to double. Between now and 2020, we're going to experience a 100 percent increase in the number of "young seniors."

Stage of Life

Beyond sheer numbers, though, the boomers represent a sea change in attitudes and lifestyle. To most of the now senior generation, preretirement and retirement meant a time to wind down. A time to enjoy grandkids, sit back and get old. The boomers, who were raised in a culture where youth has its privileges, aren't quite so ready to accept their older years as the downside of life. As they get their kids off to college (or at least out of the house), more and more of them are willing to take on new activities, start new businesses, and buy homes for getaways, vacations, and preretirement.

Pick up any magazine or newspaper that features articles on people in their forties and early fifties. What are they doing? How do they look? What are their plans? How do they think of themselves? Now, can you recall your own parents when they were that age. For most people, that comparison provides a vivid contrast in appearance, outlook, attitudes, and activity patterns. At age 50, most boomers expect to live another thirty or forty years. They want to enjoy at least part of that time at the beach, on the golf course, in the mountains, or out in the countryside.

No longer are second homes thought of as merely luxuries for the rich. Increasing numbers of boomers think of a second home just like they think of a sport utility vehicle or trip to Europe—simply one of life's necessities. In years past, seniors who displayed a "stay active, stay healthy, stay alert, stay alive" frame of reference definitely represented a small minority. In the future, the number of youngish seniors who will retain an active mindset and lifestyle will multiply five- to ten-fold—from perhaps 3 million or 4 million today, up to 15 to 30 million within the coming ten years.

Dual Incomes

When I was a kid in the 1950s, I took pride in saying, "my mother doesn't have to work." In those days, social policy and American culture held "stay at home moms" in the highest esteem. (Perhaps a little of this attitude may be returning.) But there's no doubt that when kids today are asked about their mothers, they're far more likely to say that she's a teacher, doctor, lawyer, psychologist, accountant, or executive, or that she runs her own business. She might also work as a nurse, real estate agent, or welder. The point is that more families today not only bring in two paychecks, but, in many cases, both husband and wife earn above-average incomes.

With giant leaps in the number of families who earn dual incomes, dreams of stress-reducing, second-home getaways has increased. Fortunately, millions of families (for the first time in history) now enjoy earnings large enough to make those dreams come true.

Accumulated Wealth

I recently read an article in the *Wall Street Journal* that reported the total value of all stocks had reached $16 trillion. That's an eightfold increase since the early 1980s. That money will buy an awful lot of second homes. Even if the market were to fall temporarily by 25 to 50 percent, that would still leave more of today's families and individuals with greater amounts of stock market wealth than any previous generation ever thought possible.

In addition, if (as I expect) the stock market slows its advance, at least part of that $5 billion a month of new investment that's been flowing into stocks will shift to real estate. Boomers (and everyone else) who are saving for retirement must find someplace to park their money. If stocks fall out of favor, real estate will again become the investment of choice. Housing demand and home prices will escalate.

The End of Low-Cost Land

"The cost of vacant residential land is escalating across the country," reports the *Wall Street Journal*. "Builders are paying more for lots and are incurring increased costs to deal with issues related to zoning approvals, sewer capacity, traffic, and water availability. As a result, these costs are passed along to buyers in the form of higher land prices." Here's a brief sampling:

- In northern and central New Jersey, a quarter-acre lot typically runs upward of $65,000, while move-up lots (around one acre) are priced from $125,000 to $200,000.
- In Southern California (Orange County), one-eighth-acre lots are going for $225,000, and 6,000-square-foot lots in Newport Beach (not waterfront) range between $300,000 and $400,000.
- Mountain lots in golf course communities in western North Carolina are typically priced in the $125,000 to $400,000 price range.

In Florida, land-use specialist James Nichols of the University of Florida warns that "metro areas such as Ft. Lauderdale and Orlando may have to put development into a tire squealing halt." The costs of roads, sewers, schools, and other government services necessary to support future growth are increasing faster than the taxpayers' willingness to fund them.

The Nimby (Not-in-My-Back Yard) Movement

It's not only the fact that taxpayers and current homeowners are refusing to pay the costs of growth; in many cases they want to stop growth, period. No one, of course, stands up at a public hearing and actually shouts, "We've got the good life. Let's keep it for ourselves. We can't continue to let just anyone move here. Let's jack up home prices so high that most of these people will go somewhere else." To utter such blunt language would violate the boundaries of political correctness.

No, current "nimbys" use purr words like "green space," and "managed growth." They use acceptable snarl words like "urban sprawl." They say, "We must protect the environment." William McGurn of Madison, New Jersey, writes in the *Wall Street Journal* without tongue in cheek, "First they came after the SUV's, but I drive a Taurus, so I did nothing. Then they targeted a proposed Wal-Mart, but since I own shares in K-Mart, I did nothing. Then they came for the outdoor grills and lawn mowers, and because I really never liked my wife's nagging me about mowing the lawn, I did nothing. At last they turned their attention to my plans to build a two-car garage—and there was no one left to help me."

At a recent public hearing in Manatee County, Florida, more than 100 homeowners showed up to object to a planned road expansion from two to six lanes. They said it would disrupt their neighborhoods, but, more important, the expansion would not improve traffic flow—it would promote traffic congestion. They were sure that as soon as the road widening occurred, more subdivisions would be developed. Instead of a tolerable two-lane road, residents would have to contend with a congested, noisy, and pollution-generating six lanes of traffic. At present, the Florida Department of Transportation has shelved plans for the six lanes pending further review.

"If experience elsewhere is any guide, gatherings like this hearing are going to become more commonplace in the months and years ahead," writes an editorialist in the local Manatee paper. Without a doubt, everywhere throughout the country, development faces an uphill battle. Endless rounds of hearings, court battles, and debates over, "who's going to pay?" will produce fewer homes at much increased costs. Certainly, those mile-after-mile of condo high-rises (like those that scar the landscape from Miami Beach to Boca Raton) are a remnant of the past. Granted, most resort and vacation areas will not stop development with the iron-handed ferocity wielded by the California Coastal Commission. Nevertheless, you can be sure that the cry for "managed growth" is winning (and will continue to win) an increasing number of battles. Especially in popular and desirable areas: no more cheap land, no more low-cost development.

Land Banking

Forget cheap land. In many areas, virtually little if any buildable land exists at any price. Trace the coastline around the United States from St. Andrews, New Brunswick, to Vancouver, British Columbia. My guess is that 90 to 95 percent of all the homes that will ever sit on this coastal land have already been built. Likewise for Lake Tahoe, Bainbridge Island, Martha's Vineyard, Cape Cod, Hilton Head, Aspen, Siesta Key, and many other locations.

No developer is going into any of these areas (or hundreds of others like them) to build any large-scale housing developments. Large tracts of buildable land simply don't exist. And where some chance of development does exist, more and more often residents are moving to place acreage in various types of conservation trusts, agricultural reserves, or wilderness areas.

The Main Coast Heritage Trust, the Colorado Wilderness Land Trust, and the Tall Timbers Conservation Easement (protecting 9,000 acres in the panhandle region of Florida) represent three recent examples. "I want to make sure my heirs won't put condos and strip malls on the property," say Kate Ireland, the property owner and benefactor of the Timbers Conservation Easement.

On Cape Cod, "Two well-paved roads that lead to nowhere delight Sandwich town officials," reports the *New York Times*. "Using most of its share of a new Cape Cod fund, the town will buy 275 acres blocking planned construction of seventy-five large houses that the two roads had been built to serve." Plus, with the Maple Swamp Conservation area "we'll be able to keep another 1,000 acres clear of further development forever," says Sandwich Town Selectman, Jan Teehan.

Although the land-bank movement is still wearing its baby shoes, that won't last long. All signs point to giant-size growth. Taxpayers, especially in vacation, resort, and recreation areas, would prefer to buy up any available buildable land rather than pay for the roads, sewers, and infrastructure necessary to permit development.

You Can Enjoy Fun Now and Profits Later

Every student who enrolls in Economics 101 soon learns that home prices are pushed up or pulled down according to the law of supply and demand. As never before, now's the time to put this law on your side. All market trends for second homes show upbeat signs. Like the 1970s, the boomer generation will bring millions of buyers into the housing market. Only this time around, they'll be searching for great places to vacation, retire, or just plain get away from the stresses of everyday life.

Today millions of boomer households earn historically high amounts of income. They have accumulated unprecedented amounts of wealth (stock market and home equity). These boomers enjoy far more buying power than any previous generation. And they enjoy far more buying power than when they scurried after their first homes in the 1970s and 1980s. Even better, in contrast to the high-interest 1970s, and 1980s, today's second-home buyers can arrange their mortgage financing at relatively low interest rates and on easier terms (see Chapter 11).

All of these factors together spell D-E-M-A-N-D. But will there be enough supply? The answer to that question is loud and clear: *not likely*. Environmentalists, "managed growth" advocates, and angry homeowners tired of traffic congestion, pollution, and higher taxes all stand ready to fill public hearings and fight. They stand ready to oppose any developer who plans to "pave over paradise to build a parking lot." But apart from the antigrowth ("we must protect the environment") movement, most desirable resort and vacation areas are facing severe physical shortages of buildable land.

In many instances, these areas are already built out. Drive along the coast, through the mountains, around popular lakes, and in other desirable spots. Where could developers build more homes—even if land-use law permitted it? Not all favored land is built out, of course, but the percentage that remains represents a small fraction of the amount that was available forty, thirty, or even just twenty years ago.

No one disputes the fact that two-income boomer households pushed up the prices of well-located in-city and suburban homes during the 1970s, 1980s, and into the 1990s. Now, with this history as a guide, we can confidently see the future: millions of families with income, wealth, and mortgage money who are chasing after too few second homes to meet their demands.

Yes, buy now for fun and enjoyment, but shop carefully and you also will be rewarded with a second home that will continue to grow in value. Part II provides many more tips and techniques that can help you buy smart and own profitably.

Making a
Rewarding Purchase

CHAPTER 8

How to Buy Smart

There's no doubt that an increasing number of buyers will continue to bid up the prices of homes located in the areas favored for get-aways, vacations, and retirement. Even if you bought blind, market trends *almost* guarantee that after several years, you will come out ahead. However, I must emphasize that a rising tide will not lift all boats equally.

Some areas will beat the market averages. Some will sail on an even keel. Some will fall behind. And, in a few cases, some may get swamped. Even in an overall strong market, some homes may sell for less in the future than they do today. So how can you tell the difference between the potential sinkers and the near certain winners? That's what this chapter can show you.

Evaluating the Market

Although since the early 1980s home prices have experienced strong gains, we also have lived through several market downturns. Within the not too distant past we have seen home prices decline in the oil and gas states (Texas, Oklahoma, Colorado, and Louisiana). We've seen over-building depress home prices in Arizona and Florida. We've watched the raging bull markets of Southern California, Washington, D.C., New York City, and New England turn into corralled sheep. With these market experiences lingering in our memories, it's no wonder why many media "experts" have popularized the idea that "you should buy a vacation home if you want a place to enjoy, but don't mistake it for a bank account with a white picket fence."

The Real Estate Cycle

Like most investments, home prices move in cycles—sometimes up, sometimes down. Unfortunately, most people incorrectly base their forecasts on whatever has happened recently. If home prices are galloping ahead at 10 to 15 percent a year, the predominant forecast will be for home prices to continue running at that pace. If home prices are declining, stable, or showing slow growth, most people will color the future bleak.

Yet the brief glimpse of history illustrated by the quotations cited in Chapter 7 show that home price trend lines don't extend from the past to the present as straight, smooth, and constant. They look more like the ragged peaks, plateaus, and valleys of a range of mountains. And mountain climbers always go through a series of ups and downs as they steadily move to higher and higher levels. The same is generally true for home prices.

You see periods when the market is marching up. You see other periods when it's taking time for rest and recovery. And, on occasion, markets might snowball downhill. Fortunately, by keeping your eye on the following five market signals, you can tell what direction home prices are heading:

1. Length of time on the market
2. Asking price/selling price
3. Number of homes up for sale
4. New construction
5. Type of buyer

Length of Time on the Market

In most areas of the country, Realtors keep tabs on how long it takes for listed properties to sell. When the real estate cycle starts to cool, homes sit unsold for greater periods of time. If last year, homes sat with "For Sale" signs in their front yards for an average of 77 days, and now the time on the market stands at 132 days, be careful.

As the time on the market lengthens, the slowdown is signaling that sellers are asking too much for their homes. What is true of the market in general is also true of particular homes. Before you put in an offer for a property, find out how long the home's been up for sale—not just with the realty firm that has the current listing, but also whether the home was previously listed unsuccessfully with some other firm. As a general rule, the slower the market and the longer a specific home has sat unsold, the more carefully you should weigh your buying decision.

Asking Price/Selling Price

In very strong markets, homes sell quickly at (or sometimes in excess of) their asking prices. Bidding wars and multiple offers create buyer panic. On the down cycle, the reverse occurs. Not only do homes take longer to sell, on average, the eventual selling price might fall to, say, only 80 to 85 percent of the listing price. Either of these types of markets should cause you to step back and evaluate where the market is likely to head in the near future.

Caution in a slowing market is obvious. But why caution in a super-hot market? Because buyer panic, bidding wars, and multiple offers often push prices up too quickly. Once the buying fever passes, prices get a dose of reality. When I put a home up for sale in 1984 I owned in Dallas, I got three offers right at the asking price. Buyers were in a frenzy. Eight years later, the people I sold to put the house back on the market at the same price they had paid. In contrast, I had picked up a 30 percent gain in two and a half years of ownership.

Number of Homes Up for Sale

In slowing markets the inventory of homes for sale steadily piles up. Buyers tend to disappear. Everybody wants to sell. During San Diego's most recent down market, the local M.L.S. accumulated more than

18,000 listings. By the time the area's recovery was in full swing, the number of listings had shrunk to less than 14,000 homes.

Recently, most of the areas favored for getaways, vacations, and retirement are crying for inventory. Scarcity rather than surplus seems to be the norm. "We're not yet in a sellers market, but inventory is depleted and prices are tending to go up," says a Vermont sales agent. "In 1991, I had a ski resort condo complex with fifty-two units on the market. Now only seven are for sale. I'm begging owners to list with me," he adds.

In Connecticut, Realtor Andrea Gabel reports, "Buyers are becoming frustrated by the lack of properties for sale. We're selling out of everything. Little is being built, too. Second-home owners from New York, when they have the chance to buy land contiguous to their properties, snap it up so they can be sure it doesn't end up being developed."

Keep an eye on the number of homes for sale. A growing inventory indicates that prices may be above the levels buyers are able and willing to pay. When realty agents first begin to beg for listings, the market typically is signaling, "buy now," and price increases are nearly certain.

New Construction

In most areas, the politics of antigrowth will hold new housing construction in check, but progrowth forces will win some battles. When that happens, take measure of the new development. How many homes will be built? Over what period of time? Does the number represent a high percentage of the homes that have sold recently?

Too often, new housing construction is given a completely positive spin. "It's great. Our area is really prospering. Look at all of the growth." Politicians who have supported the development point to the new jobs that the new construction is creating: jobs for the building trades, real estate agents, mortgage lenders, lawyers, appraisers, insurance agents, architects, and all of the merchants who will receive a boost in sales because of the new paychecks.

The downside of new construction is this: History shows that many builders behave like lemmings. They build themselves into bankruptcy. As long as government gives them permits, and as long as lenders provide the construction financing, they will continue to bring new product to market.

That's what happened in Dallas, Houston, and Lubbock, for example, during the 1980s. Those housing markets experienced an avalanche of newly built houses, condominiums, and apartments. During a three-year period in Houston, new home construction went from 4,371 to 48,368 units. Similar overbuilding has occurred in South Florida (especially high-rise condominiums), some Colorado resort areas, and New England. In all of these markets, home prices (and rents) plummeted.

Today, we're not likely to witness such grand overbuilding. Environmental controls and tighter construction lending (for developers) have built a fence around the cliff that builders in the past tended to jump off. Developers, too, have become smarter (or at least sturdier). In a survival of the fittest business, those that survive today haven't paid a retainer to Jack Kevorkian—they're not looking to commit suicide.

Nevertheless, who would deny that history repeats itself? Will some area at some time again suffer the plight of overbuilding? Probably. When it happens, will you get caught in the avalanche? Not if you watch the market signals and count the number of new homes being built. Then ask: Does it stretch common sense to believe that all of this new construction will get sold without massive price cutting? Yes, no, or maybe? As a rule, don't worry much about overbuilding, but people who buy smart do weigh the possibility.

Type of Buyer

In the mid-1980s, the Colorado ski resorts hit their downturn. They had built their hopes on a never-ending stream of oil-rich millionaires from Texas, Oklahoma, and Mexico. Alas, when the price of crude oil slipped from $40 a barrel to around $10 a barrel, those oil millionaires disappeared.

In 1987, the bloodbath on Wall Street reverberated throughout the resort, vacation and getaway spots of New England. As investment firms and brokerage houses slashed jobs, this prime source of second-home buyers vanished as quickly as the one-time oil barons had abandoned their Rock Mountain condos. In the early to mid-1990s, the so-called Asian flu spread to Hawaii. The Japanese who had been snapping up Honolulu houses and condominiums ended their buying spree.

What do each of these areas (Colorado, New England, Hawaii) share in common? They became heavily dependent on a single type of buyer. When those buyers hit tough times, so did the housing markets that had taken their free spending for granted.

Before you buy (especially on the tail end of a rapidly escalating market), find out who else is buying. Are they newly minted high rollers? Are they concentrated in a particular business or industry? Do most originate from a specific part of the country or the world? Is their good fortune secure, or does their income and wealth fall into the "here today, gone tomorrow" category?

An area that enjoys a stable, growing, and diversified base of buyers will offer less risk of price decline. As I write, San Francisco home prices are shooting up. Much of the money fueling this fire comes from the high-tech industry, especially newly minted money from IPOs (initial public stock offerings). Over time, I'm confident that the Bay Area will yield strong growth in home prices. But if (when) "hot" tech cools, San Franciscans may again feel the chilly winds of a down market.

Market Direction

Most housing markets go through cycles. Some fluctuate in between boiling hot and freezing cold. Others tend to warm and cool moderately. While moderate markets don't present much cyclical risk, you're still wise to check the market signals before you buy. A slow or slowing market means that negotiating power shifts to buyers and you usually can get a better deal.

On the other hand, if you plan to buy in an area that has experienced big ups and downs, find out why (loss of buyers, oversupply, economic recession). Look at market signals. Where is the market now? Year after year of double-digit price increases, or prolonged slump? How long has it been there? Are there signs that sales activity and home prices are turning for better or worse?

Buying smarter means paying attention to cycles. It means that you won't get caught in a buying frenzy that tempts you to overpay. It means that you will recognize a great buying opportunity (like Aspen of 1987, San Francisco of 1995, or New England of 1997). Thinking in terms of the real estate cycle will give you an edge over other buyers and sellers who focus excessively on the present. Reading cycles helps you think clearly about the direction home prices will be marching during the coming twelve to thirty-six months.

Cycles versus Decline

Cycles occur when the flow of homes for sale increases or decreases faster than the number of people who are seriously looking to buy. A short-term imbalance may push prices up excessively or pull them down temporarily. Over time, though, prices steadily increase as a growing total population of buyers presses against a relatively fixed supply of land.

Up and Down, or Down for the Count?

In 1995, San Francisco home prices were languishing in a temporary trough. Everyone with an understanding of cycles knew that sometime soon San Francisco home prices would come roaring back. San Francisco remained a great city. Bay Area population was up, incomes were up, wealth was up, and the number of existing homes (houses, condos, apartments) had actually fallen. (The Oakland-Berkeley fire of 1992 destroyed 3,300 homes, most of which had not been rebuilt.) Close-in land is 98 percent built out.

In contrast to the real estate cycles of San Francisco, and other desirable areas, home prices sometimes head down and stay down for long periods of time. These areas are in decline. They become undesirable; they become places you want to avoid. (Two examples were Atlantic City, New Jersey, and South Beach, Florida.) An area in decline doesn't come back naturally. People must step forward to rescue and rehabilitate it.

Avoid Areas in Decline

Generally, you don't want to buy in an area that's suffering a decline in popularity and desirability. So, don't mistake an area that's down for the count with one that's merely passing through the ebb of a real estate cycle (a buying opportunity). However, as has now happened in Atlantic City and South Beach, community action can return an area in decline to one of popularity. In that case, recognizing an area on the cusp of turnaround can offer you a good chance for strong gains in appreciation. Consider the turnaround experience of South Beach.

The Possibilities of Potential

The South Beach Example: From Derelicts to Fashion Models

In the mid-1980s, the South Beach area of Miami Beach (SoBe, as locals call it) had deteriorated to the point where crack dealers and prostitutes openly sold drugs and sex. Derelicts and criminals from the Marial boat lift filled SoBe streets, alleys, and flophouses. Tourists visited the area at their own peril. Most locals wrote off the neighborhood to urban decay. But visiting New Yorker Tony Goldman saw things differently. "I took a ride around the area and it was love at first sight. I was smitten," recalls Tony.

Instead of problems, Tony focused on potential. In his mind's eye he imagined rehabbing the neighborhood buildings to highlight their art deco architecture. He envisioned sidewalk cafes and restaurants. He saw a tree-lined, beautiful Ocean Drive, the main thoroughfare of SoBe. He saw streets free of criminals. He saw vacationers, second-home owners, retirees, and the in-crowd replacing the derelicts and debauchery.

Community Action Works

To bring this dream to life, Tony, along with friends, investors, and civic leaders, formed a community action group. Acting together, the members of the group brought pressure on the police to rid the neighborhood of crime. They began a clean-up and rehab campaign. They convinced the city to float a $3 million bond issue to fund public improvements. They generated a new enthusiasm and community spirit.

How successful were they? As one resident has remarked, "Tony put the chic back into SoBe." Within just a few years, SoBe became one of the hottest (no pun intended) neighborhoods in the Miami area. Condo sales and prices have jumped. Restaurants, outdoor cafes, and clubs fill the neighborhood. On top of it all (or because of it), SoBe has become one of the foremost locations in the country for fashion photography shoots. Hundreds of former New York models now call South Beach home. The delightful Jules Asner of E! (the Entertainment Channel) recently shot one of her exciting *Wild on . . .* specials at South Beach. For many of the in-crowd, SoBe has become the place to be.

You Can Change a Location

As the South Beach experience proves, you can change the quality of a home's location. Remember, the concept of location's appeal actually includes all kinds of things such as:

- Accessibility and convenience
- Esthetics (natural beauty, noise level, landscaping, cleanliness, architectural styles)
- Zoning and environmental controls
- The people (ages, incomes, family size, wealth, lifestyles, attitudes, and other characteristics)
- Community spirit
- Recreational facilities and activities
- Weather
- Restaurants and entertainment
- Traffic congestion
- Crime rates

Every one of these characteristics can be changed for the better through human effort, enterprise, and creativity. In fact, a great deal of community debate often centers on whether various proposed changes will enhance (or detract from) neighborhood quality. As South Beach illustrates, people who buy smart sometimes identify areas that are poised for turnaround.

Does This Buying Strategy Appeal to You?

Do you know of any neglected area that is brimming with possibilities? Are there private and community efforts underway to make the area more desirable? Would such efforts make sense? Does the area possess some "hidden value" that polish and publicity could bring back into popularity? Throughout the country, many once-popular vacation, resort, and rural areas have fallen out of favor. While they may not have deteriorated as much as Atlantic City or South Beach, their futures don't look bright.

Or do they? Maybe some deserve a second look. Do any market signals spell t-u-r-n-a-r-o-u-n-d? Is the local economy awaking from a long sleep? Have any new types of buyers rediscovered the area? Have any cities within a convenient drive experienced jumps in job growth? Are any new facilities or attractions in the works?

If you answer yes to at least two or three of these questions, decide whether the area appeals to you. Does it possess many of the locational advantages that you're looking for? How does it rank in affordability? When you locate an area that meets these criteria, you may have found a place you can enjoy, as well as a place that is primed for strong appreciation.

"You Can't Build It at That Price"

When you hear someone say—"You can't build it at that price"—take notice. A home that is priced below replacement cost often offers good potential for appreciation.

Replacement Cost versus Market Value

Usually you estimate the market value of a home by comparing its size, features, and location to the sales prices of similar homes that have sold recently. That approach is called the market sales data technique. It can tell you whether you're getting a good price based on today's values, but it doesn't tell you where home prices are headed.

To help with that task (along with the other market signals presented earlier), you can use replacement cost. When the market values of homes currently sit well below the land and construction costs necessary to build them, that's a positive sign. Home prices probably will increase. Conversely, if a hot market has pushed up market values well beyond today's building costs, that's a negative sign. The following story provides a good example.

The Dallas Experience

When Suzy Wilson and Carrie Sloan bought their townhouse in a hot Dallas market, they paid $123,000 for a 1,100-square-foot, two-bedroom, three-year-old unit. That price works out to about $112 per square foot. Since the market was booming, Suzy and Carrie's real estate agent had found quite a few similar townhouse units that had sold recently. Based on the selling price of these units, this couple got a good price.

But Suzy and Carrie focused too much on rapidly escalating market values of the past year. In doing so, they missed two critical market signals: (1) The Texas economy was showing signs of slipping; and, more to the point for our purpose here, (2) townhouses similar to the homes these women bought could be built at a total cost of approximately $85 a square foot (including land). That meant condo developers could expect to construct new units, sell them at their market values (over $100 per square foot), and make a profit (killing) of $20,000 to $30,000 a unit.

Naturally, this fact did not escape the attention of condo developers. With banks and savings and loans shoveling money out to developers (who frequently owned the S&Ls), the condo market became glutted with new units. As the oversupply of condos ran head-on into the weakening Texas economy, a severe shortage of homes for sale quickly turned into a surplus. Condo prices crashed.

The Next Stage

After the oversupply became obvious and home prices reversed direction, builders stopped building. Many construction lenders foreclosed on money-losing condo projects. Forced sales temporarily pulled market values well below replacement costs. The market became "depressed." Nearly everyone was afraid to buy. No developer could afford to build.

Eventually, though, economic recession turned into recovery. Growth in jobs, income, and population increased demand for homes. But market values still sat below replacement costs. So builders couldn't build and sell new units at a profit. Smart buyers saw a great opportunity. Buy now at less than replacement cost. Receive virtually guaranteed appreciation. As the market strengthened home prices had to increase. Growing demand was chasing after a diminishing supply. The upside of the real estate cycle was off and running.

Reading the Signal

You can protect yourself against value losses by talking to builders, contractors, or knowledgeable real estate agents. Ask them what it would cost per square foot to construct the type of home you're thinking about buying. Then do some rough calculations. If, after allowing for land (lot) value and home conditions, your home-to-be is priced high relative to new construction costs, don't count on short-term appreciation. When home prices are, say, 15 to 25 percent higher than construction costs, they probably have hit their short-term peak.

Consider, too, that when market values fall below new construction costs, builders won't build new homes. As the local economy strengthens, growth in incomes, employment, and population will push home prices up.

At any specific time, market values can rise above (or fall below) a home's building costs. Except in declining areas, though, home prices eventually keep pace with the costs of new construction. Today's costs of construction may not tell you much about today's market values, but they do signal whether home prices are headed up or down.

Discover the Next "Hot" Area

As areas that attract second-home buyers increase in popularity, their home prices shoot up. But when these areas lack sufficient buildable land (as many do), the developers can't build a competitive supply of new homes. Prices remain too high and unaffordable for large numbers of hopeful buyers. These buyers must look elsewhere.

Alternatives

As previously discussed, buyers who can't afford the premium $150,000 to $400,000 lots typical of the Cashiers-Highlands area, might go searching in nearby Franklin County where you can get an acre or two for $25,000 to $30,000. New Yorkers who can't afford (or don't want to pay) the high prices of getaway homes in upscale Litchfield County, Connecticut, are choosing the less expensive rural retreats they've discovered to the west of the Hudson River near Woodstock, New Paltz, and in the Catskill Mountains.

Only two hours from the city, these areas offer "lovely houses for less," the cultural history of Woodstock's artists' colony, and reasonable privacy and quiet. A little more to the west lies Delaware

County that offers nearby summer recreation (hiking, fishing, bicycling), as well as winter skiing. Prices? A three-bedroom, two-bath ski house on five acres listed at $125,000; a log home on 10 aces at $154,000; and, a farmhouse with barn, pond, and 46 acres at $240,000. "Although prices have gone up, they are still relatively low," report local brokers.

Relative Prices and Benefits

"What can we get for our money?" In one way or another, all smart second-home buyers ask this question. Its answer provides the key to discovering the next up-and-coming areas that promise "beat-the-market" rates of appreciation. When hopeful buyers are priced out of a market they prefer, they search diligently for an area with benefits that nearly match their first choice, but at substantially lower home prices.

When found, they quickly snap up these *relatively* bargain-priced properties. As other buyers also discover these relative bargains, home prices start heading up. The next hot area comes to life. Here are some recent examples drawn from international second-home markets:

- "The Irish property market has seen a sharp rise in prices over the past year, which means that it does not offer quite such exceptional value as it did. . . . [Now] areas nearest the border with Northern Ireland represent the best value for the money. The countryside is lovely and there are some excellent properties." (*Sunday Times* [London], October 18, 1998)
- "The value of prime cottages in rural locations straddling the M4 corridor west from London has rocketed . . . although there are a few bargains if you are prepared to travel further west. . . . Unfortunately, this drives up prices for second-home buyers who don't live in London. Cottages in Wales, the traditional cheap weekend retreat are now averaging (pounds) 145,000. . . . Those whose resources are more limited will find East Anglia their best bet." (*The Independent* [London], June 7, 1998)
- "There's better value in some lovely unspoiled areas just south of Norwich. One pretty three-bedroom house just sold for £110,000. The area is still affordable because it hasn't been colonized yet by the second-home brigade." (*The Independent*, June 7, 1998)

- "As the Costa del Sol becomes overrun with sun-seeking holiday makers, people searching for a peaceful second home start to look elsewhere. . . . One less frequented area is the Costa Blanca . . . Orihuela Costa is a well-kept secret. Thousands of Britons have purchased in Spain, yet few have found this part of the coast." (*Sunday Times,* September 20, 1998)

- "Italy's housing market is emerging from recession as overseas investors pour in millions of dollars. . . . Brick for brick, like for like in location and quality, Italy is relatively cheap compared with France and Spain. . . . Some British buyers also were snapping up homes in Marche, close to [higher-priced] Tuscany, where prices were lower. . . . In Sicily, a new studio flat . . . can cost as little as £20,000." (*The Times* [London], August 17, 1998)

If you can't afford your preferred location, discover something similar (or perhaps even better in terms of peace, quiet, esthetics, or other amenities). Buy your second home at a relatively low price. Then watch your investment grow in value.

What is true for general areas also stands true for neighborhoods. Can't afford the specific spot you want? Get out your binoculars. Survey affordable alternatives. Buy in the neighborhood that offers the most for your money. As more buyers follow this same path, they will bid home prices up.

More Smart Buying Tips

To discover areas that will beat the market rate of appreciation, here are a few more ideas that smart buyers can put to use: (1) Buy on the bad news; (2) stay alert to publicity; (3) look for improving accessibility; (4) watch where international money is flowing; and (5) look forward, not backward.

Buy on the Bad News

Smart stock market investors have long followed the adage of buying on the bad news, but the principle applies to real estate, too. When "blood is running in the streets," don't call an ambulance. Closely follow the health of the victims. When the hemorrhaging stops and you can feel the pulse of life get stronger, start buying quick. That advice was true for Aspen in 1987 and New England in 1996, and it's true for Hawaii today.

Down, But Not for the Count

A prolonged slump in tourism and the loss of Asian buyers has kept Hawaii from prospering during the recent economic good times shared by most Americans. The mood is glum. Yet, a quick survey of Hawaii's strategic location, near-perfect weather, and beautiful resorts, beaches, and island paradises leave no doubt. Today, anyone who buys a value-priced property in Hawaii will certainly enjoy large gains within the coming decade. When Japan recovers from its recession and as California coastal home prices continue to escalate, the attractiveness of Hawaii will once again bring planeloads of vacationers and second-home buyers.

Even in good times, some areas will lag overall trends. Any localized economic problem such as a decline in tourism, cutbacks by a major employer, an oversupply of new construction, or even adverse weather can generate enough bad news to temporarily scare away potential homebuyers.

After Hurricane Mitch swept through Honduras, the bad news (more than the actual hurricane damage itself) killed business. Hotel and restaurant operators saw revenues fall by more than 60 percent. This popular Caribbean location for vacation and retirement living suffered mass tourist cancellations. Potential homebuyers fled the real estate market. Home prices reversed their upward trend. All of this negative fallout occurred even though the most favored Honduras tourist destinations such as the diving resorts, Maya ruins, and beaches remained relatively untouched by Mitch's fury.

With prices stalled, hundreds of millions of dollars of insurance proceeds and international aid flowing into the country, you can safely bet that a new, improved, and more expensive Honduras will eventually emerge. After the Oakland-Berkeley fire and after Hurricane Andrew destroyed much of South Florida, the same pattern was experienced: At first, home prices and lot values fell, then rebuilding went forward, and then home and lot prices hit new highs.

Bad News/Good News

Throughout the country from Jackson, California, in the Sierra foothills to Woodstock and the Catskills in New York; throughout the world from Honduras to coastal South Africa, from Bangkok to Kuala Lumpur, once high-flying areas are suffering under a deluge of bad news of one sort or another. Can you locate any similar resort or vacation spots that appeal to you? By following in the wake of bad news (where long-term trends spell renewed growth and prosperity), you are buying smart. The good news is that you can expect to enjoy large gains through appreciation.

Stay Alert to Publicity

They say that advertising pays, but publicity pays even better. When former President Gerald Ford bought a condominium at Beaver Creek, Colorado, the media gave the then-new resort a full press coverage. More recently, Vail has received publicity as former astronauts John Glenn, Scott Carpenter, and Wally Schirra each has bought second homes in the Vail valley. Montana and Utah have become more popular since famous actors and corporate moguls such as Robert Redford and Ted Turner have bought ranches in those states. In the Florida panhandle, Seaside and Rosemary Beach ("Son of Seaside") are gaining publicity. HGTV (the cable network) is giving away a $600,000 house at Rosemary Beach, and Seaside provided the setting for Jim Carrey's movie, *The Truman Show*.

Home Prices Jump

After a burst of publicity, vacation and second-home buyers often pour into an area and bid up prices. By bringing an area into the spotlight, publicity piques the interest of prospective buyers. It draws them in for a closer look. In other instances, people like to own homes in areas that display so-called star power.

The recent book and movie, *Midnight in the Garden of Good and Evil*, renewed the popularity of Savannah, Georgia. Increasing numbers of tourists and second-home buyers have driven up its home prices. In fact, if you would like to own the home where Clint Eastwood stayed when he was in town to direct the movie, it's on the market. The expected selling price is around $2 million, up more than 50 percent since *Midnight* was filmed.

Whether it's rock stars buying second homes in Ireland, Bill Gates picking up a $1.3 million vacation-home lot in Palm Desert, California, or Tiger Woods laying out $1 million for a second home south of Los Angeles at Huntington Beach, publicity and celebrity spark interest. Following interest, more lookers. Following more lookers, more buyers and higher prices. So, smart second-home buyers pay attention to coming hot spots that make the news. Whether driven by star power or something else, a place that becomes "the place to be" often shows strong growth in home values.

Too Much of a Good Thing

Of course, at some point, publicity proves itself too much of a good thing. So, only buy relatively early. Don't wait until every Brad and Janet decides to include the area on their "must-see" list. On occasion, areas become so crowded that no one goes there anymore. In other words, the place evolves into more show than substance. An overflowing number of lookers and tourists spoils the area for residents and homeowners, and property prices fall.

In recent years the once chic Cannes has suffered that fate. All along the French Riviera, traffic jams, crowded beaches, and overpriced restaurants are pushing serious second-home buyers into other locales. In fact, some say that prices have slipped so far in Cannes that bargain hunters might want to take a closer look. You can apply the "Cannes principle"—one-time winners can become sinkers—to any area where a growing number of tourists and vacationers so impairs the quality of life that homebuyers flee and home prices falter.

Look for Improving Accessibility

Here's another way to spot properties that will yield higher than average rates of appreciation: Look for areas that are becoming more convenient to reach. "It's an hour and 50 minutes door-to-door from our home in Atlanta and not a bad drive now that Ga. 400 is finished," says Lawson Spence, who with his wife, Mimi, has watched their Lake Burton getaway home jump in value. "When we bought" says Mimi, "the price seemed outrageous. But now we know we got a bargain." Easier access has delivered more potential buyers.

Convenience Means Appreciation

Madison, Connecticut, a Long Island Sound waterfront town of 15,000, is increasingly attracting second-home buyers from New York City. Blue-water vistas, appealing locally owned shops and restaurants, and a small village ambiance all contribute to the town's growing popularity. But these smart-buying New Yorkers also have their eye on another soon-to-come advantage. Within the next year or two, a high-speed rail line will cut the NYC to Madison travel time from over two hours to around eighty minutes.

In addition to better highways and faster rail, improved air service also can boost property values. "You can now get direct flights to Eagle Airport (Vail) from La Guardia. If you leave at 10:00 A.M., you can arrive in Vail by noon and be on the slopes by 1:00 P.M.," says RE/MAX president Daryl Jesperson, as he explains why vacation home sales are booming—even in places once considered "remote." Likewise, cheap, frequent, and nonstop flights to Florida from major U.S. and international cities gives the sunshine state a growing number of buyers for retirement, vacation, and getaway homes.

Any type of improved accessibility can bring more potential buyers to an area. A road widening, added ferry service, a new bridge, anything that speeds travel (or reduces its cost) will help boost property values. If you should learn of planned improvements, stay tuned for further developments. As construction moves toward completion, prices are sure to increase for homes that will benefit from the improvements. Quicker commutes mean higher home prices.

Watch the International Money

"British expatriates helped to revolutionize the French housing market with 'English-speaking areas,' such as the Dordogne," reports the *Times*. "A few years ago the price for a traditional farmhouse was about Fr 100,000. Now, you would have to pay five times that amount, if you can find a property," says Deputy Mayor Maurice Lagarde of a Dordogne village. "But I do not know of any farmhouses for sale around here any more. They all have been bought up by the British and the Dutch," the Deputy Mayor adds.

"In truth," Lagarde continues, "if you want to buy a property in this area you have to go for a home that has been renovated and you're going to pay more than Fr 1 million." In the foothills of the Pyrenees, one of the poorest regions in France, holiday home prices have climbed to Fr 400,000. (Of course, the fact that Tony Blair chooses the Pyrenees for his annual vacation has contributed to the price escalation in the area.)

Global Buying Is Growing

In our rapidly emerging global economy, money flies around the world on a moment's notice. And people with money seem to fly almost as fast. "Much as Vancouver, Canada, became a magnet for the Hong Kong Chinese, Perth in Western Australia is now attracting thousands of Chinese Indonesians," reports the *Los Angeles Times*. In the United States, "Colorado resorts believe their biggest future growth will be international," reports the *New York Times*. Copper Mountain has reservationists who speak Japanese, Spanish, and German. In South Carolina, a Kiawah Island vacation-home builder reports recent sales to buyers from Spain, Portugal, and Canada.

About half the new condos going up in Miami-Dade high-rises are being sold to foreign buyers, mostly Latin Americans, but also a growing number of Europeans. Real estate firms now regularly send sales agents to market South Florida vacation homes throughout Colombia, Brazil, Venezuela, and other points south and east. "We're becoming much more international," says Alicia Cervera, owner of a Miami realty firm.

U.S. Prices Still Cheap

By international standards, the United States offers some of the highest-quality and lowest-priced homes in the world. In a major article on Florida, the *Sunday Times* (London) writes, "British buyers are usually surprised at the value for the money they get in the States. American homes are far more spacious than those we are used to. It is not unusual for a 3,000-square-foot house—which in our terms is a large five- or six-bedroom property—to have only three or four bedrooms . . . . In the Orlando area, a magnet to British family holidaymakers and second-home owners . . . you can buy a four-bedroom house with two-car garage and pool [for only] about £115,000."

In 1995, near the bottom of the most recent California recession, I encouraged Californians to "buy now." In my book, *Stop Renting Now*, I wrote, "Relative to other world-class cities like Hong Kong, Tokyo, Vancouver, London, Paris, and Sydney, home prices in Los Angeles and San Francisco still look downright cheap. And that's even more apparent for noncoastal cities such as Sacramento, Bakersfield, and Santa Rosa. In the year 2001," I forecasted, "many renters will regret the California housing bargains they missed during the mid-1990s."

In fact, it hasn't taken until 2001 for regret to set in among renters. As of 1999, home prices in popular California locations were up 30 percent (or more) over their 1995 levels. Although I would like to claim the forecasting skills of Nostradamus, in reality, the signals were so clearly in place that anyone who can read a map should have been able to see the direction the market was heading.

The Signs Are There

Relative to other advanced countries, U.S. home prices (and our cost of living) remain cheap. Look for increasing waves of international buyers. Not just in the familiar places, but as foreigners shop the world and the United States for the best values, they will discover other areas like Kiawah Island and Copper Mountain. "I see a lot of potential for Fort Lauderdale in attracting Latin Americans," says realty agent Raul Sierra. "It's not as expensive as Miami, and it has the amenities and security they want. Some Latin Americans, too," Raul adds, "are buying less expensive condos on Galt Ocean Miles and in Pompano Beach."

Given the Japanese passion for golf and the paucity of affordable golf courses (not to mention housing) in Japan, will these people soon start buying retirement and vacation homes in the mainland United States? Who else might join the international brigade of buyers marching to America?

Look Forward, Not Backward

When most people look at home prices, they compare today's prices to those of the past. With that perspective, they conclude that "prices are outrageous," or that "homes are no longer a goal investment." Smart buyers interpret history differently. They see an historical pattern of ever rising prices. Yes, they see peaks and valleys, but they realize that successive peaks nearly always top those that have preceded them.

In looking forward, smart buyers also differ from the crowd. Smart buyers know that the future prices of homes are foretold by emerging demographics, lifestyles, incomes, and wealth. They pay attention to market signals. They look for overbuilding. They look for evidence of antigrowth sentiment and shortages of buildable land. They buy the best value they can find. They buy smart because they shop smart.

CHAPTER 9

How to Find Bargain Prices

Some smart buyers don't merely wait for market forces to grow the value of their home equity; they buy their home at a below-market value bargain price. In real estate—unlike the stock market—you not only can make money when you sell, you also can make money when you buy.

Focusing on a Bargain Price

For our purposes, I emphasize that the term "bargain price" means buying a home for less than its current market value. This type of buying advantage applies only to real estate. You can't do it with stocks or bonds. Here's what I mean: Imagine calling your stockbroker at Merrill Lynch and saying, "I see that Microsoft is selling at $180 a share today. But I don't want to pay that much. I am looking for a bargain price. I'm willing to pay $140 to $160 a share tops. Find me someone who will sell within that price range." Of course, on hearing those instructions, your stockbroker would think you were nuts. Your instructions wouldn't make any sense. No sane stock market investor sells at a price less than a stock's quoted market price. Yet, if you told a sharp real estate agent to find a home that you can buy for say, 15 to 30 percent under market, you probably would get your home. Even if the agent failed, you're free to cruise the real estate market without a broker. You can find and negotiate bargain prices on your own.

Do You Want to Buy at a Bargain Price?

Again, the issue of priorities arises: "You can have anything you want, but you can't have everything you want." Although on a few occasions I have been lucky enough to achieve nearly everything I wanted in terms of location, home features, *and* a bargain price, such good fortune remains rare. As a general rule, when you elevate bargain price to must-have status, the home you find may not match up with other of your ideal characteristics.

Nevertheless, buying at a bargain price does provide some strong advantages: (1) You gain an instant boost to your net worth. This additional home equity can help you trade up later to a vacation or retirement home that better matches your personal wants; (2) buying at a bargain price also might help you afford a location or neighborhood that would otherwise prove too expensive; and (3) quite often homes that can be bought at a bargain price also offer great possibilities for value-boosting improvements.

Before you pass up a bargain opportunity, mull over these advantages. Look at homes and talk to homeowners who might be willing to give you a great deal. Who knows? You may get lucky and find almost everything you would like. One fact is clear, though. You'll never know unless you look.

Why Can You Pay Less (or More) Than Market Value?

When you think about it, you can see why homes often sell for less (or more) than their market value. In home buying, a market-value transaction requires that a sale meet five criteria:

1. Buyer and seller are typically motivated. Neither is acting under time or money pressures.
2. Buyer and seller are well informed and knowledgeable about the features of the property and the selling prices of comparable homes.
3. The home has been well advertised. Potential buyers can easily learn that the home is for sale.
4. The seller hasn't enticed the buyer with unusually easy credit or low-cost seller financing.
5. No exceptional sales concessions were made by either the seller or the buyer.

Fortunately for bargain hunters, the world includes many sellers who don't fit the mold of a perfectly informed, unpressured, completely reasonable, precisely calculating, unemotional human being. In fact, just the opposite often occurs. Sellers (and buyers) act out of ignorance, emotions, pressure, confusion, subjective opinions, unreasoned analyses, and a multitude of other human imperfections. Following are some common conditions that often result in a bargain price.

Owners in Distress

Every day people hit hard times. They are laid off from their jobs, file for divorce, suffer accident or illness, experience setbacks in their business, and run into a freight train of other problems. Any or all these calamities can create financial distress. For some, their only way out of a jam is to raise cash by selling their home (or other real estate) quickly at a bargain price.

Owners in distress are especially plentiful when good times turn sour, especially owners of second homes used for getaways or vacations. In good times, sales boom. As the economy slows or enters recession, highflyers get their wings clipped. People who splurged beyond their means now find they must sell fast or drown in a sea of debt.

As noted earlier, shifting exchange rates can also cause distress. During the past several years, many Canadians who own second homes in Florida and other states have suffered a large increase in their costs of ownership. Since the Canadian dollar now buys around 65¢ U.S., a $500 U.S. monthly homeowners fee, maintenance costs, property taxes, and utility bills require Canadians to pay the equivalent of around $675 a month. If the Canadians also owe a monthly mortgage payment, the historically low Canadian dollar exchange rate hurts even more. In addition, the Canadian economy has shown weak growth and high unemployment. As a result, at least a few Canadians are likely to become distress sellers.

Now you might find it unethical to prey on the down and out. Yet, I suspect that a majority of sellers who find themselves in financial distress are quite anxious to get rid of their sleepless, toss-and-turn nights. If that means selling their property for "less than it's worth," then that's what they're willing to do. These people aren't just selling a house, they are buying relief.

Under these circumstances, as long as the sellers believe they have gained from the sale more than they've lost, it's a win-win agreement for both parties. If you are willing to help someone cope with a predicament—as opposed to taking advantage of the person—looking for distressed owners could give you a good deal.

The "Grass-Is-Greener" Sellers

One day Karla Lopez was sitting in her office and in walked the executive vice president of her firm. "Karla," she said, "Stein in the Denver branch just gave us two weeks' notice. If you want the district manager's job you can have it. We will pay you $12,000 more a year plus a bonus. But you have to be relocated and on the job within 45 days."

"Do I want it?" Karla burst out. "Of course I want it. Hope for promotion like this is why I've been working sixty- to eighty-hour weeks for these past four years." Now, in this situation, would Karla think, "Well, the first thing I must do is put my house up for sale and go for top dollar"? Hardly. More than likely Karla would be willing to strike a deal with the first buyer who gave her any type of offer she could live with.

Grass-is-greener sellers stand in contrast to the financially distressed. Whereas distressed owners sell on bargain terms or price to relieve themselves of pain, grass-is-greener sellers are willing to accept a less than top dollar offer so they can quickly capitalize on better opportunities that lie elsewhere. With so many entrepreneurial people today entering self-employment and growing small- to medium-size businesses, your chances for finding grass-is-greener sellers have never been greater.

Stage-of-Life Sellers

When shopping for bargains, you can also find good deals among stage-of-life sellers. These sellers' lifestyle now conflicts with their property. They may no longer enjoy traveling back and forth from their principal home to second home. They may want to return full time to another area closer to kids or grandkids. If they are selling a house, they may have tired of maintenance and security problems. As a result, they may be eager to move to that condo on the fourteenth green at the Bayshore Country Club.

Whatever their reasons, stage-of-life sellers are motivated to make a change in their lives. Former owners of boats often say "the two happiest days of my life were the day I bought my boat, and the day I sold it." Many stage-of-life homeowners express the same feelings. In areas populated by large numbers of older retirees, you can often find stage-of-life sellers who are struggling with the infirmities of old age, serious illness, or death of a spouse and no longer want the responsibility of property ownership.

Disappointed Buyers

For some sellers, that time between euphoria and "we've got to get out of here," is very short indeed. These people are often vacationers or retirees who buy a home without careful thought. As soon as they learn that the reality of their new area contradicts their illusions, they're ready to pack their bags and move as soon as possible, preferably yesterday.

"Some people move down here [to Florida] on the basis of one or two trips to Disney World during March," says retiree counselor Marilee Tihen-Sarchet. "They don't know who their neighbors will be, what social services are available, or what the weather feels like in July." Patricia DiFore who, with her husband, returned to New Jersey after retiring briefly in Tampa says, "Talk about culture shock. We had neighbors who didn't know Donald Trump from the QE2. We couldn't find calzones or cannoli anywhere in the Tampa area. We couldn't go outdoors in the summer. We were miserable."

When I bought my home in South Carolina from some disappointed Illinois emigrants, they just wanted to get out of the state even though it meant selling their newly custom-built home at a loss. But that's the attitude of many disappointed buyers. They're willing to give a bargain price to anyone who will help them quickly bail out of what they perceive as a mistake.

Seller Ignorance

Some sellers underprice their properties because they don't know the selling price of similar homes. Or they may not know of some unique advantage their property has that would favorably distinguish it from other properties. I confess that as a seller, I once sold too low because I was ignorant of the market.

I was living in Palo Alto, California. My home that I decided to sell was located in Dallas, Texas. One year earlier, the house had been appraised for around $110,000, which at the time of the appraisal was about right. So, I thought, I'll ask $125,000. That price is high enough to allow for appreciation and still leave room for negotiating.

That first week the house went on the market, three offers came in at the asking price. Immediately, I knew I had underpriced. What I didn't know but soon learned was that during the year I'd been away, home prices in the Dallas market had jumped 30 percent. After learning of my ignorance, I could have rejected all the offers and raised my price, or I could have put the buyers into a "bidding war." But I didn't. I just decided to sell to the person with the cleanest offer (no contingencies). I was making a good profit, why get greedy?

Seller ignorance (or apathy) often occurs among second-home owners who lose interest in their properties, seldom visit them, and have not personally looked at comparable houses that have sold recently. Sometimes, too, second homes fall into the hands of heirs who know little about the housing market in the area where the home is located. Whatever the reason, ignorant sellers sometimes underprice their homes.

The "Possibility Impaired"

Sometimes you can find bargains because owners don't realize the possibilities their homes have. Earlier I mentioned the Winter Park,

Florida, home that I owned and its beautiful lake views from eight of nine rooms. Actually, though, at the time I bought the house, it suffered a closed floor plan that didn't permit views from either the kitchen or the living room. In addition, although the home was designed with vaulted ceilings, someone had installed suspended acoustic-tile ceiling in the kitchen.

For less than $10,000, I was able to completely change the appearance and livability of the home, including removing portions of several walls to open up the home and enhance the views, and removing the suspended kitchen ceiling and installing a skylight. When one of the previous owners stopped by for a visit, she was amazed. She could not believe how such relatively simple changes could have improved the home in such a dramatic way. "If we had been able to think of these kinds of changes," she said, "we probably would not have sold the house."

I call these types of owners the "possibility impaired." They live with their home's unappealing features for so long that they consider them a natural part of the universe. They don't realize they've got a diamond in the rough. As a result, they price their home for sale without regard for its true potential. They inadvertently let some smart buyer cash in on their creative blindness. Smart buyers look for possibility-impaired sellers. These types of sellers provide a steady supply of bargain-priced homes.

Off-Season Sellers

Although many resort and vacation areas are trying to develop themselves into year-round destinations, most still go through high and low seasons. In the high season, buyers usually outnumber sellers. In the off season, sellers typically outnumber buyers. Given the law of supply and demand, you can probably negotiate a better deal when fewer buyers are competing for a surplus of homes.

As part of your smart buying strategy, learn the time of year when homes for sale outnumber potential buyers by the greatest margin. You will not only enjoy a broader selection properties, you will get a chance to explore the area in the off season to see how it differs in appearance, activities, and living costs. Another good time to buy may be just near the end of peak season. Sellers who haven't yet sold their homes may begin to get anxious about leaving the area with their units still on the market.

Check with realty agents. Every resort and vacation area experiences somewhat different patterns of buying and selling. With the right timing, you increase your chances of finding a bargain.

Bargains Abroad

If you're thinking about buying a home in another country, you face all of the same types of bargain opportunities just discussed. In addition, you might locate a bargain for two other reasons: (1) lower housing costs or (2) favorable exchange rates.

Lower Housing Costs

In most industrial countries, housing prices exceed those in the United States. However, thousands of Americans have bought homes at bargain prices in Mexico, Costa Rica, Honduras, the Dominican Republic, and other (predominately) south-of-the-border locations. One recent hot spot has been the Yucatan area of Mexico. "Here in the Yucatan," reports the *Wall Street Journal*, "are hundreds of turn-of-the-century palaces begging to be restored. Interest is just picking up in the deserted estates, which can offer buyers a good deal. For the most part the estates were built in the late 1800s when Merida, Yucatan, was home to a large thriving class of millionaire ranchers and farmers."

A recent buyer, David Taub, a doctor from South Carolina says, "I love this place because it's so peaceful and remote." Dr. Taub's 100-acre spread features a hacienda, pool, orchards, and a chapel where the local residents still come for private services. Although he refused to disclose his purchase price, Dr. Taub says that the price was so low that he can visit the property only three or four times a year and still feel like he got a bargain.

"The Yucatan is hot right now; people are buying like crazy," says Margaret Andrews, whose Illinois family first bought in the area decades ago. "It's fantasyland," she adds, "Here we live like multimillionaires which, believe me, we are not." The low living costs carry through to the labor and materials necessary to restore and renovate the homes to modern standards. "Fifty thousands dollars, tops, would bring the most gutted manor home back to life," reports a local realty consultant. Also, adding to the attraction of the area as it becomes increasingly popular as a tourist destination are cheap direct flights to Merida from the United States.

Home Prices Low, But Going Up

Following the general pattern, prices for Yucatan estates are up considerably from five or ten years ago when the area was first "discovered." But they're still "bargains" by U.S. standards and, quite likely, very good bargains compared to the prices they will fetch during the coming ten years.

Roberto Hernandez, a prominent Mexican banker and real estate investor, has bought thirty of these homes at prices ranging from $100,000 to $150,000 (up from less than $50,000 during the 1980s). "In the next ten years," says Hernandez, "50 million baby boomers are going to retire. No place offers what the Yucatan offers." Although Hernandez is off somewhat on his demographics, he is right on with his investment strategy. As more people learn that they can own a landed estate in Mexico (albeit one that needs work) for less than the price of a decent Miami condo, estate prices will take off—especially considering that the Yucatan offers lower crime rates and better weather than Miami.

The Good Life at Low Cost

The Yucatan is just one location in Mexico and throughout the world where middle- to upper-middle income Americans can "live like millionaires." And just as the English have colonized a rural area of France that at one time offered bargain prices, many more foreign locations likely will be colonized by Americans. As popular U.S. vacation and retirement areas continue their price escalation, Americans will take their satellite dishes, computers, and AOL connections to parts heretofore unknown. Who cares about home delivery of the *Times* when you can grab it (and the *Drudge Report*) off the Internet? Or an even better question is, Who cares about the *Times* or the *Drudge Report*, period, if you can find a bargain-priced paradise of warm sun, ocean breezes, and a laid-back lifestyle?

Favorable Exchange Rates

The flux of international exchange rates also offers second-home buyers the opportunity to find bargain-priced properties in other countries. When the U.S. dollar strengthens against other currencies, Americans can get more house for their money. This condition exists right now for homes in Australia, New Zealand, and Canada. In just the past year, too, the dollar has strengthened dramatically against the cruzeiro (Brazil) and somewhat against the pesos of Mexico and Argentina. Of course, with the give and take of exchange rates worldwide, the principle of getting more house for the money applies universally.

Exchange Rate Risk (The Downside)

After renting for a while in Florida, Canadian retiree Roberta Way-Clark decided to buy a small place in Clearwater. But with the continuing slide of the Canadian dollar against the U.S. dollar, Roberta is fearing that she might not be able to hold on much longer. "I'm going to have to cut back my winter stay from the five months I'd planned," she says. The $325 U.S. monthly space rental for her mobile home now costs her $500 a month Canadian. "I don't want to give it up, but I may have to," she laments.

In addition, due to Canada's economic weakness, Roberta's Canadian investment portfolio has lost value. She, like many other Canadians, may become one of those distressed sellers mentioned earlier. Roberta's plight illustrates the exchange rate risk problem. If you plan to pay your costs of second-home ownership with funds from your home country, those costs can go up substantially. When a once favorable exchange rate turns adverse, you get squeezed.

You can protect yourself against this risk in two ways. First, simply shift part of your savings or investments into the peso, cruzeiro, punt, or whatever denominated account is appropriate. Or, second, although somewhat more complex, you can enter the currency futures market (a topic that clearly goes beyond our discussion here). Either way, with foresight, you need not experience the "exchange-rate poverty" now felt by Roberta Way-Clark.

Exchange Rate Advantage (The Upside)

On the positive side, if the U.S. dollar falls against the currency of the country where you own a vacation or retirement home, your wealth will increase. Say you buy a False Creek (Vancouver) condominium at a price of $300,000 Canadian. You pay $200,000 U.S. Then the Canadian dollar strengthens to a ratio of $1.25 C $ to $1.00 U.S. (from 1.5 to 1). If you sell your condo for the price you paid in Canadian dollars, you would be able to convert it into $240,000 U.S. Your net worth increases by $40,000 U.S. If you sold your condo for more than you paid (as would be likely due to a strengthening Canadian economy), you pick up even greater gains.

Growth Market

Although buying a vacation or retirement home outside the United States may still not appeal to a majority of Americans, the trend will continue to grow. Europeans, Canadians, Mexicans, and other nationalities have long-standing traditions of buying homes abroad. Americans are sure to follow suit. In addition to possible bargain prices and lower living costs, many "soon-to-be-discovered" foreign locations will undoubtedly show strong rates of appreciation during the coming decade. Think Aspen 1987, Kiawah Island 1990, or even Eugene, Oregon, as late as 1993. Up-and-coming foreign locations offer even stronger potential for gains in value.

Search Proactively

How many times have you found a $100 bill lying on a sidewalk in plain view? Quite likely, never. Free money doesn't sit around waiting for takers. The same goes for bargain-priced properties. Once they're discovered, they don't last long. (Recall my home in Dallas that I underpriced. Three offers in the first weekend.) So, to improve your odds of finding a bargain, try searching proactively.

Practice Networking

The best time to find a bargain is before the owners have put their property up for sale. Not only do you save the owners the hassle of the selling process, you greatly reduce the threat of competitive bids. Plus, owners who haven't yet formally committed to selling may lack good information about the market value of their homes. This possibility increases if the owners haven't visited their property recently.

A Bargain Price for Less Hassle

Even people who accurately know the market value of their property may be willing to give you a bargain price. They gain a quick sale. But also they eliminate the selling hassle and the 6 percent or 7 percent real estate agent's commission. If, say, the home is reasonably valued around $200,000, the owners would probably come out ahead by selling to you at a price of $180,000 to $185,000 or possibly lower if the idea of a quick and easy sale strongly appeals to them. Especially when the sellers have owned the property for a number of years, and now aren't using it much, they may see your offer as found money.

Publicize What You Want

Tell everyone you know that you're looking to buy. Ask people you see who they know that might be willing to sell. Publicize this interest at your church, clubs, activities, and employer. Tell clients and customers. Promise a home entertainment center to anyone who refers you to a property that you eventually buy. Publicize your interest in those locations that may appeal to you. Post your interest on electronic bulletin boards and chat rooms.

When I was buying rental houses, I told every seller that I was an active buyer. Just that slight attempt at networking paid off with several referrals and property purchases. When I sold my South Carolina home, I hosted a faculty and graduate-student party. When party attendees complimented me on the home, I told them that I was planning to sell. It didn't take long for the word to spread. I received two expressions of interest and subsequently a sale. Networking works.

"Cold Call" Owners

In their effort to obtain listings, real estate agents "cold call" potential sellers, that is, they contact people who haven't yet decided to sell. Agents' cold-call techniques typically include telephoning property owners with names gathered from a criss-cross directory, which lists addresses and corresponding telephone numbers, walking the neighborhood and talking to residents, circulating flyers by mail or doorknob hangers, and by taking part in neighborhood or community-sponsored events. By cultivating a listing "farm," an agent hopes to become known in the area. He or she tries to be in position to be the first person to learn of a potential owner's wish to sell.

You might take a lesson from the real estate agent's book. Try to cultivate a farm in the neighborhoods or communities where you would like to buy. You could circulate a flyer that reads: "Before you list your home for sale, call me. I would like to buy a home in this neighborhood directly from the owners. Let's see if we can create an agreement that will benefit both of us." As with networking, if property owners can save time, effort, and money by selling direct, they may be willing to offer you a favorable price (or terms).

Contact Out-of-the-Area Owners

Undoubtedly, your farm area will include some properties (vacant or tenant occupied) that are owned by people who don't live in the neighborhood. These owners may not see your flyers, nor will they be listed in a criss-cross directory. To learn how to reach these potential sellers, you may have to ask neighbors of nearby properties or talk directly with tenants in the units occupied.

If this research doesn't reveal the owners' names and addresses, you can next contact the county property tax assessor's office. There, you can learn where and to whom the property tax statements are being sent. It's not unusual to find that these out-of-the-area property owners are the "sleeping sellers" that you are looking for. They would like to sell, but haven't as yet awakened to that fact. With luck, you could be their alarm clock.

Utilize Newspapers

Most homebuyers only use newspapers one way: They read the for sale ads placed by property owners and real estate agents. This approach presents two serious drawbacks: (1) If a property isn't advertised, you won't learn about it and (2) if the ad for a property you might be interested in is not written effectively, you may pass by the ad without serious notice.

To counter these drawbacks, run your own advertisement in the "wanted to buy" column. Describe the type of property and terms you're looking for. You'll invite serious sellers to contact you. When I began buying real estate, I used this technique to locate about 30 percent of the properties I bought.

As another way to use the newspaper, read through the "houses for rent," "condos for rent," and "apartments for rent" ads. Not only will this help you gauge rental levels, quite often you'll see properties advertised as "lease-option" or "for rent or sale." These kinds of ads generally indicate a flexible seller.

To search for potential bargain sellers in the newspaper, don't limit your search to the classified real estate ads. You might also locate names of people from public notices, births, divorces, deaths, bankruptcy, foreclosure, or marriage. Each of these events can trigger the need to sell real estate quickly. If you contact these potential sellers before they have listed with a real estate firm, you stand a fair chance of buying a bargain price.

Consider Agent Services

In addition to your own search, you will probably want to rely on the services of a real estate agent. Consider this advice from a career real estate investor and renovator, Suzanne Brangham. In her excellent book, *Housewise*, she says:

> *Real estate agents are invaluable. You need them as much as they need you. After you have narrowed your choice to one or two neighborhoods or towns, enlist the aid of an expert. Your real estate agent will be your guide so you can sit back, take out*

your notebook, ask questions, and learn. . . . Good agents know what properties are selling for, which areas are strong, and which neighborhoods are getting hot. . . .

If you let your agent know that you really plan to buy, he (or she) will do everything short of breaking and entering to show you the properties that are available. . . . I'd been lusting after a beautiful two-unit building, but it had never been up for sale. My agent called me the minute it was listed and I bought it in less than an hour. In fact, I soon become notorious for signing offer forms on the roof of her car. When there's a race to get in your bid on a particularly juicy piece of property, a faithful agent who knows exactly what you want can make all the difference.

In addition to showing you properties and neighborhoods, your agent should:

- Research comp sales and rent levels so you can better understand values.
- Act as an intermediary in negotiations.
- Recommend other professionals whose service you may need (lawyer, mortgage broker, contractor, designer, architect, property inspectors).
- Handle innumerable details and problems that always seem to pop up on the way from contract to closing.
- Clue you in on what types of interest and market activity have developed around various properties.
- Give you an insider's glimpse into an area to let you know who's doing what and where.
- Disclose negatives about a property or neighborhood that otherwise might have escaped your attention.

Your key to getting topflight service from a real estate agent lies in knowing what services to request and what questions to ask. If your agent believes that you will accept "order taker" service, that's all you may get. Instead, tell the agent you want answers and analyses that flow from the topics discussed throughout this book. Smart buyers control and direct their agents; they don't let their agents control them.

Beware of Stale and Expired Listings

For any number of reasons, many properties listed with real estate agents don't sell during their original listing period. When this situation occurs, the listing agent will try to get the owners to relist with his or her firm. Quite likely, agents from other brokerage firms will also approach the sellers. However, here's a technique you can use to possibly arrange a bargain purchase. When you notice a listed property that looks like it might fit your requirements, *do not* call the listing agent, and *do not* call or stop by to talk to the owners. Instead, write the owners a letter stating the price and terms that you would consider paying. Then ask the owners to contact you after their listing has expired. (If a seller goes behind his agent's back and arranges a sale while the property is listed, the owner is still legally obligated to pay the sales commission.)

Consider this scenario: A property is listed at $200,000, which is a reasonable estimate of its market value. The listing contract specifies a 6 percent sales commission. The sellers have told themselves that they will accept nothing less than $192,500, which means that after selling expenses they would net around $180,000. Your offer is at $175,000. Would the sellers accept it? Or would they relist, postpone their move, and hold out for a net of $5,000 to $10,000 more?

The decision, of course, would depend on the sellers' finances, their reason for moving, and any other pressures they may be facing. But you can see that even though your offer is low relative to the value of the house, it still provides the sellers almost as much as they could expect if their agent found them a buyer. (Naturally, your letter offer would not formally commit you to the purchase. It would simply state the price of terms that you have in mind.)

Maintain Buyer Loyalty

If you choose to work with a real estate agent, you should deal fairly and squarely with that agent. If you do plan to search on your own, tell the agent what you are doing. Don't take, take, and take from a hardworking agent, then cut the agent out of an expected fee with an unagented purchase from an FSBO (for sale by owner). At times, the best way to snag a bargain is to go it alone. But treat your agent fairly. Inform her of your actions. Let her know up front that if you find a bargain on your own, you will buy it. Then, the agent can decide how much time, effort, and research she wants to invest in you. As a general rule, prospective buyers who show the most loyalty to their agents get the best service. These loyal buyers also get called first when a "juicy piece of property" hits (or is about to hit) the market.

Search the Web for Bargains

I originally planned to include a section describing how you can use the World Wide Web to search for a vacation, retirement, or getaway home. However, the Internet is changing so fast that anything I write could be out-of-date tomorrow, not to mention next year. So, for the latest on using the Internet to search for a second home, go to my website (www.stoprentingnow.com). Although I set up this site specifically for first-time homebuyers, I am now adding pages and links to serve buyers of retirement, vacation, and getaway homes.

I have used the Internet to look at properties everywhere from Kenya to Western Australia. In the future, the Web will become a beginning (but never exclusive) resource for all smart second-home buyers as they search to discover homes, locations, and bargain prices.

Not All Bargain Prices Are Bargains

Although good deals go fast, remember that not all so-called bargain-priced properties are good deals. You have received a good deal only if you could sell the property for substantially more than you have put into it. Beware of environmental problems (e.g., lead paint, underground storage tanks, asbestos, contaminated well water). Temper your eagerness to buy a bargain-priced property with a thorough physical, financial, market, and legal analysis. Especially in the case of very attractive seller financing, don't jump at a what looks like a great deal without subjecting it to rigorous scrutiny. While sometimes you must act quickly, keep in that mind the less you know about a property or the more you assume without verification or inspections, the greater your risk. Until you're confident about a property, don't let a seller's apparent eagerness to sell become your pressure to buy.

Lines of Defense

That house you bought at a bargain price may not seem like such a great deal after you learn the roof leaks, the foundation is crumbling, and termites are eating away the floor joists. If the next-door neighbors behave like an unruly mob of loud ruffians, you also may find that you can't enjoy the R&R that you were looking forward to. There are three lines of defense to guard against these problems.

1. Thoroughly inspect the property, talk to nearby residents, walk the neighborhood, and make sure you're working with a knowledgeable and trustworthy real estate agent.
2. Get the property checked out by a property inspector, a structural engineer, a pest control expert, or other specialists who can professionally judge the condition of the property.
3. Ask the sellers to complete a seller disclosure statement.

The Disclosure Revolution

Most states now require sellers to complete a seller disclosure statement that lists and explains all *known* problems or defects that may plague the property. But even if the state (or country) where you are buying doesn't mandate seller disclosure, you still should obtain a disclosure form (most major realty firms keep blank copies on hand) and ask the sellers to fill it out. As you review this completed disclosure statement, remember the following:

- Sellers are not required to disclose facts or conditions of which they are unaware.
- The disclosure is a statement of the past, not a guarantee of the future. By completing the statement, the seller does not warrant the condition of the property.
- Many questions require somewhat subjective answers; for example, are playing children a neighborhood "noise" problem? Is a planned street widening an "adverse" condition?

- Disclosure statements may not require the sellers to disclose conditions that are readily observable to you.
- Pay close attention to any seller (or agent) statements that begin, "I believe," "I think," "as far as we know," and other similar hedges. Don't accept these answers as conclusive. Write a note to yourself to follow up with further inquiry or inspection.

Seller disclosure statements reduce the chance for unwelcome surprise after you buy a property. Even so, be sure to independently check out the property to satisfy yourself that you know what you are buying.

CHAPTER 10

How to Negotiate a Bargain Agreement

Chapter 9 focuses on buying at a bargain price. Essentially, you achieve a bargain when you buy a property you want at a price less than its market value. Or, sometimes you might look at it another way: You know you've achieved a bargain when you can sell your second home at a much higher price than you paid. But there's still another way to define a bargain. With this view, you focus on the entire agreement, not just the purchase price. Although you win when you buy a home for less than its worth, you also can win with an agreement that gives you nearly everything else that you want. In other words, as a practical matter, you never negotiate only price. You also must agree on other parts of the contract. So with this holistic view in mind, here are some tips that can help you negotiate a great buy.

Don't Play Hardball

Even many experienced homebuyers approach purchase negotiations with uncertainty and nervousness. They don't quite know what to expect. Others falsely believe that a skillful negotiator dips into a bag of tricks and pulls out deceptive techniques like lowballing, weasel clauses, running a bluff, shotgunning, "dressing to impress" (pretending to be something you're not), bad-mouthing (deflating the owners' high opinion of their home), asking for the moon and the stars, and eleventh-hour surprises (at the last minute before closing, insisting on contract changes in your favor). One book on real estate negotiating even advises, "Remember you are in a war and you must use every weapon available to win." These hardball tactics might seem to make sense to those who use them, but experience shows that they most often backfire.

Develop a Cooperative Attitude

Bob Woolf, agent, attorney, and past negotiator for many well-known figures including Larry Bird, Gene Shalit, Larry King, and Joe Montana, says, "When I enter a negotiation, my attitude is, 'I'm going to make a deal.' I don't start with a negative thought or word. I try to foster a spirit of cooperation. I want the other party to feel that I'm forthright, cheerful, confident, and determined to reach their goals. If I'm sufficiently sensitive to the other party, I firmly believe they will be predisposed to make an agreement with me. To a degree, your attitude will become a self-fulfilling prophecy."

Bob Woolf's professional advice applies whether you are negotiating a big-time sports contract or a purchase agreement for a home—especially a purchase agreement for a home. You're usually wise to display a cooperative "Let's reach an agreement" attitude. Act in good faith. Play by the rules of courtesy. You want to buy a home. The sellers want to sell a home. Your best chance for success comes when all parties cooperate to help each other.

Learn the Sellers' Objectives

To find common ground for cooperation, find out as much as you can about the sellers' needs. Why are they selling? What time pressures do they face? Have they planned a moving date? Have they agreed to buy another home? Are they in a position to carry back financing? How much equity do they have in their home? Find out the sellers' fears, wants, and "have-to-haves." Are they really motivated to sell?

Everyone knows that buying a home arouses strong emotions. But so does selling a home. The sellers may be leaving friends and neighbors. Their children may be losing friends and classmates. Over the years, the sellers may have invested heart and soul to maintain their home, cultivate a flower garden, or redecorate and remodel. They may have years of fond vacation memories attached to the home. The more you learn about the sellers' financial, personal, and emotional needs, the better you and your Realtor can steer a cooperative path for negotiations.

One last point: Note that people from different cultures and countries approach negotiations from different perspectives. If you are buying a home from sellers whose ethnic, religious, or national background differs from yours, stay alert to how these differences may affect their expectations. Celia Young, a consultant in cross-cultural business etiquette and negotiating skill, says, "When doing business cross-culturally, we need to be aware of our own reactions and interactions. . . . That way we will be more sensitive to possible misunderstandings."

Clarify Your Own Goals and Priorities

After you have learned as much as possible about the sellers' needs and selling objectives, make sure you clarify your own goals and priorities. You can't get what you want unless you know what you want. Do the home's features and location help you satisfy nearly *all* of your most important buying goals?

Order Takers Revisited

I emphasize the importance of knowing your goals because many real estate agents that you will deal with simply want to "take your order." They ask you to describe what you're looking for exclusively in terms of features, location, and price range (one-bedroom, two-bath villa on a golf course at a price less than $125,000). At first glance, such an approach may seem reasonable. But if you're thinking in terms of multiple goals and potential trade-offs (see, for example, the list discussed in the Introduction), such a narrow description limits your focus. You will miss seeing other properties that might offer a far better combination of features and benefits. While the one-bedroom units may serve your personal needs, on inquiring you may find that the two- or even three-bedroom units rent out much easier and at substantially higher rent levels.

As you bring into view a variety of financial and personal objectives, the short-sightedness of defining "features, location, and price range" becomes even more apparent. So, before you set out to negotiate an agreement, revisit the goals you would like to achieve. Avoid order-taker agents. Work with an intelligent agent who displays the ability to listen and understand. To find the property that's best for you, tell your agent the package of benefits that you would like your second home to provide. Then, encourage the agent to use his or her market savvy, experience, and creativity not only to suggest specific properties, but also to formulate a good negotiation strategy.

Introducing the Selling Agent

The "selling agent" represents a type of realty agent who also can steer you wrong. Such an agent basically ignores or downplays your needs and wants, and focuses on why you should buy the property he or she most wants to sell. (In the trade this selling technique is called "overcoming objections.")

I recently encountered a selling agent in a resort area where I was tentatively shopping for a second home. Here's what happened: I walked into an open house and told the agent that I was just in the preliminary stage of gathering market information. I further told her that I was trying *to learn* the various property types, features, and price ranges that I might want to consider. In other words, I was conveying the fact that I needed far more market information before I would even begin to think about writing up an offer for a property.

Alas, did my intent and purpose motivate the agent to change her tactics from selling to helping? No, she just pressed harder: "Well, this house is really a bargain. The owners are really motivated. They're even willing to consider owner financing. You don't want to wait too long on this one." In later follow-up phone calls and letters, the agent continued to press the same theme of bargain price and motivated sellers. She never tried to determine my buying motives. Yet, she almost hooked me. I confess that two of my hot buttons are "bargain price" and "owner financing."

And therein lies the danger for all home buyers: If you don't identify and keep in view your full complement of goals, you, too, might be tempted to yield to selling pressure. Whether the agent presses "bargain price," "owner financing," "fantastic view," "won't last," or another type of hot button, some skillful agents can pull you into a purchase agreement. They can make the feature they're selling seem all-important, while at the same time they divert you from thinking about the broader range of benefits that better match your total needs and wants.

When it comes to negotiating your agreement, stand for something, or, as a popular country song tells us, "you'll fall for anything." Make your priorities clear to yourself and to realty agents. Don't fall prey to agents who would rather earn a quick commission by pushing you into an offer than help you sort through a variety of possibilities and trade-offs. To find and negotiate the best property agreement, you must vaccinate yourself against both the lazy order-taker and the high-pressure selling agents.

Do Your Homework

To negotiate effectively, you must understand the home and the current market. Know the features of the home, its relative desirability, recent selling prices of other homes in the neighborhood, recent sales activity (buyer's market or seller's market), normal terms of financing, and typical closing costs and procedures. Negotiations won't center exclusively on either your needs and wants or the sellers' needs and wants. Negotiations will operate within the context of market conditions.

Occasionally sellers say something like this: "We spent $20,000 to add on a den and remodel the kitchen and bathrooms. We have to get our money back from these improvements." But if you don't think the sellers' improvements add $20,000 of market value to the home, don't pay it. The sellers aren't real sellers. Until they price their home in line with the market, they are wasting everybody's time, including their own.

Good negotiators tie their wants to reality. When either buyers or sellers unrealistically inflate their expectations, they usually end up disappointed. Understanding market realities not only helps you shop for home, it helps you negotiate a good agreement.

Make a Solid First Offer

What price should you first offer for the home you've chosen? In theory, the answer to that question is easy: Don't make your first offer too low or too high. Sellers often have their emotions and their self-image wrapped up in their home. They're likely to take an unrealistically low offer as an insult. It destroys goodwill and shuts down their urge to cooperate with you. "Since it's quite obvious a 'lowballer' is trying to take advantage of the sellers," says Realtor Brenda Flagg, "the sellers don't come back with any counteroffer at all."

Just as you don't want to offer too little, neither do you want to offer too much. Ideally, you should aim for an opening bid that's high enough to pique the sellers' interest, but somewhat less than the price you actually expect the sellers will accept. You want the sellers to see you as a serious buyer. In other words, your first offer should look like a solid, yet conservative, offer.

As a practical matter, though, you can't draw a fine line between a lowball offer and a solid, conservative offer. The difference between a lowball offer and a solid offer depends on local market conditions, local negotiating practices, and the sellers' needs, motivations, and perceptions. Also, it depends on how badly you want the home. The lower your offer, the more risk you run that the sellers will not respond. They may even tell you to get lost. However, if you really don't care whether you lose the home, then lowball offers make more sense.

Nevertheless, even with a lowball offer, don't display a crude and rude "take it or leave it" attitude. To the best of your ability, explain why and how the sellers might gain by taking a low price. What are you willing to give in return?

Don't Just Compromise—Conciliate

Throughout your negotiations, never forget that you are not only negotiating price, you are negotiating an agreement. Don't let negotiations focus on price alone. Don't just compromise—conciliate. Look for other parts of the agreement that may be important to you or the sellers. Besides price, following are some other negotiating points you can use to get the sellers to accept your offer.

Anxiety Relief

Sellers worry that their sale won't close for some reason or another. The more you can assure the sellers that you're a solid buyer who is willing and able to close, the more they may be willing to accept a lower price. To relieve seller anxiety, try one or more of these eight techniques:

1. Increase the amount of your earnest money deposit.
2. Produce a preapproval letter from a mortgage lender (if you are financing the purchase).
3. If you're paying cash or making a large down payment, emphasize that fact. Cash counts. If you've got it, use it to boost your position.
4. Get your Realtor to emphasize the strength of your character, stability in your job and community, how well you will take care of the home, or other positive personal factors.
5. Avoid weasel clauses in your offer. A "weasel clause" is any clause that lets you weasel out of, or escape from, a contract without obligation. One of the easiest and most obvious weasel clauses states, "This offer is subject to the approval of our attorney." If you need to consult an attorney, do it before you begin negotiations. (In some states, by custom, attorneys routinely get involved in negotiating home purchase agreements. Nevertheless, the same advice holds. The firmer your offer, the more likely the sellers will treat you as a serious buyer and make concessions toward an agreement.)
6. Avoid indefinite contingency clauses such as "Offer subject to borrowing $10,000 in a home equity loan"; or sometimes retirees write into their offer, "Subject to the sale of our current home." Clauses like these raise the sellers' doubts, increase their anxiety, and generate reluctance to accept your offer.
7. When you do write a contingency clause into the contract, make it definite and as short-term as possible. "Buyers will secure a property inspection report within five days." Or "Buyers agree

to submit mortgage loan application within forty-eight hours."
Or "Sellers are released from obligation if buyers do not produce
a letter of mortgage loan approval within thirty days." These
clauses indicate you're not going to drag your feet through the
transaction.

8. Make your contingency clauses realistic. Don't condition your
   purchase on finding mortgage money at 7 percent if market
   rates are at 8.5 percent. Don't require a twenty-seven-year-old
   house to be free of all defects. The firmer your offer, the more
   willing the sellers may be to accept less than they originally had
   in mind. Plan your offer with no more escape hatches than you
   need (but no fewer either). Many sellers will trade a lower price
   for the peace of mind of a near-certain sale.

Possession Date and Closing Date

How soon do the sellers prefer to close? When do the sellers want to
give possession? Home buying and selling often calls for a balancing
act. Sometimes sellers need to speed things up. On other occasions they
may want to close quickly, but delay turning the house over to you until
after they have bought another home. Or the sellers may want to keep
their children in the same school until the end of the term. It's possible
the sellers may even want to give possession before they close. Prior to
negotiating, find out whether the sellers strongly prefer any specific
dates for closing and possession. If they do, you may have found a bar-
gaining chip for a reduced price.

Nominal Price versus Effective Price

Some sellers may be tough to negotiate with on price. They know the
lowest price they will accept and won't budge further. Sometimes price
stands as a symbol of the sellers' egos. If you run up against sellers like
this, you might agree to the price they insist on. At the same time, you
can ask the sellers for concessions that reduce the effective price you'll
pay. For example:

- The sales price could include personal property such as the washer
  and dryer, kitchen appliances, window blinds, an oriental rug, or

that antique buffet that's too large for the sellers' new condominium. Maybe the sellers will throw in that 21-foot Winnebago
that's sitting in the garage.

- The agreement could shift more of the closing costs to the sellers,
  including some of your mortgage points. Or you could ask the
  sellers to buy down your interest rate.
- The agreement could give you an escrow credit for repairs or dec-
  oration. Some lenders may even let you use this money as part of
  your down payment.
- In exchange for the price they want, the sellers could agree to
  carry back some or all of the financing. If seller financing saves
  you money on points, closing costs, or interest rate, it might make
  sense for you to trade off a higher price for favorable terms.

Leave Something on the Table

As you conciliate the terms of your agreement, don't push for everything you can possibly get. Negotiating pro Bob Woolf points out, "A
successful negotiation isn't one where I get everything. I haven't done
a single contract where I couldn't have got more money. I always leave
something on the table." Why? "Because," says Woolf, "it's possible to
push too hard so you create antagonism. If someone feels you held
them up, they're going to try to get back at you later. The idea is to
make an agreement that works."

You and the sellers may run into unanticipated snags concerning
any number of things: closing date, credit check, mortgage approval,
closing costs, property inspections, property condition, seller disclo-
sures, property repairs, appraisal, title search, survey, moving date, personal property, or fixtures. If you and the sellers both feel good about
each other and your basic agreement, you should be able to resolve any
surprises or setbacks that come up. Leaving something on the table can
help you and the sellers pave over any potholes you may hit on the way
to a successful closing.

Win-Win Negotiating

Throughout the entire negotiating process, never stray far from the
idea of win-win. Pay close attention to the sellers' needs, wants, and

expectations. Make sure, too, the sellers understand and appreciate your situation.

You and the sellers should see each other "as working side by side to attack the problem, not each other," advise Robert Fisher and William Ury of the Harvard Negotiating Project, and authors of *Getting to Yes*. Focus on underlying interests and potential benefits. Try not to get bogged down in ego battles by arguing things like, "Well, our position is. . . ." Forget about your position. Look for possibilities. "Invent options for mutual gain," say Ury and Fisher.

With good knowledge of the market, cooperative sellers, a "let's make a deal" attitude, and a realty professional skilled in possibility analysis, you and the sellers can achieve the goal you need most: a win-win purchase agreement.

CHAPTER 11

How to Save Thousands on Your Financing

"**L**enders are offering vacation-home mortgages with more flexible terms. In the past you would have to put down 20 percent or 30 percent of the purchase price," says Tom Halley, an executive vice president at Countrywide Funding, "but we can now do a vacation home loan with 10 percent down."

To that "flexibility," now add relatively lower interest rates. "In a sharp break from the past, interest rates for vacation homes are now generally no higher than for primary residences. At current levels, these rates are a significant factor in what has become an explosive convergence of demographics and finance," reports the *New York Times*. With this "explosive convergence," no wonder *U.S.A. Today* headlined a recent front-page article, "Vacation Getaway Sales Going through the Roof."

Financing Rules Differ across the Country

There's no doubt that easier and lower cost financing is helping to drive second-home sales "through the roof." But "easier" and "low cost" don't apply to all lenders, or to all borrowers. In upscale and growing Vero Beach, Florida, "Local banks fight each other for business," reports Joe Weibel, a development company executive. "In this environment lenders are likely to be flexible on down payments, interest rates, points, and closing costs, particularly if you walk in with a wad of cash."

For second homes in Michigan, though, the *Detroit News* reports, "Demand is driving property values in southern Michigan as high as $150,000 for even the most rustic [nonwinterized] lakefront cabins—with year-round waterfront property selling for much more. However, those prices don't seem to deter buyers, nor do the *stricter guidelines* [italics added] on second-home mortgages. These include higher interest rates than those for primary homes and down payment requirements of 25 to 35 percent."

Easier or Tougher?

So which is it? Easier or tougher to obtain a mortgage on a second home? The answer is, it all depends. Among other things it depends on:

- The lender you select
- How you present yourself to that lender
- The property you select
- How you plan to use the property
- The local economy and the competitive lending environment

As a general observation, today, increasing numbers of mortgage lenders are bending over backwards to make loans on second homes. Steep competition is leading them to make deals like never before. But lenders are also showing a bit of schizophrenia. They realize that if economic conditions turn south, borrowers tend to walk away from their second-home mortgages faster than they would their primary home loans. Also, property values in some vacation and resort areas have tended to boom and bust roller-coaster style. Add to those negatives, the increased risk of damage that results if you leave the home unoccupied for much of the year. Taken together, you can see why lenders might want to apply tougher standards to mortgages on second homes.

Hope and Fear

In other words, mortgage lenders think the same way most people think. They smell hot profit potential and want to taste it. But they fear getting burned. So, unless you're a no-risk borrower, who would like to finance a no-risk property, in a no-risk location, don't assume the lenders you talk with will automatically "fight each other for your business."

To help you get the best rate and terms possible, then, this chapter reviews some mortgage basics. Even though your past mortgage experience already has taught you much of what follows, you still might profit from a quick review. Borrowers who give more thought and planning to their mortgage decision often can slice their financing costs by thousands (sometimes tens of thousands) of dollars.

Your Borrower Profile

The lender wants to answer one primary question about you: Are you a manageable credit risk? Fortunately, you can greatly influence the answer that the lender comes up with. Although the rapid spread of electronic credit scoring (see "Credit Scoring" as follows) has introduced an element of mystery into the mortgage lending decision, some common rules still apply.

Common Rules

Monthly Debts

The lower your monthly outgo, the more money that will remain to pay the mortgage on your second home. So, first list all of your monthly payments such as:

- Credit cards
- Department store accounts
- Car no. 1
- Car no. 2
- Car no. 3
- First mortgage
- Country club due
- Child care
- Home equity loan

- Old student loans
- Child support
- Alimony
- PITI (principal, interest, taxes, insurance)
- Homeowners' association fees
- Cosigner obligations
- College tuition

Look through your checking account records. Where is your money going? What expenses can you eliminate? Which ones can you reduce? Which ones can you consolidate? Can you sell a car and pay off any loans? Can you refinance your car or your house to get lower payments? Can you apply for a new higher limit, lower rate credit card and then can you roll all of your credit card balances into that single account to obtain a lower monthly payment?

Lenders love borrowers who show frugal spending patterns and low (or no) monthly debt. Anything you do to achieve those ends will help strengthen your borrower profile.

Cash Reserves

Lenders also love high cash balances. If your income falls or stops temporarily, will you be able to continue making the mortgage payments on your second home? In our era of downsizing, freelance consulting, and self-employment, lenders would like you to maintain a large financial cushion that can soften any setbacks. Do you have any idle assets that you can convert to cash (car, boat, recreational vehicle, antiques, artwork)? Even if it's a car or boat that you need (or want), you still might sell it now. Put the cash in the bank. Then reacquire it after your second-home loan has closed.

When you show your net worth in possessions, lenders never quite know how much weight to give to the dollar amounts you show. Lending experience proves two truths: (1) Borrowers overstate the value of their possessions (from houses to business interests to home furnishings) and (2) even when the assets are valued fairly, those values may not be easily realized (illiquidity) and their prices may fall in hard times (volatility). To a lender, nothing counts as much as cash. The more you have, the better.

Income: Quantity, Stability, Growth

In these good (but uncertain) economic times, how can you prove to a lender that your income is as much as you say it is? You show W-2s and tax returns. If you have trouble documenting the amount of your income, you may face trouble getting your loan. Beyond verification of amount (which is primarily a problem for the self-employed), lenders want to know whether your income goes up and down like a yo-yo. Or is it as stable as a G-14 employee of the federal government? Have you worked for the same company for sixteen years? Or have you changed jobs more often than you've traded cars?

What about your career path? Upward without limit—or dead end? Ideally, lenders like to see the best of all worlds: a high income (relative to your monthly obligations); little or no downside risk (layoff, downsizing, a drop in your fees or commissions); and, a rising- (rather than shooting-) star career.

Credit History

You've heard it a hundred times and it's true: Before you apply for a mortgage loan, get copies of your credit records from Equifax (1-800-685-1111), and Experian (1-888-397-3742). Check for errors. Get mistakes corrected. With 120 million names on file, one billion accounts, and tens of billions of data entries each year, mistakes happen. And they happen all too frequently according to every consumer group and government agency that has looked into the problem. Don't wait until you need credit to discover errors. Check your credit records now.

Naturally, your credit records report whether you have paid your bills as scheduled. But lenders also take interest in the following:

- The number of accounts you currently have open
- The number of accounts with outstanding balances
- How many account balances are pressing against their limits
- The number of credit inquiries registered by other lenders

In every instance, more is worse. If credit history could present a problem for you, get to work on it early. Close accounts, pay down balances, don't go around applying to six or eight lenders for a new car loan. If you suffer credit dings, dents, or total collisions, be prepared to explain them. A one-time total wreck won't prove fatal if it resulted from a one-time-never-to-happen-again circumstance—especially one that was beyond your immediate control—but an accident-prone life looks bad.

Credit Scoring (FICO)

Today, many mortgage lenders are adopting electronic credit scoring programs (often called FICO scores after the Fair, Isaac and Co., Inc., whose scoring has become an industry standard). This approach might be called "lending by the numbers." Strictly applied, it means that if your credit score is 700 and the lender's cutoff is 680, your application probably will be approved without question. On the other hand, if your score comes in at 600, your loan shouldn't be automatically rejected. Instead, the application should be kicked out for personal review and you may be asked to submit more documentation, explanations, or compensating factors.

Unfortunately, some by-the-book loan officers may fail to follow up a low credit score with a second-look personal review. In that case, your application might be automatically turned down. If you find yourself in this situation, ask the loan officer what credit scoring factors contributed to your low score. Then see what you can do to convert a "no" into a "yes."

Even better, before you formally submit all of your application documents and figures, try to learn as much as you can about the lender's credit scoring criteria. If you've got some weak spots, work to strengthen these items before your application is moved forward in the approval process.

Credit Scoring: Pro and Con

On the positive side of credit scoring, someone who has a strong borrower profile (according to a lender's criteria) will fly through the mortgage approval process with very little paperwork, documentations, and verifications. This streamlining saves the lender and the borrower time and money.

Unfortunately, many good credit risks don't fit the lender's profile. Even worse, the computer scoring criteria are guarded secrets. Although everyone in mortgage lending knows generally what counts, no one can say exactly how various factors are weighed. As a result, I have heard of cash-rich, job-secure, perfect-credit borrowers who were turned down on the basis of a low FICO score. And no loan officer in the institution was willing to step forward and overrule the computer.

Profiles with Problems

By strengthening your borrower profile, you reduce the chance that you will fail your FICO exam. So, your first line of defense is a strong offense. Get as much detail as you can about the lender's scoring criteria and how the lender weighs them. (As credit scoring is used more widely, mortgage brokers and others familiar with the lending process will begin to crack the code.) Once you've got as much inside information as possible, see how you rate.

If you still fail, look for a lender who does not rely on credit scoring, or one that uses a different formula. In the coming years, a low FICO (or other similar) credit score will make it more difficult to borrow mortgage money on the best terms and at the lowest rate. At present, though, many lenders still rely on the judgment and experience of seasoned loan officers. When you have built a strong borrower profile that doesn't register high enough on FICO, ask a mortgage broker to recommend a lender who is more likely to appreciate your strengths.

Fortunately, even if your borrower profile misses the mark because of real (and unremedied) weaknesses, you don't necessarily face defeat. The so-called subprime mortgage market now offers a huge variety of second-home financing plans for nearly all types of borrowers. These loans probably will extract an arm and a leg in costs and fees, and they typically will require a higher down payment, but they are available.

In addition to subprime products that are specifically aimed at the credit or income impaired, borrowers with weak profiles might also turn to several other home buying techniques such as mortgage assumptions, seller financing, lease-options, and bringing in partners. (Each of these options is discussed later in this chapter.)

When Not to Change Your Borrower Profile

Once you get your loan approved, don't change your borrower profile until after the loan closes. Especially don't change anything that could affect any of the following:

- Installment debt (you celebrate your purchase of a mountain cabin with the purchase of a $35,000 sport utility vehicle that requires a $550 monthly payment)
- Job security (you quit your job of twelve years to start a new business)
- Credit record (you fail to pay your income taxes and the IRS slaps you with a lien)
- Cash reserves (you enroll your eighteen-year-old at Princeton and write a check for $25,000)
- Net worth (you favor your church with a large donation for the new building fund)

Sometimes lenders run a preclosing review of your finances. If any changes you have made subsequent to your application weaken your borrower profile (according to the lender's view, not necessarily yours), the lender may withdraw its loan approval.

Loan Pricing and Grading

In today's highly competitive mortgage market, most mortgage originators work on commission. They want to find you a loan. Otherwise, they don't get paid. That's the good news.

The bad news is that loan originators earn higher commissions when they place you into higher-cost loan products. In other words, to a certain degree, the interest rate, points, and fees that you pay are subject to negotiation. If your loan officer says, "The best I can do is a rate of 8.25 percent and two points," don't take that as his or her final quote. Just like a car salesperson (or any other types of salesperson), the loan officer may be testing you.

If you accept, great, for the loan broker. If you balk, then the broker can say, "Oh, wait a minute, I've just thought of something else. Maybe

I can get the lender to shave a point off those origination fees. They owe me a favor."

Protect Yourself

To protect yourself against paying too much, ask to see the loan officer's rate sheet. The rate sheet shows the "wholesale" cost of the loans. The bigger the spread between the wholesale rate and the interest rate and fees you pay, the larger the loan officer's commission. In fact, ask the loan officer straight out, "What's the amount of your commission on this loan?" If it's, say, $4,000 on a $150,000 loan, you know that more than likely you've been placed into a high-cost loan. If the commission is $400, there is far less chance you're being taken for a ride. (Typical commissions run about 1 to 1.5 percent of the amount you borrow.)

Of course, neither the wholesale–retail spread nor the amount of the loan officer's commission—taken together or separately—provides the entire picture as to whether you are getting the best possible loan given your needs and financial qualifications. But that information is one important piece of the puzzle. Don't simply accept your loan originator's quotes at face value. Do some investigating. Then negotiate, negotiate, and negotiate. The stronger your borrower profile, the more power you have to persuade a mortgage broker to reduce your costs of borrowing.

Credit Blemishes

In the language of mortgage lenders, homebuyers have been traditionally classified into the credit categories of A, B, C, and D. The lower your grade, the more you must pay for your mortgage. But, just like in school, the grade you receive depends on who's doing the grading. Whereas, even with credit blemishes, one mortgage lender might give you an A, another might downgrade you to B or C status—and, correspondingly, try to persuade you to pay a higher interest rate and fees. (At the same time, of course, the loan rep earns a higher sales commission.)

If you get downgraded because of credit blemishes, don't meekly accept that category. Ask why. Is the loan rep bamboozling you so he or she can make more money? Or do you really deserve the downgrade? Also, try to learn how long it will take—or what you can do—to reach A status. Maybe you should defer buying for a while until you can qualify at a lower rate.

Also, talk with other mortgage companies. If your blemishes consist of nothing more than a few late payments, you can probably find an A-grade mortgage somewhere. Even when you've suffered more serious setbacks, sometimes it's possible to provide an excuse that will move you into an A category.

Just keep in mind that loan originators earn higher commissions when they persuade borrowers to accept higher fees and interest rates. If your credit is severely blemished, you may face little choice. You may have to pay more for your loan than A borrowers (but still subject to negotiation). Still, don't passively accept the downgrade. Learn the specific reason and then seek second, third, fourth, or even fifth opinions. (One mortgage company recently told me that 50 percent of B and C borrowers could have qualified for an A grade.)

Loan Term: Thirty Years Versus Fifteen Years

Mortgage lenders joke among themselves about the many telephone calls they receive where the caller asks, "What's your best rate?" Nine times out of ten, the caller really means, "What's your best rate on a thirty-year, fixed-rate mortgage?" Yet, the thirty-year, fixed-rate mortgage is nearly always the most expensive loan over the short run—and it's far more expensive than the fifteen-year, fixed-rate loan over both the short run and the long run. Consider the comparisons on a $200,000 (zero points) loan shown in Table 11.1. The original monthly payments on a thirty-year loan cost less than the payments on a fifteen-year loan, but that's where the advantage ends. After five years you would still owe $190,122 for the thirty-year loan (compared to a $156,188 balance on the fifteen-year loan). And after your first ten years of ownership, you would owe $79,862 more on your thirty-year loan as compared to the fifteen-year loan ($175,385 − $95,523 = $79,862). After fifteen years, your fifteen-year mortgage would be paid off, but you would still owe $153,507 on your thirty-year loan. In total, the thirty-year loan not only will cost you a much slower payoff but also $194,400 in additional interest expense.

Why do so many borrowers choose the higher-cost thirty-year loan? Some combination of unthinking habit and the lower monthly payment

Table 11.1 **Comparison of Thirty-Year and Fifteen-Year Fixed-Rate Outstanding Mortgage Loan Balances**

	Thirty Years Fixed-Rate at 8%	*Fifteen Years Fixed-Rate at 7.5%*	*Difference*
Monthly Payment	$ 1,467	$ 1,854	$ −387
Balances			
5 yrs	$190,122	$156,188	$ 33,934
10 yrs	175,385	95,523	79,862
15 yrs	153,507	0	153,507
20 yrs	120,911	0	120,911
30 yrs	0	0	0
Total Interest Paid	$328,120	$133,720	$194,400

for the first fifteen years is usually the reason. Not only does the original lower payment help borrowers qualify for a larger mortgage, many borrowers say they don't want to pay down their loan quickly. They would rather invest their "extra" money in stocks. Or they say, just for safety, that they want the thirty-year loan's lower payments, but that they plan to make larger payments to get rid of the debt faster.

Only you can judge whether and to what degree such reasons may influence your choice of loans. Before you decide, compare the fifteen-year versus thirty-year numbers very closely. Experience proves that for many (if not most) homebuyers, the fifteen-year choice proves far less costly.

Choosing an ARM

In today's relatively low interest rate environment, most borrowers not only choose the higher cost thirty-year mortgage, they also choose the higher cost, fixed-rate loan. Many mortgage brokers tell me that a majority of their customers won't even consider an adjustable-rate mortgage (ARM)—even when it would almost certainly save them thousands of dollars. Are you one of these headstrong, "I-don't-want-to-think-about-it" borrowers who are fixed on their preference for a fixed-rate loan? Are you someone who likes to throw away money? If not, then ask yourself these six questions:

1. Is there a strong probability you will sell the home within seven years?
2. Do you expect your income to increase during the coming year?
3. Would you like to increase your price range by $10,000 to $40,000, or even more?
4. Would you like to cut your closing costs by $1,000 to $3,000?
5. Do you expect to keep the home for more than seven years?
6. Do you enjoy a financial cushion in your budget and savings accounts?

If you answer yes to at least three of these questions, you should fully explore your ARM options.

Save Money

The shorter the length of time you plan to own your second home, the more you should consider an ARM because nearly all ARMs cap your monthly payments. You can almost always find an adjustable that will cost you less than a fixed-rate loan if you plan to sell within seven years. As a minimum, take a look at 5/25 or 7/23 (sometimes described as a 30/5 or 30/7) adjustables.

These types of ARMs fix your interest rate and monthly payments for the first five or seven years of the loan. Then they periodically adjust to keep your rate in line with the market. Even this limited type of adjustable may save you between .5 and 1.5 percent in interest rates as compared to a fixed-rate mortgage. For instance, when thirty-year fixed-rates were at 7.25 percent, I saw several 5/25 ARM plans with interest rates as low as 5.75 percent.

On a $100,000 loan, your payments for a 7.25 percent thirty-year fixed-rate loan would have cost $682 a month. If you selected the 5/25, your payments would drop to $583 a month. Although the precise cost differences between thirty-year fixed-rate loans and various types of ARMs change daily, it pays to explore the market. When you plan to sell within seven years, the chances are good that you can find an ARM that limits your risk at the same time it reduces your monthly payments. You have the best of both worlds.

Lower Points and Fees

To further encourage you to use an ARM, some ARM lenders cut their loan origination fees and closing costs. This benefit, however, may not be the advantage it once was. To meet competitive pressures, some lenders also have been offering low cash-to-close (no points, no costs) deals on their fixed-rate loans. Nevertheless, don't forget to at least compare adjustable- and fixed-rate mortgages on the basis of cash you need to close

Longer-Term Cost Savings

Nearly all experts agree that ARMs may save you money if you plan to sell within seven years or less. But you also might save money over the longer term. Here's why: Say you're faced with a choice between a thirty-year fixed-rate loan at 8 percent and a 7/23 that starts at 6.75 percent. You want to borrow $100,000. With the fixed-rate plan, your payments will cost $733 a month. With the 7/23, you'll pay $648. So, for at least the first seven years, you'll save $85 a month, for a total of $7,140.

Instead of pocketing this monthly savings of $85, though, let's say you add it to your mortgage payment. Even though you're only required to pay $648, you go ahead and pay $733 ($648 + $85 = $733). This tactic causes you to pay down your outstanding mortgage balance much faster. By making these extra payments, your mortgage balance after seven years would have fallen to approximately $83,000. With the fixed-rate plan at 8 percent, your mortgage balance would have dropped to just $92,480. Obviously, if you sell at this point, you're way ahead of the game with the ARM.

But what if you don't sell? As long as your new adjustable rate stays below 9.5 percent, your monthly mortgage payments would increase only to $798 a month. Now, what if interest rates are lower when your loan adjusts after seven years? Not only will you have accumulated an additional $9,480 in home equity, but your monthly payments won't increase. They may actually go down.

ARM Assumptions

When you finance with an ARM, you gain another potential advantage. In contrast to fixed-rate loans, most ARMs may be taken over (assumed) by someone who buys your vacation home. This option provides two benefits to your buyers: (1) assumptions typically require far lower points and closing costs than most new loan originations and (2) in some situations, your ARM may provide the buyers a lower interest rate than they could get on a new mortgage. Taken together, these two benefits could give your home a competitive edge when it's time to sell.

Making the Choice

No one can answer the question, "which type of loan is best?" once and for all. The *relative* costs of ARMs and fixed-rate loans change daily. In some periods, the yield spread between ARMs and fixed-rate loans falls within a narrow range. At other times, steep differences occur. Yet, even in periods of narrow spreads (a flat yield curve), some lenders may offer a super ARM deal. Either they want to balance their loan portfolio or they might want to pull market share away from competitors.

Whatever the reason, such practices mean thousands (maybe tens of thousands) of dollars in savings for you. But first, you must open your mind to the possibility. Then, search the market and really work through your mortgage options. More often than you may realize, an ARM will not only cost less, it can also protect you against unwise risk.

When shopping for a loan, keep your mind open to various alternatives. I know of borrowers who have picked up super-priced ARMs even though they had mentally committed to a fixed-rate product. It's just like going to a restaurant with your appetite set on sirloin steak. Then you learn the lobster–prime rib combo is on special at $9.95. In that situation, why pay $12.50 for sirloin? It always makes sense to look at the menu before you order.

More Cost-Saving Tips

Sometimes it seems like lenders complicate the mortgage process and price their loans to maximize customer confusion. And even though a number of lender and lending innovations are aiming to simplify borrowing decisions, there's still a long way to go. As it stands, borrowers who want the best terms and lowest costs must remain alert to the tricks of the trade.

Understand Prepayment Penalties

Some borrowers choose the high-cost thirty-year mortgage with the idea of refinancing into a fifteen-year loan later when rates drop or when their income goes up. Be careful, though, if you are adopting this strategy. Some lenders place prepayment penalties into their mortgages. This contingency means that if you pay off your loan early (say within the first three to five years), the lender may stick you with a $2,000 to $4,000 penalty (maybe more).

In some cases, loans with prepayment penalties aren't necessarily bad. These loans can be originated at slightly lower interest rates. In other words, you might be offered a thirty-year fixed-rate loan (no penalty) at 8.25 percent, but with a prepayment penalty, the rate drops to 7.75 percent. In addition, some of those "no points, no closing costs" loans that you see advertised include a prepayment penalty.

Unfortunately, some loan reps don't fully explain these choices. Nor do they automatically give you the interest rate break that loans with prepayment penalties warrant. Once again, a word to the wise: Ask your loan rep to fully advise you concerning the features and costs of the mortgages that you are considering. If your loan includes a prepayment penalty, make sure the lender discounts your interest rate.

Figure Points versus Interest Rates

Nearly all lenders offer a broad variety of trade-offs with respect to points (fees paid at the time the mortgage money is loaned) and interest rates. For example, let's say you're looking at the choices shown in Table 11.2. The question is, which of these choices is the lowest cost? The answer: It all depends on how long you keep your mortgage. Clearly, if you keep your loan more than three years (thirty-six months), the 6.75 percent/3-point loan will save you the most money. Although you must pay an additional $3,000 at closing to get this lower rate, this loan will save you $85 a month over the 8.0 percent/0-points loan. In

Table 11.2 **Illustration of Different Payback Calculations for a $100,000 Mortgage over Thirty Years**

Interest Rate (%)	Points/Amount	Monthly Payment	Months to Break Even
8.0	0/0	$733	0
7.75	1/$1,000	716	58
7.5	1.5/$1,500	699	44
7.25	2.0/$2,000	682	39
6.75	3.0/$3,000	648	35

other words, in comparison to the 8.0 percent mortgage, you'll earn back your $3,000 in points in just over thirty-five months ($3,000 ÷ $85 per month = 35.29). Although these figures only serve to illustrate (the actual trade-offs you see will differ), this type of calculation does provide a good method (though not precisely accurate) to select the lowest loan *based on your circumstances.*

A trustworthy and competent loan rep will go over interest rate and points trade-offs with you to figure out which look best for you. A greedy loan rep will steer you into an interest rate and points combination that yields the largest sales commission. Don't make the mistake of asking your loan rep which one is best. Instead, ask him or her to work through the numbers to calculate the lowest costs for your circumstances.

Be Prepared to Deal with Closing Costs and Fees

At the time you apply for a loan, your lender will provide a so-called good-faith estimate of the closing costs and fees that will be charged at settlement. In addition to points (just discussed), closing costs may include charges for an appraisal, credit report, prorated taxes, mortgage application, flood insurance, title insurance, mortgage insurance, homeowner's insurance, garbage fees, and numerous other expenses that in total can run into the thousands of dollars.

First, before you apply for a loan, get some idea of the closing costs that buyers typically pay. Then, in your home purchase negotiations, shift some of these costs to the sellers (or at least keep this tactic in mind). Second, in some markets and for some loan products, lenders differ greatly in the costs they levy against buyers. When shopping lenders, compare costs and fees as well as points and interest rates. And third, if the closing costs seem high (or even if they don't), ask that the lender reduce or eliminate them. It is perfectly reasonable for you to question and negotiate a lender's costs and fees.

Surprise Costs

In 1977, Congress enacted RESPA (Real Estate Settlement and Procedures Act) to stop surprise overcharges at closing. It hasn't worked. When Kathy and David Binninger recently closed their refinance, they were socked with $8,300 of fees and closing costs. Their good-faith estimate had showed $4,000 in expected costs. If they had refused to close, they believed (erroneously) that they would have lost approximately $3,000 that they had given the lender in "prepays."

However, if instead of a refinance, the Binningers had been buying a home, their refusal to close probably would have not only lost them the house they wanted, but also their earnest money deposit. Unscrupulous lenders know that when homebuyers realize at the last minute that they've been had, they can't easily walk away from the closing table.

As always, lenders want the highest yield, whereas borrowers shop for the lowest rate. High, undisclosed closing costs permit deceptive lenders to boost their return while still quoting borrowers what they want to hear. A revised RESPA is now being debated. When (if) a new law passes, you can find the details at my Website, www.stoprenting-now.com.

[Note: Under current law the Binningers could have walked away from their closing *and* legally required their lender to return all monies they had paid—even those costs the lender calls "unrefundable." People who refinance are given three days after closing to rescind their loan agreement and receive a full refund. Homebuyers (for very practical reasons) do not enjoy the right of rescission.]

What to Do

Naturally, dealing with trustworthy lenders is your first line of defense against excessive, unexpected charges at closing. Second, if overcharged, raise a ruckus. Threaten a lawsuit in small claims court.

Threaten to tell everyone you know. Threaten to write a letter to the president of the lending institution with copies to every regulator and legislator who drafts bank rules and laws. Third, at the beginning of the transaction, head the lender off at the pass. Don't accept a good-faith estimate; get a firm and fixed amount in writing. Fourth, you can skip fees and costs altogether by dealing only with a "no points, no closing costs" lender.

Watch Out for Tricky Tactics

Bait and Switch

In addition to undisclosed closing costs, some mortgage companies use another tactic to boost their yield above the rate and costs originally quoted. These lenders will quote you one amount for costs, fees, points, and interest rate. Then, after they get you into the loan approval process, they will "discover" a credit blemish or some other so-called defect in your application. "Sorry," such a lender might say, "we're going to have to charge you more because. . . ." At that point, don't give in without a fight. You may be a target for the old bait-and-switch sales tactic. If you do suspect this type of unethical (perhaps illegal) behavior by the lender, tell them to honor their commitment or you will file a complaint with the various regulators. Also, you could switch lenders and demand that the offending lender forward your file to the new lender. That way, your new approval process won't have to start over from square one.

Bad-Faith Lock-Ins

Some unethical lenders also play tricks with lock-ins. At the time you apply for a loan, the lender may (for a fee) lock you into an interest rate of 7.5 percent for, say, forty-five days. Then, if market interest rates head up, the lender may "discover" problems in your application that delay settlement beyond the forty-five days. "Sorry," the lender says, "rates have increased, and we have to bump you up to 8.0 percent." If you believe that the lender has purposely dragged its feet to push you into a higher rate, don't accept it. Complain. Demand. Threaten to go the regulators. More than likely you'll get the original rate restored.

False Float-Downs

Some lenders will lock in your maximum mortgage interest rate, yet will also give you a float-down if rates fall between the time you apply and the date your loan closes. "Good news," your loan rep tells you, "rates haven fallen and we can now close your loan at 7.25 percent instead of 7.5 percent. You're going to save $26.30 a month."

Well, yes, that's good news. But it may not truly reflect the full drop in rates that has occurred. If market rates are really at 7.0 percent, by fooling you into accepting 7.25 percent, your loan originator is going to pocket a nice-size overage commission. Even with float-downs, take care. Make sure you're receiving the full float-down to which you are entitled.

Be Realistic about APRs

When you compare the costs of mortgage loans, you will undoubtedly see the term "APR" (annual percentage rate). To comply with government truth-in-lending laws, nearly all mortgage interest-rate advertising includes this figure. Except for "no points, no costs" loans, the APR is always higher than the stated interest rate because it reflects your total cost of borrowing (interest, fees, points, prepaids, and certain other expenses). Presumably, by comparing APRs among various loan products and lenders, you will be able to select the lowest-cost loan.

APRs and ARMs

Alas, life is not so simple. In the first place, APRs that apply to ARMs make no sense. Under the law, they are calculated as if the ARM interest rate will not change during the life of the loan (except for the scheduled boost up from the teaser rate to the initial contract rate). Yet, the very idea of an ARM means that the interest rate will change. An APR for an ARM gives mathematically precise, yet totally irrelevant figures; true APRs for ARMs cannot be calculated in advance.

In its effort to force lenders to tell the truth about the costs of their mortgage loans, the government misleads borrowers. When comparing ARMs, you cannot rely on the stated APRs. You may find a COFI (cost of funds index) ARM with an APR of 7.86 percent and a one-year treasury ARM at an APR of 7.21 percent. But since no one knows how these respective ARM indexes will change over time, no one can accurately predict which one represents the lowest-cost loan.

Fixed-Rate APRs

Although it might appear that the APR would apply accurately to fixed-rate mortgages, that is true only in the unlikely event you pay off the loan balance precisely according to schedule over the full life of the loan. If you pay ahead (or behind) of schedule, your actual APR will increase. Similarly, if you sell your house or refinance your mortgage, your actual APR will exceed the APR figure the government requires lenders to calculate.

To figure out a rough APR, you must return to the calculations shown in Table 11.1. If you're contemplating a "loan for life," it's *generally* better to trade off higher points for a lower interest rate. In situations where you might sell or refinance "tomorrow," it generally makes sense to accept a higher interest rate in exchange for lower up-front points, costs, and fees. In either case, you will still want to calculate a years-to-break-even figure. Then evaluate the results according to your circumstances.

Look for Hot Products and Hot Lenders

In highly competitive mortgage markets, mortgage costs such as points, rates, and closing expenses may not vary much among lenders. However, on occasion, some mortgage lenders decide to "buy market share" or push a "hot" loan product in an effort to strike a desired balance within their total portfolio of mortgage product. In these cases, if you're in the right place at the right time, you could score a real bargain loan.

Summing Up: Loan Costs and Possibilities

Getting the best loan at the lowest cost can't be left to chance. Nor can you simply "dial for dollars" and ask lenders, "What's your best rate?" Instead, learn the many ways that unscrupulous (or inexperienced) loan reps can lead you into paying more than you should. Work through your many loan possibilities. Know why you need to ask questions. Assert yourself and negotiate. Most important, work with a trustworthy loan rep who demonstrates savvy, knowledge, competence, patience, and concern. Just as a top real estate agent does far more than "show houses," a top loan rep does far more than "give rate quotes and process applications." Put a top loan rep on your side, and you'll get the loan that's right for you.

Collateral (Riskiness)

In addition to the all of the issues mentioned so far, the costs and terms of your loan will be influenced by (1) how you plan to use your second home, (2) the amount of your down payment, and (3) the type of home.

Type of Use

The easiest home to finance is your principal residence. Lenders see little risk in lending to homeowners. Next in line is a personal-use only vacation home. Although traditionally thought to be more risky than a primary home, increased competition for this business is eroding cost and rate differentials. The highest risk use (from the lender's perspective) is a vacation home that you plan to rent out on a regular basis. Lender experience shows that rental properties go into foreclosure more often than principal residences or personal-use vacation homes. As a result, if you must rely on rental income from your vacation home to help pay for it, your lender will likely put your borrower profile under a microscope; require a higher down payment (20 to 30 percent); and charge a higher interest rate.

Of course, second-home buyers who rent out their vacation homes find that the more costly financing is a small price to pay. To offset a higher down payment and maybe a point or point and a half interest rate premium, they are able to bring in thousands of dollars of extra income.

Also, if you originally finance your second home as a principal residence or personal-use vacation home, you can later change the home to a rental without disturbing the favorable financing. In fact, if you're going to spend considerable time at your second home, check the lender's definition of "principal, owner-occupied residence." Should you be able to slip within that definition, you can make your home financing easier and less costly.

If you have built up a large equity in your current primary home, you have a better option: Do a cash-out refinance and use the proceeds to pay for your vacation home.

Amount of Down Payment

In today's market, you can finance a primary home with a down payment of 5 percent (or less). A personal-use vacation home will usually require at least 10 percent down. And a rental property typically requires a minimum down payment of 20 percent. However, if you are willing to increase your down payment above the minimum required, you will generally receive a lower interest rate or more lenient qualifying standards.

Even better, in many cases that extra down payment to achieve favorable mortgage terms needn't be paid in cash. In reality, the lender is concerned with exposure to risk, which is a function of the lender's loan-to-value (LTV) ratio. When you pay 30 percent down, the lender loans you 70 percent of the home's purchase price for a very safe LTV. But if you pay 15 percent down and the seller carries back 15 percent of the purchase price in a second note, your mortgage lender still maintains a 70 percent LTV. Yet, you didn't have to pay the full 30 percent in cash.

These "piggyback" loan arrangements may be completed in any variety of combinations such as 80-10-10, 75-10-15, or 70-20-10. In each case, the percentage of your actual cash down is represented by the last number in the series.

Type of Property

As another loan factor, the lender will judge the riskiness of the property you are buying. A five-year-old brick home in a beautiful gated community that's well located for appreciation probably would be welcomed as collateral by your lender.

If you're buying a one-bedroom, one-bath condominium in a twenty-seven-year-old building where 50 percent of the units are rented out, you may find that many lenders won't even talk to you unless you're putting down 25 or 30 percent. If you're buying a rustic cabin in the deep woods of Michigan that's located on 150 acres of land, you'll probably have to find a specialty lender who will accept that kind of property as collateral.

When newspaper and magazine articles talk about easier financing for second-homes, they typically forget to ask: What are the characteristics of the home and land that you are buying? All lenders apply tougher rules and higher costs to certain types of properties. (Farm houses on large acreage, for example, also have proved more difficult to finance than, say, a contemporary beachfront villa on a one-acre lot.)

Before you assume that you can borrow mortgage money with "relaxed terms" and a "low" interest rate, verify whether the type of property you're buying qualifies for such favorable treatment. Lenders not only judge your borrower profile, they also rate the "profile" of the property.

Alternative Ways to Finance Your Second Home

Up to this point, I have written as if you were going to finance your second home with a newly originated mortgage loan. However, in addition to this method of financing, you might also choose from a variety of other alternatives as described in the following. Each of these methods frequently offers lower costs and easier qualifying than a new loan.

Mortgage Assumptions

If the home you are buying already has a mortgage in place, see if you can assume it. Mortgage assumptions typically require little up-front costs. Plus, if they carry a below-market interest rate, you can save thousands more through lower payments. The most common assumable loans include all mortgages that are insured (or guaranteed) by the FHA (Federal Housing Administration) and VA (Department of Veterans Affairs), and nearly all adjustable-rate mortgages. On rare occasions, you can even run across fixed-rate mortgages issued by credit unions or other mortgage lenders that are assumable.

Seller Financing

People who can't qualify for new financing know they must turn to some type of seller financing or mortgage assumption. But even if you can qualify through a bank, you should still consider negotiating a completely seller-financed purchase. Here are four reasons why seller financing can save you time and money:

1. You can often get the sellers to accept a lower interest rate than typical mortgage lenders.
2. Sellers don't charge application fees, "garbage" fees, or loan origination fees. You need less cash to close.
3. Seller financing involves less paperwork and a quicker closing.
4. You can tailor the exact terms, amounts, and payment schedule to your and the seller's needs. You don't get stuck in the red tape of lender rules and regulations.

More than 40 percent of the homeowners in the United States and Canada own their homes free and clear. These homeowners are prime candidates to carry back all or a substantial part of your financing. But sometimes you have to do more than ask. You have to make seller financing an essential condition of your purchase offer. Then itemize and explain the benefits.

For older sellers, OWC (owner will carry) financing often makes sense. They frequently need income more than cash. Given the low yields banks offer to savers, as well as the volatility of stocks and bonds, a 6 or 7 percent return from a mortgage loan can look relatively attractive. As the nationally syndicated expert Robert Bruss emphasizes, "Where's the best place to get a mortgage? The best source of financing for a home is the seller."

Amen. I have received seller financing in more than half of my home and rental property purchases. This financing has always carried better terms and rates than lenders were offering. But in many of these cases, the owners didn't volunteer. First, I had to make it a part of my written offer.

Lease-Option

Robert Bruss also frequently advocates the use of another seller-assisted buying technique called the lease-option. "One of the best kept secrets in real estate is the lease-option," Bruss writes in a recent article. "Most home buyers, sellers, and real estate agents have never heard of this technique. But every year, thousands of people use lease-options to buy and sell homes. . . . As an investor," Bruss adds, "I've used lease-options for at least twenty years."

Essentially, a lease-option is nothing more complicated than a lease (with whatever terms and conditions are agreed to) coupled with a right to buy the home at some agreed price within a specified period (say, one to three years). You can use a lease-option with any type of home (condo, co-op, mobile home, townhouse, single-family house). Although few *second-home* buyers that I know of have used this buying technique, I believe that it offers a number of potential advantages:

- You can obtain your vacation home with a relatively low amount of cash.
- During the lease period, you can get to know the home, neighborhood, and location better to see if they are really right for you.
- If during the lease period the home's value increases above the option price, you win regardless of whether you go ahead and buy the home. If you do buy, you achieve an "instant" gain. If you don't buy, you can sell the option for a profit to someone else.

Typically, lease-options are used by people who need time to shape up their credit or save for a down payment. For second-home buyers, those same reasons may apply. But more important for most, the lease-option gives you the opportunity to "try it before you buy it."

Likewise for retirees who are moving to a new area. If you just rent for a year or two, you're throwing away money. If you buy and then decide not to stay, you may have wasted thousands in real estate fees, costs of financing, and other expenses. In contrast to both of these choices, the lease-option gives you a comfortable place in the middle. You immediately gain most of the benefits of owning, but if you leave, changing your mind won't cost you so dearly.

For more information on the pros and cons of lease options, write for the $4 special report by Robert Bruss (who is an attorney), "How To Quickly Buy or Sell a Home with a Lease-Option" (251 Park Road, Burlingame, CA 94010). As with other types of seller financing, many landlords and homeowners don't know they are lease-option sellers until someone approaches them with an offer.

Reverse Annuity Mortgage

A type of loan called the reverse annuity mortgage (RAM) offers older homeowners a great new financing option. You can borrow money and never have to pay it back

Here's how it works: If you're at least age 60 (possibly age 55) and have accumulated a large equity in your primary home, you qualify. No credit, bad credit, no job, no income, nothing matters except your age and the amount of equity in your home. With a RAM the lender will advance you a sum of money or monthly payments for life. You can spend or invest the money any way you like. Then, upon the death of you and your spouse, the lender sells your home, pockets the balance outstanding on the RAM loan, and turns the remaining amount (if any) over to your heirs.

The disadvantage of the RAM is that the interest rate and fees required to close this loan exceed the costs of most cash-out refinances or home equity loans. But those types of loans qualify borrowers according to credit and income. Plus, they must be paid back in monthly installments. Since the RAM suffers neither of these drawbacks, it can provide an excellent source of "worry-free" cash that you can use to pay for a vacation or second home.

For more information on RAMs contact the FHA, the American Association of Retired Persons (AARP), or the National Home Equity Conversion Center. Each of these organizations publishes booklets that describe the pros and cons of RAMs in more detail. They also list potential RAM lenders.

Partnering

Even though San Francisco apartment roommates Jennifer Bossin, 32, and Kelly Donnely, 33, don't own a primary home, they decided the time was right to buy a vacation home in Lake Tahoe. With a price of $238,000 and a 7 percent mortgage, their costs of ownership split two ways provided a very affordable purchase.

Jennifer and Kelly represent a growing trend. Many renters in unaffordable cities enjoy "bargain" rents due to rent control or some other happenstance. They want to own but they don't want to lose their "low-cost" housing. So, they are joining together to buy a "second" home in resort and vacation areas.

Going in together with friends or family to buy a vacation home makes sense for a number of reasons:

- Studies repeatedly show that most vacation and seasonal homes go unused during the greater part of the year.
- High prices in many popular areas push many of the more desirable homes out of reach for most people buying on their own.
- Good times often involve friends and family.

Combined, these facts spell opportunity for partnership buyers. By partnering, the home gets used more often (less wasted money); the ownership and maintenance costs become more manageable; and everyone who benefits regularly from the home shares the responsibility for upkeep and monthly payments (fewer freeloaders). If you can't afford, or don't want to pay, the full expense of owning a second home, put together a partnership team. Experience proves the benefits far outweigh the disadvantages.

Creative Partnering

Boston attorney Bernard Borman wanted a second home in Maine, but didn't want the upkeep responsibilities that went along with ownership. Shirley Hale wanted a primary home in Maine, but couldn't swing the deal by herself. The solution: Borman buys the house and Hale lives in it full time and undertakes a restoration and improvement project. Borman visits on weekends. When the home is sold Shirley and Bernard will split the profits.

When Bernard visits the home, he knows that "the lights will be on, the heat will be working, and the woman of the house will either be making dinner for him—or waiting for him to do the same once he arrives." Although Hale and Borman dated many years ago, their partnering relationship today is strictly social and business. "Basically," Shirley says, "our agreement states that Bernard does exactly what I say, immediately, no matter how hard it is or how much it costs—that's the secret of a good house share."

While Bernie and Shirley's partnership may not fit your ideal, it does illustrate creative partnering. To make an agreement work, everyone need not contribute everything equally. Each partner can give and receive in whatever way works for all other partners. You're limited only by imagination and preferences.

Two for One: The New Tax Law Helps

"It's amazing what a little downsizing can do. As my property in St. Albans, Hertfordshire, increased in value over the years, I came to realize," says Graham Norwood, "that cashing in these gains and buying a smaller house would release enough capital for me to buy a cottage in South Devon as a second home."

Do you own a larger-size home where upkeep chores outrun your time and effort? Would you like a seasonal or getaway home where you can enjoy cooler summers, warmer winters, or R&R weekends? Then, sell the "big house"; buy a luxurious smaller home or condo and invest the remaining proceeds of sale in a second home. You will make your life easier and happier.

Prior to 1997, homeowners who used a two-for-one buying strategy would have paid dearly for the privilege. The IRS would have claimed a nice chunk of those sales proceeds. Today, though, you can pocket up to $500,000 of home ownership gains without bother by the tax authorities. As more people realize the tax-free advantages of two for one, I expect this trend to shoot up. It will fuel even greater demand for second homes. (See additional discussion in Chapter 14.)

How Much Home Do You Want?

Nearly all books and articles on home financing ask, "How much home can you afford?" But that's the wrong question. The real question is, "How much home do you want?"

As you have read in this chapter, you can choose from a broad variety of financing options. You can take many steps to make your financing easier and less costly. You can use a home equity loan, partnering, a two for one strategy, or some combination of these and other tactics.

You can boost your buying power with rental income. You can create value through restoration and improvements.

Although most people face some buying limits, they also enjoy a larger world of possibilities than they realize. Do you want a second home for vacations, getaways, or seasonal use? Then put the techniques in this chapter (and others) to work. "Affordability" is not a genetic trait. It depends on your knowledge, your will, and, most importantly, on whether you spend and invest according to your top priorities.

CHAPTER 12

Timeshares, Condominiums, Mobile Homes, and New Construction

Are you thinking about buying a timeshare, a unit in a condominium complex, a mobile home, or perhaps a newly constructed home? If so, take care. Smart buyers realize that these types of properties present some unique risks (and opportunities).

Timeshares Hit Their Stride

Without a doubt, timeshares represent the fastest growing type of vacation home "ownership." Just since 1990, the number of owners worldwide has jumped from 1.8 million to around 4 million. The timeshare industry forecasts that within the coming decade, another 10 million to 20 million people will hop on the timeshare bandwagon. At present, timeshare buyers can choose from more than 5,000 domestic and international resorts. Hundreds of new timeshare projects are coming on stream every year. In addition to real estate development companies, timeshares are being operated by name-brand hoteliers and entertainment giants such as Disney, Marriott, Hilton, Westin, Embassy, Ramada, and, in Europe, Thomas Cook (the travel agency who gave us the Cook's tour) and the De Vere hotels.

Reasons for Rapid Growth

The quick pace of recent and forecasted timeshare growth is being driven by a number of market developments. Included among the most important are affordability, demographics/psychographics, convenience, and strong marketing campaigns.

Affordability

At a typical lump sum price ranging between $3,500 and $25,000, nearly anyone who's financially solvent can afford to buy a timeshare unit. Add to this low one-time price, a yearly owner's fee of $350 to $800, and timeshare costs still fall well below the purchase price and annual expenses of even the most modest second home. But most timeshare units aren't modest. They frequently offer vacationers beautifully designed and landscaped resorts; popular (and often premium) locations; and a package of services, amenities, and activities that can fulfill your every wish. Many timeshare buyers are convinced that timesharing provides them with a champagne vacation on a beer budget.

Demographics/Psychographics

Those tens of millions of baby boomers who are stoking demand for all types of second homes also are joining the timeshare crowds. With Club Med now passé, the Royal Resorts Club (Cancun) is in. Unlike an expensive stay in a hotel or at Club Med, timeshares offer buyers pride of ownership, a feeling of community, and the status of permanence. A week spent in a hotel is just that—a week *spent*. With a week (or longer) stay in your own place, you gain a sense of belonging. Looking into the future, the number of people who fit the age, lifestyle, and emotional profile of timeshare buyers will continue to increase.

Convenient Exchange Privilege

Don't want to vacation in Cancun or Key West this year? No problem. Take a look through the resort catalogue. Click on www.rci.com. Where in the world would you like to go? It's your choice. The arrangements will be made for you. Only a small fee required.

No question about it. The exchange privilege of timesharing is helping to boost the number of timeshare buyers. With the click of a mouse or a simple telephone call, you can plan to vacation at any resort around the globe that participates in an exchange pool with your timeshare development. No hassle with travel agents. No (or little) risk of disappointment. You can even check out the resort and accommodations prior to committing. Just phone or e-mail other members (owners) of your timeshare community and ask them to give you the lowdown.

Strong Marketing

Affordability, lifestyle, convenience—individually and collectively (through industry trade groups), timeshare marketers are pushing those three benefits. Plus, the snowball effect applies. As the number of timeshare buyers increases, timesharing attracts more favorable publicity, and word-of-mouth referrals from owners expand geometrically. In total, the momentum for timeshare growth is continuing to pick up speed.

The Basics of Timesharing

Timesharing originated in the French Alps in the 1960s. The price of ski resorts had skyrocketed. Developers and operators were trying to figure out how to expand affordability. Someone got the bright idea of sharing ownership. Since most people don't visit their vacation homes all that much, why not develop a system where vacationers only pay for the time they really want?

The preceding discussion does put a positive spin on the timeshare concept, and with millions of timeshare owners, the industry must be doing something right. Since the "fly-by-night" promoters of the 1970s, the industry and most of its firms have come a long way (partially because of increased regulation). Nevertheless, as a smart buyer you still must take steps to protect yourself. Before you buy, here are some of the issues that you will want to consider.

Value Revisited

In their sales promotion efforts, timeshare promoters try to get you to compare the cost of a timeshare to the full cost of a vacation home. Or they point out the high expenses of staying in a hotel and eating in restaurants throughout your vacation. Compared to both of these alternatives, the timeshare looks cheap. But these cost comparisons leave out other comparisons that can give you an additional perspective on value. To better judge whether the timeshare price is worth the money, make these four calculations and comparisons:

1. Add up all of the per-week prices for a timeshare apartment. Say the unit is split into fifty weeks at an average price of $6,000 per week. That yields $300,000. Now compare that gross figure to the market values of similar condominium units that have sold recently. You will find that the timeshare sellout price often exceeds the value of comparable condominium units by 50 to 100 percent. In this case, you could probably buy a similar apartment at a price of $150,000 to $200,000.

2. Let's say your timeshare will cost $7,500 in cash today, plus $500 a year in fees. If you can earn 10 percent on your investments, that time each year actually is costing you $1,250 a week. If you financed your unit on a credit card at 20 percent interest, your annual total cost jumps to $2,000 per week.

3. Now, compare the true weekly cost figure to the cost that you would pay to rent a comparable vacation apartment. How much more per week of use (or less) does the timeshare cost?

4. Quite often timeshare sales reps try to pressure and control you. But don't buy until you have compared the price of the units being sold with other similar timeshare units. Too, often, prospects are hyped on all the benefits, but are never given the chance to find out what kinds of values other competing timeshare properties might be offering.

When you run through your calculations and comparisons, you can better see what you're paying relative to what you're receiving. Given the high markup on timeshare units, you might discover that renting units when and where you want them provides a more flexible and economical choice. Or maybe you can bring together five or ten friends or family members and create your own timeshare.

The Investment Question

The fly-by-night promoters used to tout the supposed investment benefits of timeshares. As a result, the state regulatory agencies nailed several timeshare operators for violations of state security laws. Since that clampdown, most operators now steer clear of any remarks that imply you'll be able to sell your timeshare for more than you paid for it. But you know what? In recent years several of the Marriott timeshare resorts actually have experienced some appreciation.

It's the bulging boomers who are pressing against a relatively short supply. At some point in the future, it's possible that *premier* resort timeshares in *premier* locations will go up in price. I'm not forecasting price increases, for I haven't studied the timeshare market locations that closely. Yet, I disagree with those so-called experts who say that buying a timeshare is like buying a car: "Buy it to use it. It can only depreciate."

A well-run timeshare is not like a car. If you get deeded rights (discussed later) to the real estate, you become a part owner of land and buildings. And even though you pay an inflated price today for that real estate, at some point, too many buyers chasing too few premier properties could push values above the price you paid.

Still, everyone must admit that historically, timeshare resales have glutted the market. To sell their units, most owners must steeply discount their prices *and* pay a 20 percent sales commission. Read the timeshare resale ads in *USA Today*. They strike a chord of desperation:

- "Bank liquidations, foreclosures, repossessions . . . call for latest listings."
- "50–60 % discounts. New year's discount."
- "Owner resales, fantastic opportunities."
- "Timeshare and campground distress sales, cheap rentals."

Advertisements like these do not inspire investor confidence. When you buy a *new* timeshare, don't count on getting your money back anytime soon. However, distress for sellers can mean bargains for buyers. If the timeshare concept appeals to you, shop the resales. In fact, as long as you buy a highly exchangeable resort and time period, it really does-n't matter where it's located. Just put it into the exchange pool and swap your week(s) for the resort that you prefer.

Inflation Protection (Vacation Ownership)

After the 1970s, when the idea of timeshare became sullied, promoters tried to hang a new moniker on the timeshare concept called "interval ownership." It never stuck. Today, they're trying another name, "vaca-tion ownership." This one might work. Vacation ownership really does describe the concept better than either the term timeshare or interval ownership.

When you buy a timeshare, you receive vacation accommodations at a *guaranteed price* for some specified period (20 years, 40 years, life, or perpetuity). Only your annual fee for services and maintenance can increase. In effect, then, you own the right to vacation at member loca-tions. No matter how high hotel or resort room rates climb, you'll always enjoy a nice place to sleep and play. Just as home ownership protects you against ever-rising rents, vacation ownership can protect you against ever-rising hotel bills.

Exchange Programs

Most timeshare (or, I should say, vacation ownership) buyers purchase their units with the idea of exchange in mind. Without the exchange privilege the timeshare industry would shrivel. To a large degree, then, the value of a timeshare unit relates directly to how well it will trade in the national and international swap meets. Essentially, "exchangability" depends on the answers to three questions:

1. What is the quality and location of the resort?
2. Which exchange system does the resort belong to? (Resort Condominiums International and Interval International operate the two largest exchange systems.)
3. How popular is (are) the week(s) you own?

The answers to these questions will go a long way toward helping you decide whether to buy a particular timeshare. Beware of oral promises and representations. Verify the exchangeability of your potential unit in writing. Here's what a Better Business Bureau publication advises:

> *Exchange programs: Offers of exchanges for other timeshares are usually an important consideration for timeshare buyers. But, there may be no assurance that the program will be able to provide the interval owner with another accommodation that is desirable or available at the time the owner wants to swap. There may be no assurance that the development you buy into will continue its contract with a given exchange, or with any exchange. Remember that exchange systems rate participating units by desirability and other factors; buyers in a project that is not highly rated by an exchange service cannot expect to "trade up" to fancier units, more appealing locations, or better times of the year.*

Clearly, the Better Business Bureau has learned from experience that many timeshare buyers assume too much and verify too little.

Although most eligible timeshare exchanges are arranged by Resort Condominiums International or International Interval, owners may arrange their own swaps directly. Or they may use an owner exchange service such as those described in Chapter 13. Nevertheless, the same caveat applies: Don't expect to trade a lemon for lemonade.

Other Considerations

In addition to the timeshare basics just discussed, a number of less frequently addressed issues also deserve attention. As is often the case, the devil is found in the details. Before you buy, ask these eight questions:

1. Who controls the homeowners' association and management contract? Can the homeowners vote to terminate the existing management, enact new rules, and bring in another management company? Or will you simply live as subjects under a prince with no practical way for democratic change?
2. Is the timeshare a "right-to-use" project? Or do you receive a deeded, fee simple ownership interest in the land and buildings?

3. What is the current financial condition of the project? Does it maintain adequate reserves for maintenance and replacement of major building components? Are any assessments looming over the horizon?

4. How much have annual fees increased during the past five years? What increases are budgeted for future years?

5. Does the resort participate in a club that gives you discounts on travel, restaurants, or other attractions and services?

6. Does the resort offer bonus weeks that give you the right to additional time at the resort at discount prices.

7. Does the purchase agreement or state (or county) laws specify a "cooling off" period—a set number of days when you can rescind the contract and receive a full refund? (A Royal Resorts Club resort in Cancun offered American buyers a twelve-month money back guarantee. "We only wanted satisfied buyers," says Mark Carney, an executive with the resort.)

8. Have you visited the resort? Have you compared its quality, price, and exchange program to other resorts in similar (and different) locations? Have you talked with other owners?

Be Wary of Satisfaction Surveys

The vacation ownership industry frequently publicizes the fact that 70 to 80 percent of owners surveyed report that they are satisfied or very satisfied with their units. Don't put too much stock in that result.

What if CBS surveyed everyone who was watching Dan Rather? Most viewers would respond "satisfied" because otherwise they wouldn't have tuned in. But on any given night, Dan Rather attracts only about 15 to 20 percent of the adult population. Evidently, *most people* prefer doing something else. The same is true for timeshares. Even though most *owners* report satisfaction, that statistic in no way implies that *you* will become a satisfied owner.

I don't mean to end this section on a negative note. Overall, I do believe that "vacation ownership" does make sense for many people who can't (or prefer not to) take individual (or joint) ownership of a second home. However, I also know that too many timeshare promoters and sales agents will use that "satisfaction" statistic to pressure you into buying. Don't let them. Instead, investigate wisely. Ask questions. Measure your lifestyle demands against the costs and benefits. If after making these inquiries, you like what you see and hear, go for it. Chances are you will join the ranks of the satisfied timeshare owners.

Considering a Condominium

For many second-home buyers, a condominium (or townhouse) provides the best housing choice for getaways, vacations, or retirement. Low maintenance responsibilities, generally good security for "lock and leave," and possibly a relatively low price all combine to give condominiums and townhouses high marks. In addition, many mid- to high-rise condominiums offer panoramic views that can't be matched by most single-family homes.

"We have moved 12 times in 15 years," says Major Art Shapiro of the U.S. Marines. "We have lived in all types of houses. But we like this townhouse development best. We have great privacy, the neighbors always stop to say, 'Hi, how are you doing?' and that sort of thing. As for security, we feel very safe. Even when our six-year-old grandson visits, we have no fears. The homeowners' association keeps everything in top condition, too. I've never even seen a McDonald's sack or cigarette package lying on the ground. We really don't have any complaints. We love it."

Sam Dolnick agrees: "I love taking walks around the complex and looking at the greenspace and realizing I don't have to mow all that grass. We've got swimming pools, an exercise gym, courts for tennis, badminton, and basketball, and 11 acres of landscaped grounds. It's a great way to live."

The Community Association

Are you thinking of buying into a condominium or townhouse that is governed by one of America's 150,000 private homeowner or community associations? Then do your research on the community association and neighbor relations. Like Art Shapiro and Sam Dolnick, most people respect their homeowner associations for doing a good job. But don't trust your fate to chance.

Although community living is the fastest growing type of residential development in the United States, some homebuyers in these developments have experienced disappointment and unexpected costs. Before you buy, check out (1) fees, assessments, and services; (2) rules, regulations, and neighbor relations; and (3) the resale package.

Fees, Assessments, and Services

"We've got a great deal," reports Vicki Duryea. "For $268 a month we get a swimming pool, racquetball courts, health club, jogging paths, yard care, exterior maintenance, cable TV, and trash pickup twice a week. As to special assessments, we've never seen one. Up to now anyway, the association has always set aside enough money in the budget to cover reserves and replacements."

As you shop homes in different developments and community associations, look at the monthly homeowner's fees *and* what services you get for your money. In developments like Vicki's, you may enjoy a full complement of amenities and services at a reasonable price. In other projects, you may come to believe the association is burning the money you pay every month.

Rules, Regulations, and Neighbor Relations

Whether it's yapping poodles or cars parked where they don't belong, a community must police itself. Without proper rules and enforcement, the quality of community life deteriorates. But to a certain extent, one person's necessary rules may be felt by someone else as an assault on their right to live as they please. To angry neighbors a "noisy poodle creates a nuisance that must be quieted or disposed of." To the dog's owner, the pet is a loving companion that "barks only on rare occasions." Where does the truth lie? What rules should govern? What penalties should be levied? Who will enforce them?

When it comes to community issues that stir up disputes (pets, parking, noise, privacy, architectural compliance, children, lifestyle values, renting out units, use of recreational facilities), the quality of life in a development will result not just from the rules themselves, but also from how well owners agree to voluntarily live within those rules. Without widespread mutual agreement, community living breaks down. Life becomes perpetual bickering.

Fortunately, owners in most community associations realize that through cooperation they can nurture a pleasant living environment and boost property values. These are the types of developments to look for. In contrast, be wary of those developments where individual owners (or factions of owners) can't agree on much of anything. These are the types of community associations to avoid.

Ask yourself, too, what rules can you live with? After retirees, Chuck and Margaret Kane bought their new townhome, one of the first things they wanted to do was to put in a yard. So Chuck spent one weekend planting grass seed. Two days later a representative of the homeowners' association stopped by to tell Chuck the bad news. Grass seed was not permitted in the development. To comply with association regulations, the Kanes would have to sod their yard. And to encourage the Kanes to follow all other rules, the association fined the Kanes $400.

Once Chuck and Margaret really started to look over the rules they would have to live under, they learned:

- Their homeowner's association would have to approve any exterior design changes or painting they planned for their home.
- Chuck couldn't park his antique Chevy in his driveway while he worked on it.
- The Kanes couldn't put a Sears storage shed in their backyard.
- No outside clotheslines or television antenna or satellite dishes were permitted.

Homeowners' association rules and regulations can touch on nearly anything you might want to do. Before you choose a development, closely review the "laws" you will have to live under. It is true that homeowners' associations are run democratically and that most rules and regulations operate to enhance the value and livability of the development. Yet, for some homeowners, democratic rule means "tyranny by the majority." The rules imposed are just too "socialistic." Would you want to live under rules such as the following?

- No more than one pet is allowed per unit. Maximum weight of a pet shall not exceed 15 pounds.
- A pet deemed by the board to be noisy or uncontrollable must be disposed of within three days' notice.
- No automobile mechanical work whatsoever will be permitted on the premises.

- Bicycles must be stored in designated areas. They must not be left on the grounds, in hallways, or stored on patios or balconies.
- Personal conduct and attire in the common areas are subject to approval of the board.
- No signs ("for sale" or "for rent") shall be displayed in any manner whatsoever.
- No owner/occupant shall install drapes or curtains within any unit unless such drapes have a white liner visible from outside the unit.
- No entertaining of more than ten persons within a given unit shall be permitted.
- Any owner who wants to offer his or her unit for rent must first obtain the approval of the board. All tenants also must be approved by the board.
- No leases beyond a duration of one year are permitted.
- The board retains the right to disapprove a new purchaser in the development for any lawful reason it deems appropriate.
- No driveway basketball hoops and playing areas are permitted.

Compared to some Draconian homeowner association rules I have seen, these seem rather mild. But you will have to judge for yourself what rules you are willing to live under. Just make sure you review them before you buy.

The Resale Package

As an additional safeguard, when buying a home governed by a private homeowners' association, ask for a resale package. A resale package (required by law in many states) should include the legal documents and financial reports that set the operating, voting, and policy procedures of the association. From this resale package, you (with aid of the sellers, an attorney, or an association officer) should be able to answer these eight questions:

1. Are the financial reserves and insurance coverages adequate to cover repairs, replacements, and potential losses?
2. Does the annual budget allow enough money for maintenance, upkeep, and daily operations?
3. Is the association involved in any lawsuits? What are the potential financial consequences of this litigation?

4. What method is used to calculate each unit owner's monthly fees or special assessments? Are the sellers current in all of their fees and assessments? Are any new assessments scheduled in the near future? If so, will you or the sellers pay them?

5. What method is used to determine each unit owner's voting rights? What methods are used to select property managers, board members, officers, and committees? How can homeowners remove association officers from their positions?

6. What are the association's existing rules, regulations, and bylaws that govern homeowner conduct within their homes and community property?

7. What methods are used to change the rules, regulations, or bylaws?

8. What areas of the building and grounds fall within the direct ownership, responsibility, and control of individual owners? Which areas of the building and grounds fall within the direct ownership, responsibility, and control of the homeowners' association?

Millions of Americans now own homes that are governed by a private homeowners' or community association. This trend continues to grow as developers build more gated communities, townhouses, co-op, and condominium developments. People are finding that they want more say over their neighbors and their neighborhood. As homebuyers seek sanctuary, private communities are springing up to meet this need. But buying into a private community—whether a condo, townhouse, co-op, or even a single-family development—means shared responsibilities. To get the most out of their communities, homeowners must cooperate with each other.

Only through a well-managed association and a "let's work together" spirit can homeowners realize the quality of life, carefree living, and property appreciation that private communities promise. I have lived within several communities governed by private homeowner associations. Each of these homeowning experiences was pleasant and profitable. Yet, before you buy, get the facts. Check out the financial, social, and legal issues that will affect the community. Choose carefully and like Sam Dolnick, you, too, may agree, "It's a great way to live."

Condominiums as Investments

Several years back, Paul Maglio bought a two-bedroom condominium located near Boston Harbor. He paid $120,500 for the unit. At the time Paul bought, 200 other potential buyers had put their names on the complex's waiting list. Everyone wanted this sure-fire investment opportunity. With appreciation rates running at 2 percent *a month*, condominiums were the geese laying golden eggs.

Then, the geese died. Throughout Massachusetts, other states in New England, New York City, much of the Southwest, and Southern California, many condominium (and co-op) prices fell 30 to 70 percent off their peaks. Bruce Hopper, another Bostonian who lost a bundle on his condominium, sadly regrets his decision to buy. "It's too bad," Hopper says, "because condos were the ideal situation for a lot of people. But it didn't pan out and now we're stuck." With experiences like these in mind many second-home buyers hesitate to buy a condominium. They'd rather not take a chance on getting "stuck" with a condo that can't be sold for anywhere near its purchase price.

Don't Prejudge: Weigh Risks against Potential Rewards

It's true that since the early to mid-1970s many different condominium markets throughout the United States have seen their prices escalate wildly and then nose-dive. Between 1973 and 1975, condo markets crashed in the Southeast, especially South Carolina and Florida. After a steep run-up in condominium prices in Chicago in the late 1970s and early 1980s, condo prices there fell more than the 1987 stock market crash. Between 1978 and 1983, many condos in Dallas and Houston tripled in value; by 1987 these same units were selling for 50 cents on the dollar. From the early to mid-1980s to 1988, Boston condo prices shot up without restraint; by 1989 the market had hit the skids. By 1993 nearly one-half the condominium homeowners' associations in the state of Massachusetts were approaching insolvency. In the Burbank Street complex in Boston, units that originally had sold for $50,000 were subsequently sold for as little as $5,000.

Even today, for example, there are condominiums in Fort Meyers, Florida and Honolulu, Hawaii, that are worth less than their owners paid years ago. That's the bad news.

How to Spot a Condo Bargain

Let's now turn to the bright side. First, in nearly every case, the major groups of condo buyers who have lost money have been those who bought within a year or two of the top of the market. Longer-term owners *generally* have come out ahead. Second, condo owners who could see the crash coming and sold out near the top of the market often made tens of thousands of dollars. Third, buyers today who can learn to spot opportunity (and smell potential danger) stand to make good profits.

By learning the lessons of history, you can reasonably judge whether condo prices in the area where you're buying stand a good chance of going up (or down). To spot opportunity here are the signals to look for:

- Nearly everyone is pessimistic about appreciation rates. (Yes, contrarians frequently do make money.)
- The monthly after-tax payments for principal, interest, property taxes, insurance, and homeowner fees total less than monthly rentals on comparable apartments.
- The market values of the units are substantially below the cost of constructing similar new units (see Chapter 7).
- Vacancy rates for rental apartments are less than 5 percent.
- Local economic indicators (number of people working, retail sales, new car sales, bank deposits, tourism, new business starts, etc.) show increasing strength.
- The units you are considering enjoy some *unique and highly desirable* advantages (design, views, location). Recall the high-rise units on Longboat Key mentioned in Chapter 7.
- Very few new apartment or condominium complexes are being built. No major conversions of apartments to condominiums are under way or planned. Government restrictions limit apartment conversions and new construction.
- Compared to single-family homes, condo prices (especially when calculated on a price-per-square-foot basis) sit relatively low.
- The complex you are looking at is stable: strong financial reserves for repairs and replacements; no pending litigation; very few units occupied by renters (fewer than 20 percent is good, less than 10 percent is excellent); relatively little turnover of owners and resi-

dents; well-maintained common areas; and harmonious relations among owners.

On the downside, history shows that, in most cases, a drop in condo prices usually is foreshadowed by one or more of these danger signals:

- A steep downturn in local employment or tourism.
- Large numbers of apartments being converted to condos, especially when accompanied by easy-qualifier financing.
- Large amounts of new condo or apartment construction.
- The current monthly cost of owning greatly exceeds the monthly cost of renting.
- More than 30 to 40 percent of a complex's units are occupied by renters or even worse, are vacant.
- Everybody "knows" values are going up at least 10 to 15 percent a year. The market is rampant with speculation.

Past experience has taught lenders, investors, and homebuyers that a condominium isn't a printing press for money that's disguised as a place to live. Nevertheless, with most speculation now squeezed out of the market, condos in many resort and vacation areas (as well as many cities) once again offer good long-term investment potential.

Mobile-Home Communities

"'Griswald!' Bill Henrich barked. 'You know they don't like loose pets.' The offending dog scurried back onto the porch, having run up against one of the many rules that regulate Mr. Heinrich's pristine community. Lawns must be kept mowed. Cars cannot be repaired. Drivers must carefully obey the 7 mile-per-hour speed limit. Potential residents must undergo strict financial scrutiny." (From the *New York Times*, January 31, 1999.)

Mobile Home Communities Move "Upscale"

In popular lore, trailer parks attract trailer trash. But not anymore, or at least, not necessarily. The preceding quotation describes a mobile home community, not an elite gated community. As so many others, this mobile home park has moved "upscale." But in this sense, upscale doesn't mean upper income. It means upscale in terms of behavioral standards. The residents of this community all own their own homes. They all watch carefully to make sure no one else is violating the resident-established rules and regulations. And, they all take pride in the community they have created.

A Lower-Cost Alternative

Would you like to consider a lower-cost alternative for your second home? Then weigh the advantages of a mobile home community. Quite often, a mobile home offers the absolute best value for your money. It's true that in many cases, town ordinances ban or restrict mobile home parks. To find one, you often have to accept either an inferior or remote location—but not always. Every now and then you can discover a park that's in a premier location.

Just recently, I discovered two mobile home communities on Longboat Key (LBK). One of the communities even enjoyed frontage on Sarasota Bay and dock space. As it turns out, these mobile home parks date back to the 1940s, long before LBK outlawed mobile homes.

If you want to buy a "low-priced" two-bedroom condominium on LBK, you would probably have to pay $125,000 to $150,000. For a single-family home, prices start at around $200,000. But you can buy one of these mobile homes with the lot it's sitting on for around $70,000. If you prefer to lease your lot for around $375 a month, you can buy an existing home for $15,000 to $35,000. Amazing! At those price levels, second-home ownership (in a premier location, no less) seems too good to pass up. Can you discover a similarly desirable and affordable mobile home community?

New Construction

With the vast growth of planned communities designed for second homes and retirement living, you may want to build or buy a newly constructed home or condominium. Many of these developments provide their homeowners with a gracious lifestyle, golf courses, tennis courts, and equestrian trails. With all of this delightful living in view it's easy to overlook some small points like, "Do we really get all of this house and its features for only $99,000?"

Get What You Think You're Paying For

When it comes to new homes, "don't make the mistake of assuming without asking," cautions William Young, who serves as a director of consumer affairs for the National Association of Home Builders. Young's advice is aimed at buyers of new homes who expect their homes will include all the same amenities and custom features they've seen in their builder's models. But, as homeowner Paul Jakulski discovered, that's seldom the case.

Paul was conducting a preclosing walk-through of his newly built $185,000 split-level ranch home when he discovered that, unlike the model homes he was shown, his home lacked skylights, which were very important to him. "Without the skylights," Paul complained to the builder, "the house is way too dark."

The builder sympathized with Paul but pointed out that in their contract, skylights were optional and not included in the basic price. Since Paul hadn't specified he wanted them, the builder didn't put them in. To do so now that the home was virtually complete would cost twice as much as if they had been installed during the construction process.

Paul's mistake happens all too frequently. If you plan to buy a new home that's not yet completed, check two things: First, don't assume those gold-plated bathroom faucets are standard features. Read your purchase contract closely. Look for those cost-increasing words such as "optional" or "upgrades." With some houses, costly upgrades and options are what transform the frog into Prince Charming.

Second, keep tabs on the construction process throughout the time your home is being built. Don't wait until final walk-through to discover the features that you wanted aren't the features you're getting. Even when you've accurately listed your options and upgrades, builders, and contractors can make mistakes. In addition, if you decide on changes during construction (as you undoubtedly will), make them as early as you can and put them in writing. The earlier you specify changes, the less it will cost you. Moreover, memories are too fragile and building sites too hectic to rely on ad hoc talks with your builder, a sales representative, or a contractor.

Watch for Defects: Even New Homes Aren't Perfect (and Some Aren't Even Livable)

"Christine Estep is weary—weary of paying for a home she can't live in," opened a front-page article in the *Miami Herald*. Christine Estep is one of the tens of thousands of homeowners whose homes were damaged by Hurricane Andrew. But instead of having her home repaired, Christine and the other 343 homeowners in her Village Homes condominium complex are about to see their homes demolished. The relatively new complex was "so riddled with construction defects" the engineers have recommended tearing down all the units and rebuilding from scratch.

Government investigators say the homes had undersized foundations, inadequately designed roof trusses, masonry walls without necessary steel reinforcement, unanchored support posts, and missing hurricane straps. Now you might wonder, aren't newly constructed homes supposed to be inspected and approved by government building inspectors? How could major defects slip by? A lot of other people are asking the same questions. But it's not the first time.

Government Inspectors Sometimes Fail to Do Their Jobs

Over the years most cities throughout the United States have been rocked by various types of permits-for-sale bribery and payoff scandals. In fact, Janet Reno, now attorney general of the United States, previously served as the state attorney for Dade County (Miami). In that capacity she spearheaded a drive to investigate the government's building inspection process. Reno never charged anyone with a crime, but her office investigation did result in charges of lax enforcement of building codes. For example, one building inspector who was followed by an investigator somehow managed to inspect and approve seven homes in five minutes. A former building inspector in Dade was quoted by the *Miami Herald* as saying, "It was a farce. The building and zoning department for years pushed quantity not quality."

Get Your New Home Inspected Privately and Professionally

My purpose here is not to point the finger at anybody. It will be years (if ever) before a complete accounting of errors and responsibilities are tallied up and assigned to the various parties involved in Christine Estep's case. But you should know that the construction defects and lax inspection practices that contributed to Christine's emotional and financial worries are all too common. Just because a home is new (or nearly new) doesn't mean it's defect free. A few builders and developers are crooks; others are careless; some need to cut corners "temporarily" to stay solvent; and others just plain make mistakes. Any way you look at it, new does not necessarily mean perfect.

Avoid unpleasant surprises. Employ a professional inspector even when you're buying a new or recently built house or condominium.

Verify the Long-Term Character of the Development

"A Power Struggle in Paradise Pits the Rich Against the Rich," headlines a recent *New York Times* article. What's causing this battle? The developer of Fisher Island, Florida (second home to multimillionaires like Oprah, Pete Sampras, Mel Brooks, and Sharon Gless) wants to "downscale" the development. He wants to construct 318 new lavish condominium units that will sell for upwards of one million dollars each. Downscale? Well, that's the view of one faction of residents led by Isadore Pines who owns a $4.5 million home.

"We bought privacy, beauty and most of all, safety, which will disappear with 318 more condominiums. . . . We did not buy traffic fumes and overcrowding," says Gerri LeBow, an outspoken member of the opposition. Other opponents say that the added development will "overwhelm the island's services, causing long lines at the restaurants and unconscionable delays at the ferry and golf club."

Think about How You Would Feel

No matter how "upscale" the development, no matter how rich the residents, there's always some chance that, over time, a new development will change its character. The pampered residents of Fisher Island imagined that they were buying into a new development where their quality of life would remain exactly as it was. Now they've learned that they are mistaken. They must share paradise with several hundred more rich people.

In some ways, the Fisher Island battle seems silly. How can anyone who lives in such grandeur and beauty complain about anything?

Rather than feel empathy, we should feel envy. Yet, how would you feel if you stood in their shoes? They've worked hard, made money, and now they want to enjoy the life they thought they had secured for themselves when they bought. Would you feel disappointment if the same thing happened to you? Would you welcome the fact that your new home development planned to add hundreds of lower-priced homes? Would you simply accept heavier traffic, longer waits for tee time, and more competition for the best tables at restaurants?

Look to the Future

If you do want to buy into a new development that will perpetually provide the high quality of life you expect, make sure you look into the future by doing at least the following two things:

1. *Ask the developer*. Check the developer's plans. How many phases are scheduled? How many units will be added, and at what sizes and price ranges?
2. *Look for legally enforceable restrictions*. How do zoning laws, environmental regulations, and deed restrictions limit the number, size, and price range of future development? Must future building go through a complete public review process with hearings and appeals?

When the residents of Fisher Island bought their homes, they paid little heed to the fact that renderings for the completed development showed that as many as 1,200 more new homes were planned. That fact they concede. Now, they are spending hundreds of thousands of dollars on lawsuits to try to block construction of just 318 units.

Don't make the Fisher Island mistake. Before you buy into a new development, verify its future plans. See if the quality of life you expect is guaranteed. With a little checking, you can improve the odds that your new home will give you years of pleasure and profit.

CHAPTER 13

How Your Second Home Can Pay for Itself

"**E**very six seeks, Baltimoreans Robin and David Matheiss head to their place on the Outer Banks of North Carolina," reports *Money Magazine*. "They relax in the hot tub, dip into the pool and revel in the fact that their place is essentially free. Their renters, who pay $2,500 a week during the season, cover their mortgage payments."

Fun *and* Rental Income

Like David and Robin Matheiss, second-home owners increasingly are finding that their vacation properties can generate substantial rental income. From the Hamptons to La Jolla, owners have seen vacation-home rents jump by 10 percent annually—year after year. At the low end, even one-bedroom condominiums can command upwards of $500 a week. When you consider that in vacation areas, run-of-the-mill rooms at the Holiday Inn often top $100 a night, a weekly rent of $500, or even $1,000, for a more comfortable and roomy condo unit looks like a good deal.

For nice to extravagant homes, rental rates can range from $1,000 up to $5,000 a week or more. In the Hamptons along Further Lane (called Raider's Row because of Wall Streeters like "Gordon Gekko" who fancied houses along the beach), three-month summer rentals have gone for as much as $325,000.

Rent monies, though, don't just flow in automatically. If you want your second home to bring in rental income, you must plan your purchase, marketing, and management of the unit. Some homes sit vacant without takers. Others get rented only during peak periods of demand. Some owners overprice their units and then have to slash their asking rents at the last minute to avoid a complete loss. To achieve the full rental potential of your second home, you must think through each step of your efforts.

Do You Really Want to Bring in Rental Income?

Maybe at this point you have doubts about whether you want to rent out your second home. Novelist Jacquelyn Mitchard (*The Most Wanted, Deep End of the Ocean*) who lives in Madison, Wisconsin, recently bought a vacation home on Cape Cod. "I never want to rent it out," she says. "I want it to be there for family and friends and their children. I want everyone to come here and relax."

Like Jacquelyn Mitchard, you may want to reserve your second home for friends and family. But before you decide, think about how frequently you, your friends, and family will actually use the home. The U.S. Bureau of Census reports that one-half of all second-home owners leave their home unoccupied for more than 330 days a year. That's an awful lot of wasted time and money. If, realistically, your second home, too, will go unoccupied most of the time, why not shop for a vacation home with the rental income in mind?

Do You Fear Renters?

Many second-home owners fear that their renters will damage their property. Or they believe that the hassles of renting outweigh the benefits. I can assure you that from my experience, these fears are greatly exaggerated.

Over the years, I have been on both sides of the vacation-home rental agreement many times, and I have dealt with others who have done likewise—with never a problem. One summer, for example, I accepted a tenant in my Winter Park, Florida, home. In turn, I rented someone else's home in Vancouver, while they rented someone else's home on Vancouver Island. The Vancouver Island homeowners let a place in Italy. On another occasion, I first let out my Dallas home. In turn, I rented the home of a University of California-Berkeley professor and his wife who (as always) were spending May through August at their summer home in Maine. That was their seventeenth year of following that practice without a problem.

Why Do Vacation Rentals and Home Exchanges Typically Work Problem-Free?

Such arrangements as I have just described typically work problem-free for several reasons: Foremost, perhaps, they work because the tenants aren't really tenants in the strictest sense of the word. When people play "musical homes," they mostly are dealing with other homeowners. They are renting to people who respect and value the property of others because they, too, own. Second, you can locate many tenants through networking—or, at the least, you can check them out through a network of contacts.

I didn't know the aforementioned Vancouver or Berkeley homeowners prior to meeting them to discuss their respective homes. However, in both cases, after briefly playing the "name game," we were able to discover some mutual friends and acquaintances. As networking advocate, Harvey MacKay (*Dig Your Well Before You're Thirsty*) would agree, "It's a small world."

Should You Try Renting Out Your Second Home?

I encourage you not to quickly dismiss the idea of renting out your second home. At today's rent levels—especially during peak rental periods—you can generate thousands (maybe tens of thousands) of dollars of extra income. But with rentals and home exchanges, you can look forward to more than money. You will make new friends; you will expand your own network of contacts and acquaintances.

As mentioned earlier, though, rental income doesn't flow in without thought and planning. To the extent that you would like to take advantage of this opportunity, choose your home and location with tenant demand in mind. With the right property, you will enjoy years of fun *and* rental income.

Exploring the Rental Market

If you've decided to pursue the idea of renting out your second home, you need to get to know the rental market in the area where you're considering a home. Basically, you need to ask three questions: (1) When are the rental seasons? (2) What do competing properties offer? (3) What do vacationers (potential tenants) want?

When Are the Rental Seasons?

In some areas (such as Orlando), a good rental market exists year-round. Some periods are stronger than others, but every month of the year brings in more than a million visitors. Your rental rates will vary somewhat, but there's always an active market for some types of rental units. Then there are areas like Augusta, Georgia, that are able to command very high rental rates but only during a brief period (the Master's Golf Tournament). During other times of the year, the area attracts relatively fewer tourists and visitors.

Some second-home owners prefer short-season, high-dollar rentals. That way, their home is available for personal use during the biggest part of the year, yet it still produces a nice-size chunk of cash. In addition, many people actually like to stay away from their homes when the crowds really begin to roll in. If this rental strategy appeals to you, look for areas with peak events (e.g., the Cannes Film Festival, Daytona 500, Santa Fe Art Festival, and the Oregon Shakespeare Festival represent a few of the well-known, crowd-drawing events).

Twin or Multiple Seasons

Some areas (especially mountain climates such as North Carolina, Colorado, and Vermont) are developing twin or multiple seasons. Many Colorado resorts are investing more money in golf courses and summer activities than they are ski lifts. "North America's biggest ski resorts are blazing new trails," reports the *Rocky Mountain News*. "They're selling building lots, constructing housing developments, creating golf courses, and carving hiking and biking trails out of the wilderness. Unable to lure more skiers to the slopes in the winter, they're hoping to turn one-season businesses into year-round operations. . . . Ski resort operators also are playing up rafting, tennis, mountain-biking, hot-air ballooning and other warm-weather activities."

Ideally, in multiple season or year-round resorts, you might choose to stay at your second home during the season you like best, then rent out the home during the other periods of activity.

College Town "Seasons"

Rob and Stacy Loman work as school teachers in the Chicago area. They own a second home in Flagstaff, Arizona. During the academic year, they rent their Flagstaff home to visiting professors at Northern Arizona University. During June, July, and August they enjoy getting away from the "hot town, summer-in-the-city, back-of-my-neck getting dirty and gritty" feeling of Chicago and into the summer fun of an Arizona mountain-college-resort area.

To further boost their finances, they rent out their principal residence during the summer. Given the consistent flow of newly relocated or temporarily assigned professionals in any metro area, Rob and Stacy have never lacked for quality tenants. Through their smart planning, the Lomans own and enjoy two homes, but, in effect, only pay for one out of their own pocket.

Vacation Bonus

As another bonus of good planning, on several occasions, the Lomans have rented their Flagstaff home to different professors during the fall and spring terms. The renting strategy frees up their getaway home for them to take an Arizona ski break over the Christmas holidays. With

Las Vegas only three hours away, they also can enjoy fun overnight excursions to the city of lights and action.

[Personal note: To further show how creative house renting and exchanging can yield bonuses, let me relate another personal experience. During a year that I served as a visiting professor at the University of Illinois (Urbana-Champaign), I rented a home from a university administrator (and his wife) who was temporarily assigned to the Chicago campus. However, during vacations they wanted to spend time in Champaign. "No problem," I said. "Since I like visiting Chicago, when you return 'home,' I will stay at your place in the Windy City." They said, "That's fine with us." Creativity and conciliation helped all parties put together a win-win agreement.]

Planning Rentals and Personal Use

To maximize fun and income, choose a location that best matches the area's rental income potential against your desire for personal use. If, for example, you insist on summering at the shore in Maine, your potential for rental income has plummeted. With practically no winter renting season, the dates of your personal use preclude opportunities for profitable seasonal rental. However, if instead you choose the Vermont mountains, you could enjoy getaway summer and fall weekends, yet still earn a nice rental sum from winter skiers.

The point is that before you commit to an area, you need to investigate the good to terrific seasonal and vacation rental periods. Your best match would provide a great situation like the Lomans have achieved. They get to enjoy their second home exactly during the time they prefer. Yet, during their "off" season, their homes provide enough income to cover the mortgage on their Flagstaff property. Choosing in this way may involve trade-offs. At first, the Lomans actually preferred Santa Fe. But once they thought through their budget and goals, they discovered that Flagstaff offered them their best value.

What Do Competing Properties Offer?

When you plan to participate in the rental market, you must blend your personal likes, dislikes, and indifferences with the preferences of potential tenants. Before you buy, get out and look at the units with which your home-to-be will compete. What are the features of the top rental units? (And by "top rental units," I don't necessarily mean those units that command the highest rents, but those types of units that always seem to carry a long waiting list of tenants.)

Competitive Market Survey

No matter what type of business or profession you work in, you probably keep tabs on what your competitors are up to. In marketing, we call this type of research a "competitive market analysis." The same principle applies to the "vacation-rental business."

Ask realty sales and rental agents for the names and addresses of the most popular buildings, complexes, or developments. Which rent best: small, medium, or large units? How many bedrooms, and other amenities characterize these units? What are their locations, views, accessibility, and vacancy rates? Essentially, you want to discover the "must haves," "most preferred," and "no-no" features that spell rental success or failure. You might find a great buy on a one-bedroom, one-bath condo that fits your needs just fine, but if it's tough to rent those units at any price, maybe it would pay you to look for something else.

Beware of Puffery

In conducting your market survey, guard against puffery. In their efforts to make sales, some agents forecast a rental flow the size of the Mississippi, when, in fact, you could expect something more in line with the trickle of a mountain brook. You must be sure to verify realistic rental amounts for each seasonal or vacation period. Also, verify vacancy rates. How many nights, weeks, or months a year can you count on getting the unit occupied?

Beware of Overestimating Rentals

"Like other people, I got greedy," says William Sokolin. Through the cocktail-party circuit, William had heard of fat rentals for homes like his Long Island, four-bedroom villa that provide views of the vineyards in Water Mill. After six weeks of advertising in the local papers, still no takers. "I think it's time to drop the price," he said.

"Hundreds of Hampton landlords may be thinking the same thing," reports the *New York Times*. "High hopes for their rose-covered bungalows are wilting. . . . Several rental brokers say that they have at least 40 percent of their inventory left. . . . Where are the missing tenants? More and more people are heading not only to Martha's Vineyard and Nantucket, but also to the Maine coast and parts of Litchfield and Fairfield Counties in Connecticut, with or without the beach."

High Rents Bring More Homes to Market

"Across the board," says rental agent Charlotte Cotton, "prices are up 5 to 10 percent over last year, and because of that, more people have listed their houses for rent. In Westport, alone, the number of available houses has jumped from 60 to 90. . . . Many people who bought with the intention of renting haven't been able to this year."

Although your rental home can pay for itself, don't let your hopes outrun reality. Rental vacation homes must compete with other properties in terms of features, location, and rent levels. So, before you buy, get reliable information on past rentals. Think where the market might be heading. Are vacationers increasing and the number of properties decreasing? Or is it just the opposite? Too many owners chasing too few renters drive vacancy rates up and rental rates down.

What Do Vacationers Want?

In the end, of course, to get the most rental income with the fewest vacant days, you must "get inside of the customers' minds." Your survey of competing properties will give you a good idea of what people are buying. But to go further with your investigation, try to find out the "hot buttons" that really motivate tenants to choose one property over another.

Differences That Make a Difference

As you shop for a home, you undoubtedly will run into a number of features that are "turn-offs" and "turn-ons." Renters act in the same way. Find out what turn-ons light their fire. Look for ways to make your property stand out from the crowd. Would renters be drawn to a gourmet kitchen, a beautiful flower garden, a deck, fireplace, king-size beds, hardwood floors, a sauna, hot tub, jacuzzi, child-safety features, skylights, or what else?

Ask rental agents to tell you the kinds of rental requests they receive from tenants that they find difficult to fill. What turn-on features have you noticed that remain in short supply? When you travel, pay attention to new ideas that you can incorporate into your home. Look through home decorating magazines. Visit home centers. Stay alert to learn those differences that will make a difference to your prospective tenants.

You: The Big Difference

When someone rents your home, you can provide another difference that will make a difference: Become the perfect host. Through your study of the ways other vacation-rental homes operate, try to figure out what you can do to make your "guests" feel comfortable and welcome. Anticipate their needs. Eliminate their inconveniences. Here are eight ideas:

1. Stock the home with cold (hot?) drinks and snacks, leave a full assortment of condiments, spices, and other essentials for cooking.
2. Place a flower arrangement and fruit basket on the dining room (or kitchen) table.
3. Provide a full complement of local maps, restaurant menus, art and entertainment guides, brochures on local attractions, and transportation schedules (if pertinent).
4. If local merchants and restaurants publish discount coupon booklets or advertisements, gather up several.
5. Provide notice of any special upcoming events.
6. Include a list of merchants, restaurants, attractions, and shops that you personally recommend. Tell why.
7. Give the guest a door key for every member of the household who is old enough to need one.
8. Post names, numbers, and addresses for treatment of medical emergencies.

Think of yourself as a host (and not a landlord). You're not just providing your guests a place to stay. You are helping them get the most they can out of their vacation. As you adopt this "resident-friendly" approach, you will create a competitive edge over other owners—and a cooperative advantage with your guests.

Creative Rentals

In addition to renting to vacationers (or visiting professors, as do the Lomans), many second-home owners find more novel ways to generate rental income. Keep in mind that many other types of users may need temporary housing accommodations.

Family Gatherings

"Barbara Williams has turned her fondness for family gatherings into a novel business venture," reports *Newsday*. "She rents out her North Haven vacation home by the week to families coming together to attend a wedding or celebrate a wedding. . . . Williams knew that when large families from out of town unite for a family gathering like a wedding, they don't like renting a bunch of motel rooms. It's too confining, especially when younger children are involved. But finding a nice home that owners will rent by the week is not easy."

Barbara's creative rental use shows the basics of market analysis: Find a market gap and fill it. First, she noticed that especially during the summer months, many large weddings take place. Second, she knew that very few homeowners were serving this market, so competing properties consisted almost exclusively of hotels and motels. Third, because hotels and motels charge high rates for a small amount of space, out-of-town wedding guests and family members weren't really getting what they wanted.

Although some potential wedding parties object to the somewhat rural and inconvenient location of her home, Barbara turns that negative into an advantage. If it were closer-in, she points out, the home would be more expensive. Moreover, it wouldn't offer the privacy and solitude that her 2-acre, wooded lot provides.

Barbara's idea has brought in a good response. She rents to eight or ten wedding parties a year at a rental rate of $4,000 to $8,000 per week, depending on the time of year. Her rental price may seem high. But compare it to the cost of four or five motel rooms and a week's worth of restaurant meals for, say, ten or twelve people. Plus, consider the extra space, comfort, and privacy of the home. By these standards, Barbara beats the competition by a country mile.

Filling the Gap

Ask yourself, besides vacationers, who else might like to rent your second home? Or turn the question around. What kind of accommodations would a target market like to rent? Could companies use your home as a corporate retreat? Or maybe they could award weeks of use to top employees as a (tax-free?) bonus. Does the area where you're buying frequently attract conventions, arts and crafts shows, major sporting events, or touring dance and theater companies? Do area medical facilities bring in many patients from out of town whose family members need living quarters?

"Commercial" Space

If you plan on using your second home as a weekend getaway, who might want to use it from, say, Monday noon to Friday at 6:00 P.M.? Would space in the house work well for a writer or artist who needs a place to work? Could the home double as a professional office for an accountant, lawyer, doctor, counselor, or consultant? Many vacation and retirement areas attract professionals who want to work part-time. Yet, they don't want the expense of renting and equipping a full-time office. Some type of home shared with you might really produce a win-win arrangement for everyone.

"Bed and Breakfast"

My brother's home on Sugar Mountain in North Carolina includes an accessory apartment with a full kitchen, living area, and bedroom. During both the summer tourist season and the winter ski season, he can rent out the apartment for $80 to $100 per weekend night. In a sense, he and his wife offer a "bed and breakfast"—but the guests prepare their own breakfast.

If you buy (or remodel) a vacation or seasonal home that likewise includes an accessory apartment, you can enjoy the best of several worlds. You maintain the privacy of your own living quarters while you generate substantial rental income. And, during the off-season(s) when you're away, you can rent the accessory apartment to someone who will serve as caretaker for the home. Based on my brother's experience, I am convinced that more second- (and primary-) home owners, should search out homes that include (or could be remodeled to include) an accessory apartment, guest cottage, or mother-in-law suite. Except for people with unlimited money, the benefits clearly outweigh the slight costs and inconvenience.

Bed and Breakfast Business

If you are willing to enter the bed and breakfast (B&B) business, you can really push up your income potential. But, of course, you also add considerably to your workload. Running a B&B involves far more effort than the occasional rental of an accessory apartment. Still, a B&B does give you the advantage of being able to live in your second home—even during peak seasons. For someone who wants to enjoy peak seasons in a high-cost resort or vacation area, the B&B business could provide the ticket to affordability.

More Than Money

In her book, *How to Open and Operate a Bed and Breakfast*, Jan Stankus points out that running a home-based (as opposed to an inn or lodge) B&B can yield good supplemental income. But to gain success, you can't focus on money as your chief motivator. According to Jan, here are her six key ingredients:

1. You must enjoy meeting people from all walks of life.
2. You must maintain the home in top repair and spotless condition.
3. You should like to cook.
4. You should display an open, cheerful, and easy-to-get-along-with personality.
5. You should like the role of host(ess).
6. You should think of the money as a nice extra.

Based on my experience in staying in home-based B&Bs, I agree with Jan. B&Bs achieve a competitive advantage over hotels and motels (as well as other B&Bs) only to the extent that their owners provide guests with a truly unique, warm, friendly, and comfortable residence along with a breakfast feast of foods prepared from "special recipes." Ten years after, I still recall the B&B where I stayed in Mendocino, California, that scored five stars on all counts.

To make a B&B work well, you must provide guests with far more than a roof, a bed, Hills Brothers coffee, and a box of stale Dunkin' Donuts. Nevertheless, even though a B&B means work, the rewards far exceed the effort. If your personal characteristics fit the profile, read Jan's book.

Home Exchange

You don't need to buy a timeshare to enjoy "free" stays around the world. Your second home not only can earn you extra income, it can save you from paying thousands of dollars in hotel bills and vacation rentals. While home exchanges have always taken place directly among home owners, since 1996 home exchangers have been able to turn to Vacation Link for assistance.

Vacation Link

In 1996, E. Wade Shealy founded Vacation Link because he "saw a big void in the marketplace." "For second- [or principal-] home owners," Shealy says, "Vacation Link offers a nice marriage of what people really want—a second home with a little diversity." Operating from Atlanta, Georgia, Vacation Link mimics the service that Resort Condominiums International provides for time-share owners. Second-home owners choose the weeks that they plan to make their home available to exchangers. They then list those weeks in a catalogue published by Vacation Link that now includes more than 1,000 properties. Exchangers may select homes from nearly anywhere in the world—from New Zealand to Barbados, from Aspen to Hong Kong, from Fiji to San Francisco.

Like for Like (Sort of)

Exchangers classify their homes according to a standard rating system. The goal is to arrange swaps among properties that feature similar amenities, quality, and value. But "like for like" doesn't mean "exact for exact." "That's the beauty of it," says attorney David Batten who exchanged his Outer Banks, North Carolina, home for a five-bedroom townhome next to the ski lift in the center of Aspen. "You don't have to have a true item-for-item swap."

"In every case," relates exchanger Norman Scott, "the homes we stayed in were as nice or nicer than ours. . . . Our home in Vail was nothing like the one we got in the T&C Islands; our place is nice; but theirs was wonderful." If exchangers don't classify their homes accurately (within reason), Shealy can drop them from Vacation Link. "But so far," he's happy to report, "everyone has been pretty honest."

Have No Fear

Just as I have found in my home exchanges and home rentals, Vacation Link exchangers treat each other and each other's homes "with a high level of dignity and respect." At first, like many homeowners, Judy Cohen felt some anxiety about exchanging her vacation home. But several exchange experiences later, she says, "I totally trust these people. Everybody respects everybody else's home."

Norman Scott expresses the same feelings. "People leave gifts, as we do, too. I even leave my liquor cabinet open and tell guests that they are free to drink all they want. . . . They always leave more than they have taken." The next time Norm and his wife, Carlisle, who are professed "Italy freaks," take off for the island of Elba, they know they're leaving their Myrtle Beach vacation home in good hands.

Other Exchange Organizations

In addition to Vacation Link, whom you can reach at (800) 750-0797, a variety of other organizations also serve home exchangers. Included among the better known are:

Vacation Exchange Club
P. O. Box 820
Haleiwa, Hawaii 96712

International Home Exchange
P.O. Box 190070
San Francisco, California 94119

Intervac U.S.
P. O. Box 590504
San Francisco, California 94159

Vacation Home Exchange
Services International, Inc.
16 956-4 S. McGregor Boulevard
Fort Myers, Florida 33908

The last organization listed is run by veteran home exchangers and authors, Bill and Mary Barbour. Their book, *Home Exchange Vacationing*, covers the details of exchanging for everything from pets to plants to cars to kids. It also tells the personal stories of dozens of home exchangers. (One of my favorite stories involves an exchange couple who informed their host, who was out of the country, that the car he had left them to use was not running properly. In response, he immediately wired the couple $25,000 and asked them to buy a new one. Now that's hospitality!) I highly recommend the Barbour book.

Attracting Paying Guests

When you decide to rent (or exchange) your home, you can rely on a realty agency, a property management firm, or an exchange service. While most of these firms do a good job of finding tenants (or exchange partners), many homeowners aren't willing to sit back and delegate all of this work to others. Some second-home owners prefer to operate completely on their own, or perhaps work in partnership with their management firm.

Do-It-Yourself Marketing

Here are several reasons why you might want to locate your own tenants: (1) You can save money because vacation rental firms often collect 20 to 40 percent of a home's gross income in fees. (2) You can exercise more personal control over tenant selection. (3) You might be able to achieve higher rates of occupancy.

When your home goes into a rental pool run by a management agency, it becomes just one of dozens (perhaps hundreds) of properties in that firm's inventory. When you do it yourself, you can focus on just one task—getting *your* home rented. In addition, if you can save rental fees and boost occupancy, you can give your "guests" a break on rental rates. This "break" in turn reinforces high occupancy and repeat business.

Is Self-Marketing Practical?

Can you self-market? That all depends. When your second home is located an hour or two from your principal residence and you're renting it by the month (or by the season), certainly you can do it yourself. However, if you live in Columbus, Ohio, and your vacation home is on Maui, you would face great difficulty in trying to rent it out yourself on a daily rental basis. More than likely you will fall somewhere in between these two extremes. Then you'll have to weigh the pros and cons of self-marketing according to your personal situation and the types of rentals you're going after. (Barbara Williams self-markets her "wedding party" home rentals.)

Self-marketing doesn't mean that you do everything personally—it means you find your own tenants. Most self-marketing owners (though not all) delegate the unit's "make ready" tasks to someone who lives near the property. Other owners operate more as "assistant-marketers." These owners find all (or some) of the tenants for their homes, but they leave the specific rental arrangements (rental agreement, collections, make ready, maintenance) to a property manager.

How Can You Help?

If you want to maximize the amount of rental income you net from your property, at least think about self-marketing or assistance-marketing. Once you put on your thinking cap, you're sure to come up with many ways you can publicize your home and attract tenants. Here are six ideas:

1. Prepare a well-designed promotional brochure that displays your home's features, amenities, and locational advantages. Use the brochure to emphasize all of the benefits that guests will enjoy as residents of your home. Use this brochure to help in all of your publicity efforts.

2. Publicize the availability of the home to everyone you know. Ask them who they can think of who might like to take advantage of the wonderful home you are offering at a very competitive rental rate.

3. Make liberal use of bulletin boards at work, church, clubs, and college campuses.

4. Post your home on the Internet. Go to my Web page (www.stop-rentingnow.com) for links to "vacation home" rental sites.

5. Telephone, write letters, or personally contact special target markets such as corporations, theater companies, trade associations, convention bureaus, hospitals, or any other type of firm, organization, or group whose members (employees, clients, out-patients) need accommodations. Do out-of-town law firms frequently try cases in the area? Could the lawyers use your home? It would certainly offer more for less cost than a hotel.

6. Inform all of the neighbors near your second home that it is available. They may receive inquiries about rentals that they can pass along to you. Or maybe they have friends, extended family members, or acquaintances who would like to rent in the area.

What about Paid Newspaper Advertising?

Don't pay for advertising until after you have exhausted every technique just mentioned. If you still need more ideas, read Harvey MacKay's *Dig Your Well Before You're Thirsty*. I have found that paid advertising is the first refuge of lazy minds. In the past, I have used paid advertising successfully, but networking, word-of-mouth, and target marketing generally prove less costly and more effective. Whenever you advertise (especially in the classifieds), you surround yourself with competing homes. Through networking and word-of-mouth, you come much closer to "one-to-one" marketing.

Repeat Business and Referrals

What's the single biggest failure in marketing? The failure to keep in touch. Too many people believe that once a "sale" closes, that's the end of the matter. Not true. You should think of your guests in terms of lifetime customer value. The name of the game in sales is repeat business and referrals. Here are four easy ways to let your customers know you care:

1. Within a few days after they "check out" of your home, send a handwritten thank-you note.
2. After a week, follow up the note with a "just-checking-to-see-if-you-received-it" telephone call. Ask for comments, critique, what they liked, what they disliked, and suggestions for improvement.
3. Send a holiday greeting card during the Christmas season. (Harvey MacKay suggests Thanksgiving cards because few others send them.)
4. As the next rental reservation season approaches, call or write the guests to see if they would like to reserve your place again—or perhaps whether they can suggest the names of people who are prospective guests.

You can dramatically reduce the time, effort, and expense of marketing your home: Pay attention to details. (Little things do mean a lot.) Show gratitude. Follow up and "ask for the order." Provide all of those differences that make a difference and you'll never want for paying guests.

CHAPTER 14

How to Protect Your Investment

Through smart buying you can locate a second home that promises years of good times and financial rewards. But, in and of itself, "smart buying" doesn't complete the story. To realize fun and profits, you will need to protect your investment. Uninsured losses, excessive or unexpected repairs, vandalism, lawsuits, and taxes represent some of the common pitfalls that you should guard against.

Review Insurance Coverages and Costs

When fire swept through the Oakland-Berkeley, California, hills, Ron and Betty Bugaj lost their $500,000 home and all their personal belongings. The Bugajes were not alone. In the most damaging residential firestorm in U.S. history, more than 3,300 other homeowners suffered total losses. Twenty-seven people died. As tragic as the fire was, though, for many of these families their troubles were just beginning.

"The damage we really suffered," said Betty, "was in our negotiations with the insurance company."

Like more than 1,000 other firestorm victims, the Bugajes learned after the fire that their homeowner's insurance policy would pay far less than they expected. To get the amounts they thought they were entitled to, the Bugajes wrangled back and forth with their insurance company for more than ten months. Adding to their hassle was the $75,000 in lawyer's bills and consulting fees that their negotiations with the insurance company cost them.

In the end, the Bugajes and most of the other firestorm victims did settle with their insurers—but only after the California Department of Insurance, various consumer advocacy groups, and widespread unfavorable publicity pressured the insurance companies to give in. Although to some extent several insurers had tried to lowball their policyholders, most of the settlement problems resulted because homeowners had not purchased the insurance coverage they actually needed (or thought they had).

A Personal Experience Aside

I write here from personal experience. My home at the time was directly confronted by this inferno. When I drove out in panic, the woods and houses all around were in flames. For four days, the police blockaded the area. My home was posted as one of those completely destroyed. Amazingly, though, the posting was wrong. For some inexplicable reason, the fire jumped several houses and continued on its way. My house was one of the few that was spared.

Nevertheless, during the four days that I couldn't get to my home, I believed that it had been destroyed. I had no sleep because I "knew" I had lost years of work-in-process, files, manuscripts, computer disks, and other items that were neither insured nor backed up elsewhere with copies. To add insult to injury, in 1981, I had published an article in the *Journal of Consumer Affairs*. My research had surveyed hundreds of families and the results were clear: Most households—at all levels of income and education—do not carry the insurance coverages they need.

At least now I can say that this is no longer true for my household. But I will bet money that, like me and my neighbors in the Berkeley-

Oakland hills, your coverages need to be examined and revised. Don't wait until it's too late. Do it now.

The important lesson of the Oakland-Berkeley hills firestorm was not that most insurance companies are bad guys. Rather, it's that far too many homeowners don't actually understand their insurance coverages. They just buy a homeowner's policy and assume (incorrectly) they have the protection they need. This assumption is a big mistake.

Unfortunately, most people are told "read your insurance policy." That's not much help. Before you can make sense out of an insurance policy, you have to know what you're looking for. Essentially, that means knowing what questions to ask. It is especially important that you ask these questions of your second home's coverages because mountain, coastal, and rural properties often present dangers that differ from those you face with your principal home.

What Perils Are Covered?

In insurance language, a "peril" is a cause of loss. No insurance policy covers every type of loss. Some policies exclude losses due to hurricanes, floods, mudslides, sinkholes, earthquakes, and riots. Sometimes freezing pipes and roof collapse due to a buildup of snow and ice are not covered. If you buy a "comprehensive" or "all-risk" policy, you do not receive "all-risk" protection. These types of policies list exclusions. A comprehensive policy only gives you coverage for everything that's not excluded. What it appears to give in one part of the policy, it may take away someplace else.

If you buy a "named peril" policy, the policy will name specifically the causes of loss for which you are covered. Don't fool yourself into believing that a policy provides the protection you need. Determine what perils do and do not trigger a valid claim.

What Property Is Covered?

Do you plan to bring work with you to your second home? You should realize some of your business property or business inventories may not be covered under your homeowner's policy. Nor are your pets, golf cart, or snowmobile. Similarly, if you own any expensive antiques, jewelry, furs, artwork, or a collection of stamps, coins, or baseball cards, you'll want to find out whether they're covered, and, if so, for how much. More than likely, you'll have to pay extra to secure adequate protection. If you're a writer, store an extra copy of the manuscript you're working on with friends or in a safe-deposit box. (Dozens of writers in the Oakland-Berkeley fire lost computer disks and partially completed books and articles.) Typically, your homeowner's policy won't pay for the value of your past work, or even the market value of a finished manuscript.

Also, if you live in a co-op, condo, or townhouse, make sure you clearly determine the property covered by the homeowners' association coverages and the property coverages that remain your responsibility. For example, if a water pipe bursts within a wall and causes water and plumbing damages, who pays for what? Check your association rules and regulations.

Property Use

Most property insurance policies don't cover all property uses. If you plan to rent out your vacation home, make sure you notify your insurance agent. A "rental" property poses more risks than a home that qualifies exclusively as personal use. Also, inform guests or tenants that your property insurance *does not* cover the property they bring along with them. (Such property, though, may be covered for named perils under the guests' or tenants' own homeowner's policies as "away from premises" protection.)

"Vacant" versus "Unoccupied"

Some property insurance policies limit coverage to homes that are occupied or unoccupied as opposed to remaining vacant. This means that as long as people are coming and going regularly from the home, you've got coverage. However, if you stay away for "too long" (read the policy) or move all of your furnishings and belongings out (i.e., the house becomes "vacant"), your coverage may not apply— even though you have paid the premiums. The insurance company knows that nonuse increases the riskiness of a home. Make sure you know how long you can stay away before your insurer suspends coverage.

How Much Will the Insurer Pay?

Even when you have a covered loss, you may not be entitled to full reimbursement—or, in some cases, you can collect far more than your loss. Confusion often arises because, within the same policy, insurers may use a variety of methods to determine how much they will pay you. For example, cash: If a fire destroys $2,000 in emergency cash that you've hidden in a shoebox in the closet, kiss your money good-by. Insurers typically limit reimbursements for cash to $100.

Internal Limits and Deductibles

Policies often provide internal limits to reduce exposure to false claims. Otherwise, whenever a fire (or other peril) destroys a house, the insurer could expect to receive claims for large amounts of lost cash, precious jewelry, and unreplaceable antiques. (Just like no dry cleaners ever lost a suit worth less than $300.) Even though your policy covers those diamond earrings and your $4,000 shotgun, check the amounts. You may not be able to collect the full extent of your loss.

Check similarly for deductibles. You may have purchased a policy with a $500 deductible on losses to the home by fire. But if it's damaged by earthquake or hurricane, the deductible might jump to, say, $5,000 or more. (Several years ago, insurers in California tried to apply a $25,000 deductible to all damages caused by earthquakes.) When certain types of perils present high risk, insurers will attempt to reduce claims by using high deductibles.

As a precaution, check the amounts of all the internal limits and deductibles within your policy. You may find that you aren't entitled to the amount of coverage that you expect.

Overall Policy Limits

In addition to internal limits and deductibles, all policies limit their maximum payout in one or more ways. Typically, the policy will state dollar maximums that apply to the home, contents, medical coverage, and liability protection. For the home and contents, the policy also will specify coverage as "actual cash value" or "replacement cost."

With a replacement cost policy, your insurer agrees to pay you enough to repair or replace your house at today's prices. Under actual cash value coverage, the company subtracts a figure for depreciation from the costs of replacement. Naturally, it's better to buy replacement cost coverage. Otherwise, the older your house, the greater its wear and tear, the less you can collect. The same thing is true for contents. Thieves broke into one of my homes and stole about $1,000 worth (actual cash value) of televisions, VCRs, microwave ovens, and radios. But with replacement cost coverage, my insurer wrote me a check for $3,000—enough money to replace every item brand new.

Remember, though, to collect full replacement costs, the amount of reimbursement can't exceed your policy limit. That was one major issue that created problems for fire victims in Oakland-Berkeley. Many homeowners had not periodically reviewed their policy limits to keep them up-to-date according to today's costs of construction. Don't confuse market value with replacement value. The former refers to the likely selling price of your home; the latter refers to how much a building contractor would charge to rebuild it.

Other Payment Issues

The Oakland-Berkeley fire also provoked heated debate over several other issues that you will want to talk over with your insurance agent. You should ask the following six questions:

1. In the event of a major loss, how much will you be able to collect if you choose not to rebuild?
2. What happens if government regulations prevent repairs or rebuilding? (For example, some homes now located in coastal areas, floodplains, wetlands, or hillsides could not be rebuilt because of new safety or environmental regulations.)
3. What if new government regulations (safety codes, environmental laws, building regulations) significantly increase the costs to reconstruct (replace) your home? In the Oakland fire, many destroyed homes were thirty to seventy years old. They couldn't be rebuilt as they previously had been built. Extra regulations added as much as $50,000 or more to their rebuilding costs. Yet, homeowners' policies often exclude these types of costs because they're not really "replacement" costs. This fact came as a big surprise to many homeowners when they learned that to rebuild they were going to have to come up with sub-

stantial amounts of cash from their own pockets. (A *guaranteed* replacement cost policy is one way to meet this problem.)

4. How much will your policy pay for your home's unique architectural or historical value? (Usually nothing, unless you've requested special coverages.)
5. If your insurer drags its feet while settling your claim, are you entitled to interest payments on the proceeds when the company finally does pay?
6. If you choose an actual cash value policy, how will your insurance company calculate depreciation?

One final point: Keep a list and photographic (or video) inventory of your personal property. Under the terms of your policy, you'll be required to prove your loss. Photos or videos stored in a safe place (away from your home, of course) can serve as good proof of what you owned. Besides, without a detailed inventory of your possessions, chances are you'll forget or overlook a lot of things that you're entitled to collect for.

What Liability Protection?

In addition to protecting your home and its contents, your homeowner's policy will protect you against liability for lawsuits arising from personal injuries. Typically, it provides "slip and fall" coverage where someone is injured on your property, but it may also cover you for accidents such as running into someone while on your bicycle or hitting someone with a golf ball with your mean slice.

If you buy into a condominium, co-op, townhouse, or subdivision development where you're a member of a homeowners' association, check to see what type of liability coverage the association carries. In some states, you can be held personally liable (along with other homeowners) when someone is negligently injured on the common areas of the property (swimming pool, bike trails, tennis courts, clubhouse, hallways).

According to attorney Benny Kass, a specialist in condominium and homeowners' association law, too many homeowners' associations "are pitifully underinsured and represent a significant risk to association members."

What Are the Premiums?

Apart from fully understanding your insurance coverages, before you offer to buy a vacation, seasonal, or getaway home, determine how much adequate insurance protection will cost you. During the past ten years, property insurance companies and homeowners have suffered billions of dollars in losses (Hurricane Andrew, the Oakland-Berkeley firestorm, the Los Angeles riots, the Midwest floods, the Los Angeles-Malibu fires). As a result, some companies have raised their premiums and made insurance much more difficult to obtain in some areas with high loss potential.

In Florida after Hurricane Andrew, for example, many major insurance companies canceled tens of thousands of homeowner policies, and several insurers tried to withdraw completely from writing policies in hurricane areas. In California, many insurers have eliminated or severely limited the coverages they offer for earthquake losses. At present, no one can predict how all these troubles will work themselves out. But for these and other reasons, it does mean that you will need to check your coverages and your premiums very closely. You can't assume that you'll be able to get the coverages you need at a price you want to pay.

Buying Smart

To a certain extent, you can control your insurance costs by buying smart. That means making sure your coverage adequately protects against big losses, but you "don't sweat the small stuff." Since small manageable losses occur far more frequently than major losses, insurers give relatively large discounts in premiums to homeowners who select high deductibles. Fortunately, you can usually increase your policy's limits by tens, even hundreds of thousands of dollars, with perhaps not more than a 10 or 15 percent increase in premium.

More Good News

As *Money Magazine* recently reported, "The insurance picture is looking brighter for vacation homes. Traditionally, a second home costs up to twice as much to insure as a primary home. That's because second homes are empty much of the time, leaving them more vulnerable to burglaries, fire, and other risks. But in the past couple of years, the big Warren, N.J.-based insurer Chubb has been slashing its second-home premiums in thirteen states that contain lots of vacation homes. (Chubb plans to do the same in the rest of the country in the next two years.) Chubb's rationale: Most people have fewer and less valuable belongings in their second homes than in their primary residences. So the insurer's plan offers lower than usual coverage levels on those items in return for an annual premium bill that might run $700 a year, vs. $1,000 for a primary residence. Other insurers are expected to follow Chubb's lead."

You can also reduce your property insurance bill through loss reduction and loss prevention. "With measures like hurricane strapping, shutters, and water-resistant roof treatments, it's possible to receive big discounts on rates," says Allan Cook of the Florida Windstorm Underwriting Association.

If you buy a vacation home that's located in a peril-prone area, ask your insurance agent to list precautions you can take to "damage-proof" the property. For example, in some especially rural areas, fire and burglar alarms, sprinklers, and sensors to prevent frozen pipes can save you insurance dollars. More important, loss prevention may save your home and the lives of you and your family.

Buy Title Insurance (An Owner's Policy)

To further protect your second-home investment, buy title insurance. This coverage protects against title defects such as undisclosed liens, easements, or claims by heirs of previous owners. As with homeowners' (or rental property) coverage, though, you must determine the policy wording with respect to causes of loss, who's covered, policy limits, amount of the premium, and whether any discounts are available (such as if you take over the sellers' policy rather than change companies).

Often, a title company issues a *lender's* title policy that protects only the lender. To remedy this omission, you need to request an *owner's* policy. You also should request inflation protection that will protect your growing equity in the property due to appreciation. Otherwise, you may not be able to collect more from the policy than your original purchase price.

Say you pay $100,000 for your second home. Fifteen years later, the home is valued at $300,000. A long-lost heir to the property shows up and claims that he was swindled out of his rights by a crooked brother who forged his name to the deed. A lawsuit erupts. The judge awards the home to the heir. You're out. Lacking coverage for appreciation, the title insurer would pay you no more than $100,000.

Learn about Home Warranties and Termite Inspections

Home Warranties

In 1999, nearly one million sellers provided their buyers with a home warranty (technically, a preowned home service agreement). This coverage helps you guard against major (and minor) costs of repair and replacement for plumbing, heating, air conditioning, wiring, roofing, appliances, and other components of the home. However, not all home warranties give you "sleep-easy" protection.

Read the Fine Print

Don't count on home warranties to reimburse you for repairs or replacements unless you've first verified exactly what types of repairs and amounts of protection the warranty offers. Real estate broker Carl Steinmetz says his realty firm stopped dealing in home warranties because "we just had too many cases in which the buyers were discontented with their policy. They always thought it should have covered something, but then it didn't."

Not everyone agrees with Carl. California Department of Insurance spokesman John Fogg reports his agency gets fewer complaints about home warranty policies than any other type of insurance. And the real estate brokerage firm Joan M. Sobeck, Inc., thinks so highly of warranties that some of its agents buy the policies as a service to their sellers and buyers. Another broker says, "Many buyers often don't know much about repairing a home. . . . [As a result] those folks are really drawn to the protection of a warranty." So what's the bottom line on home warranties? Read the fine print and look for answers to these seven major questions:

1. Does the warranty cover labor, materials, and parts? Or is it limited to certain named items (e.g., roof shingles, furnace combustion chamber, air conditioner compressor)?
2. Will you receive full reimbursement? Or will payments be prorated?
3. Regardless of coverage, will you be required to pay for service calls? Some warranties charge homeowners anywhere from $50 to $200 each time a repairman is called out to the house.
4. If you're buying an existing home with a warranty, ask what items are excluded from coverage (e.g., roof, foundation, air conditioner, pool equipment, well pump, sprinkler system, plumbing, wiring).
5. How long will the warranty last? Most overall warranties with existing homes end after one year. New home warranties may cover major structural items for ten years but limit coverage on appliances, furnace, and air conditioners to just one year. (In some instances the manufacturers of these items separately warrant their quality and performance. You'll need to check these separate warranties to determine how you're protected.)
6. Does the warranty cover preexisting conditions? When you buy your home, if the pipes are rusty or the furnace is clunking and clanging, the warranty may exempt these items from coverage. Many (but not all) warranties only guard against unexpected breakdowns or malfunctions—not sure things. So don't count on a warranty to substitute for a thorough inspection of the home by a professional inspector.
7. What is the warranty company's track record for honoring claims? Does it run you through a maze of paperwork and proofs? Or does it enjoy a reputation for fair settlements?

Termite Inspections

Most mortgage lenders require an inspection for termites and other wood-destroying insects before closing a home loan. As with home warranties, though, you must read the fine print of the "service" agreement.

A termite inspector only "samples" the house. He pokes here and there hoping to spot any problems that might exist. But there's always the possibility the inspector won't hit the right spot, or the damage may be hidden and inaccessible. Either way, actual damage could exceed reported damage. (It's even possible for an infested house to receive a clean bill of health.) So protect yourself by following these guidelines:

- Tag along with the inspector as he tours the house. Did he get under the house and poke around in the crawl space? How about the attic? The foundation? Did he especially check areas where wood (treated or untreated) comes in contact with the ground? How thoroughly has the inspector actually "sampled" the home for infestation?
- Ask the inspector questions. Try to learn the areas of the house that are most vulnerable to infestation. Find out whether other homes in the neighborhood have had a termite problem. See if he discovers any signs that the house has been treated previously. If so, how extensive was the previous damage? Were there any recurrences?
- If the inspection and treatment results in a warranty, what does it cover? Will it pay for all necessary repairs? Or does it only require the company to retreat the home with another dose of pesticides?
- If the company locates infestation and estimates repairs, who bears the risk for underestimates? Is the company merely issuing a good-faith estimate? In that case—unless the firm has been negligent in its inspection—you must pay the repairs if additional damage is found after work begins. Some exterminators, though, guarantee their estimates. When they miss problems, they bear the costs to correct them.

Avoid simply accepting a termite inspection, clearance report, or damage estimate at face value. With some reports, you can sleep easy knowing you've covered (or limited) your exposure to loss. With others, you just have to hope those pesky little critters have satisfied their appetites somewhere else. Because if they haven't, you'll be the one who's picking up their dinner check.

Hire a Home Inspector

Before you offer to buy a second home, thoroughly inspect its interior and exterior. Try to identify problems and potential sources of problems. You want to make sure the home will fit not only your living patterns and lifestyle, but also your budget. Unexpected repairs and replacements can cost you dearly.

Why "waste" $300 (more or less) on a home inspection? Here are four good reasons:

1. You're buying a second home that differs in age, construction, and design from your principal home. You may not recognize problems that are obvious to the trained and experienced eye.
2. You're buying a second home that differs in location from your principal house. Likewise, problems common to that area may not be common to you. I almost bought a four-year-old house that showed extensive foundation cracks. The owner said, "No worry, just settling cracks." My inspector said, "Big worry. The home's foundation had not been properly set for the type of soil (clay)." Prior to that time, I had no experience with the damage that results when a home is built improperly on clay. Apparently neither did the builder of the house.
3. You want to maintain the home to reduce the costs of ownership. As you walk through the inspection with the professional, ask him to point out potential maintenance problems and how best to remedy or prevent them from growing into large and needless repair or replacement expenses. Another true adage: "An ounce of prevention is worth a pound of cure."
4. Your professional inspector can better recognize the "games people play" to cover up, cheaply repair, or otherwise hide their home's problems or defects.

Home warranties and termite inspections offer two needed defenses against unexpected costs. Your third defense is a professional inspection. Amazingly, though, real estate agents and mortgage brokers tell me that just 50 percent of their buyers employ a trained and experienced inspector to cast a critical eye on their home's state of repair. This mistake clearly reflects "penny wise, pound foolish."

Save on Property Taxes

In addition to avoiding losses due to casualty damage, excessive maintenance and repairs, or unexpected replacements, you can take steps to reduce your property taxes. It's not just the termites who will eat up your investment. So will the tax collectors (local, state, and federal).

Preventing Unhappy Surprises

Throughout the country, property tax laws materially differ among the many state and local taxing districts. Some assessors stay up-to-date. Others lag behind. Some home assessments are valued accurately. Others differ wildly. When it comes to property taxes, you can't assume that the tax authorities where you're buying your vacation home operate in the same way that your tax assessors back home operate. Most important, don't assume that you will pay about the same amount of property taxes that the sellers have been paying.

To prevent unhappy surprises, learn the ins and outs of the property tax system in the area where you are buying. If the home is underassessed, or if the sellers qualify for more exemptions than you are entitled to, you might see a steep rise in your property-tax bill. Here are eight major property tax questions you should discuss with your real estate agent or the tax assessors office:

1. What is the current market value for tax purposes of the home you're buying?
2. What is the current assessed value of the home? (In some tax jurisdictions, the assessed value is stated as a percentage of the home's market value. Therefore, you should look at both the tax assessor's appraised value and the assessed value before you conclude a home is underassessed.)
3. After you buy, can you expect the *assessed* value of the home to increase, decrease, or remain about the same?
4. Are you entitled to any exemptions that can reduce your property tax bill? Will you lose any exemptions that the sellers have been taking?
5. What is the local millage rate? One mill equals a thousandth of a dollar or one-tenth of a cent. A millage rate of, say, 17 would mean a property tax of $17 for every $1,000 of assessed value.
6. Will any improvements you plan to make to the home increase its assessed value? Some types of improvements will add significantly to your assessed value—if the tax assessor learns

about them. Built-ins, room additions, a swimming pool, or wall-to-wall carpeting, for example, typically increase a home's assessed value. A new roof, furnace, or hot water heater may not. Every tax assessor's office has its own way of operating. You'll have to check for the specifics as they may apply to the home you buy.

7. After improvements (if any), what amount of taxes can you expect to pay? (To calculate this figure, multiply the millage rate expressed as a decimal by the home's expected assessed value. With an assessed value of, say, $100,000 and a millage rate of 21, your property taxes would run $2,100 a year (.021 × $100,000).

8. Does the tax jurisdiction plan any major tax rate increases? Do current tax revenues cover all necessary expenses, or is government "starved for cash"? Without a tax increase, will government services get cut? Is the property tax base increasing or decreasing?

Special Assessments

From time to time local governments levy special assessments. These charges usually pay for new sidewalks, sewers, sewage disposal plants, schools, street widening, parks, or other types of infrastructure. In most cases special assessments will range between $300 and $1,000, but on occasion they can go as high as $2,000, $3,000, or even more.

Since special assessments can upset a budget, find out whether any assessments are planned for the community. Also, learn of proposed "infrastructure" changes before you buy. Better parks may add to your home's value. But widening the street through your neighborhood or in front of your home could bring more traffic. That would take away from the value of your home. In many high-growth areas around the country, residents are getting squeezed at both ends. They're paying (or can expect to pay) higher taxes and assessments for a lower quality of life.

Residents of declining areas also face the same squeeze, but for different reasons. In those cases, a dwindling tax base coupled with larger government spending on social problems (drugs, crime, welfare, social services) pushes up tax rates as living conditions worsen. (Obviously you won't invest in a declining area unless, like South Beach of the 1980s, it shows great promise for turnaround.)

Reduce Your Income Taxes

Few among us can escape paying income taxes. But as an owner of a second home, you are entitled to a number of tax breaks. Unfortunately, the mind-numbing incoherence and complexity of federal income tax law prohibits a full discussion of these tax breaks here. Instead, I can only offer suggestions that you can go over with your tax advisor. The better you protect your income and capital gains from the IRS, the more you protect the returns that you will receive from your second-home investment.

Mortgage Interest and Property Taxes

When you use your second home only for personal pleasure, you generally can deduct the amounts you pay for mortgage interest and state and local property taxes. As long as your total mortgage debt for your principal and second home don't exceed $1 million, you're within the limit. In addition, you can deduct the interest on a home equity loan up to $100,000. As to property taxes, no limits apply. Whatever amount you pay, that's the amount you can deduct.

The Original-Indebtedness Trap

Be careful, though. Apart from a home equity loan, you can only deduct mortgage interest up to the balance on your *original* mortgage indebtedness. If you pay cash for your second home, or buy with a large down payment, you can't later refinance with a larger loan and gain a full deduction for the interest you will pay.

Say you pay $250,000 for your second home, put $100,000 down, and finance $150,000. Three years later your loan balance stands at $142,000. You want to refinance and put a new mortgage on the home in the amount of $200,000. You will be able to deduct interest on only $142,000. The lesson is that if you think you might want to take out a high loan amount on your second home(or principal home, for that matter), do it when you buy the home. Otherwise, you can't deduct the total interest—even though your balance stays well below the $1 million maximum.

The Part-Time-Rental, Part-Time-Personal Trap

More complexity: You get the second-home mortgage interest deduction in total *only* when the home meets the IRS test for a personal residence. If you use the home part-time as a rental, and part-time as a vacation home, the home may lose its "personal" character. In that circumstance, only mortgage interest paid for the time the home is rented becomes eligible for deduction. (But this isn't all bad. As discussed in the following, what you lose in personal mortgage interest deductions, you may gain back in a variety of other deductions as rental expenses.)

Rental Income and Expenses

If you use your second home to generate rental income, you may lose some deductions for mortgage interest, but not necessarily. As a "gift" to second-home owners, tax law established the 14-day rule.

The 14-Day Rule

When you rent out your home for fourteen or fewer days, you get two tax breaks: (1) Your home retains its personal-use status and you get all of your otherwise allowable personal mortgage interest deductions. In addition, (2) your rental income is earned tax-free. You don't even need to declare it on your income tax return.

For second-home owners who own in areas where peak rental rates really shoot up (say, Augusta, Georgia, during the Master's Tournament), this break could mean $5,000 or $10,000 in extra nontaxable income. Naturally, though, under the 14-day rule, you can't deduct any rental expenses associated with that rental income. If you spent money for advertising, "make ready" and cleaning the home, those expenses merely reduce your net gain from the rental proceeds. In this instance, the IRS doesn't let you take the best of both worlds.

Over-14-Day Rules

Once you exceed fourteen days of rental income, all of your rental income becomes reportable to the IRS. You may also lose your full personal mortgage interest deduction. However, you ordinarily get to deduct all property and mortgage expenses associated with your "rental" property. In other words, your mortgage interest may still qualify as a deductible expense. Only now it's a rental expense rather than a personal expense.

Say you rent out your home for 180 days a year. You can offset that income with 180 days of mortgage interest. Plus, you can also deduct advertising, cleaning, utilities, management fees, depreciation, and other rental-related charges. You may also be able to deduct some travel to and from the home. If the travel is connected primarily with your duties as owner and manager of a rental property, it's deductible.

Another 14-Day Rule

When you rent out the home for more than fourteen days—and you personally use the home for more than fourteen days, or more than 10 percent of your total rental days—your home meets both the "vacation home" test and the rental property test. Under these circumstances, you are allowed a deduction for your "vacation-home" mortgage interest. To qualify for this "double break" given a rental situation of 180 rental days, you would need to "personally" use your home more than eighteen days. If you didn't meet this personal use test, you wouldn't get the vacation-home mortgage interest deduction.

Fortunately, "personal" use includes the time you let friends or family stay at the home without charging them a fair market rental.

Complexity Reigns

My basic point here is that you need to be aware and recognize that the IRS does not tax all vacation-home owners equally. Your tax status depends on: (1) how many days you "personally" use the home; (2) how many days the home sits out of use; and (3) how many days renters occupy the home. In addition, your tax status will vary according to the amount of your adjusted gross income (under $100,000 is best); how actively you participate in the management of the property (more is better); and whether you work full time in a real estate related profession (their lobby got them a special tax break on rental properties).

All of this complexity means that *before* you decide how and when to use your second home, talk with your tax advisor. Through appropriate tax planning you may be able to shield thousands of dollars of rental income from taxation. You may be able to deduct thousands of dollars in personal *and* rental deductions.

That's how the tax system works. To protect your wealth and income, you must first learn how the tax rules apply to your personal situation. Then structure your behavior accordingly. This approach doesn't mean that you always try to minimize your tax burden per se. It does mean, though, that you should act knowledgeably. You can take the breaks that work for you. You can avoid the tax traps that snare you into paying big bucks with little or no off-setting gain.

The Capital Gains Exclusion

Under the tax law act of 1997, homeowners receive a big tax break. You can now sell your principal residence and pocket up to $500,000 (married filing jointly) of tax-free capital gain. If you're single, you get $250,000 of exempted gains. Although aimed at owners of principal residences, as described in the following, this tax break has two features that favor the ownership of second homes.

The Two-for-One

As mentioned earlier, with this new break for capital gains, you can sell your "big house," take the proceeds tax-free (up to the limit), then buy two less expensive homes—a new principal residence and a vacation home. Unlike the old law, you now no longer must meet the "repurchase" rule to escape capital gains taxation. The prices of your two new residences can equal, exceed, or come in at a lesser amount than the sales price of your "big house." It doesn't matter.

Multiple Exemptions

Also, unlike the old one-time $125,000 capital gains exclusion available to those age fifty-five or older, this new tax break can be used by all homeowners time and again. It's only subject to the 2-2-2 rule. To qualify, the law says that prior to the date of sale, you must have (1) occupied the home for at least two of the past five years; (2) you must have owned the home for at least two years; and (3) two years must have elapsed since the last time you used the $500,000 ($250,000) exemption.

Thus, by making your second home your principal residence two years before you sell it, you can reap tax-free gains. In other words, you could buy a vacation home today, hold on to it for eight or ten years, watch it appreciate, and then convert it to your principal residence for two years. After those two years, you can sell it and pocket your gain tax-free (as long as you haven't taken the exemption on some other home during those two years).

Even if you have used your second home as a rental property for the past ten, twenty, or thirty years, you can still exempt your gain from taxation by converting the property into your principal residence. You will have to recapture any depreciation you've previously written off, but that's a small price to pay. And this tax-free gain gives you an added incentive to profitably improve your second home. Just think, every dollar you add in value will end up in your net worth. You don't have to pass along a big chunk of cash to the IRS. Undoubtedly, this new law will encourage tens of thousands of people to become "serial sellers."

Check with Your Tax Advisor

With tax law, nothing can ever be stated simply *and* accurately. Exceptions and qualifications always interject themselves. So, as urged before, consult with your tax advisor for details. One fact, though, remains clear. The new capital gains tax break can help owners of second homes, just as it can help owners of principal residences. Tax planning is the order of the day.

With the appropriate tax planning (income and property), home maintenance, insurance, inspections, and warranties, you can secure the fun and profits your second home will provide. Good luck and enjoy!

Index